# HOUSING RENE
# IN EUROPE

# Other titles available from The Policy Press include:

*City for the 21st century? Globalisation, planning and urban change in contemporary Britain*
by Martin Boddy, Christine Lambert and Dawn Snape
Paperback ISBN 1 86134 048 6 £16.95

**Joseph Rowntree Housing Repair and Maintenance Series**

*Make do and mend? Explaining homeowners' approaches to repair and maintenance*
by Philip Leather, Mandy Littlewood and Moira Munro
Paperback ISBN 1 86134 096 6  £11.95

*Management of flats in multiple ownership: Learning from other countries*
by Nick Bailey and Douglas Robertson with Hal Pawson
Paperback ISBN 1 86134 077 X  £11.95

*A good investment? The impact of urban renewal on an inner-city housing market*
by Rick Groves and Pat Niner
Paperback ISBN 1 86134 105 9  £11.95

*Uncommon currencies: LETs and their impact on property repair and maintenance for low income homeowners*
by John Pearce and Chris Wadhams
Paperback ISBN 1 86134 078 8  £11.95

All the above titles are available from
Biblios Publishers' Distribution Services Ltd, Star Road,
Partridge Green, West Sussex RH13 8LD, UK
Telephone +44 (0)1403 710851, Fax +44 (0)1403 711143

# HOUSING RENEWAL IN EUROPE

Edited by Hans Skifter Andersen and
Philip Leather

The POLICY PRESS

First published in Great Britain in 1999 by

The Policy Press
University of Bristol
34 Tyndalls Park Road
Bristol BS8 1PY
UK

Tel    +44 (0)117 973 8797
Fax   +44 (0) 117 973 7308
e-mail   tpp@bristol.ac.uk
http://www.bristol.ac.uk/Publications/TPP

© The Policy Press, 1998

British Library Cataloguing in Publication Data
A catalogue record for this book is available from the British Library

ISBN 1 86134 135 0

**Hans Skifter Andersen** is Senior Researcher at the Danish Building Research Institute. **Philip Leather** is Professor of Housing and Urban Renewal, University of Birmingham.

Cover design: Qube Design Associates, Bristol.

The right of Hans Skifter Andersen and Philip Leather to be identified as editors of this work has been asserted by them in accordance with Sections 77 and 78 of the 1988 Copyright, Designs and Patents Act.

All rights reserved: no part of this publication may be reproduced, stored in a retrieval system, or transmitted in any form or by any means, electronic, mechanical, photocopying, recording, or otherwise without the prior permission of The Policy Press.

The statements and opinions contained within this publication are solely those of the authors and contributors and not of The University of Bristol or The Policy Press. The University of Bristol and The Policy Press disclaim responsibility for any injury to persons or property resulting from any material published in this publication.

The Policy Press works to counter discrimination on grounds of gender, race, disability, age and sexuality.

Printed and bound in Great Britain by Hobbs the Printers Ltd, Southampton.

# Contents

| | | |
|---|---|---|
| Notes on contributors | | vi |
| List of tables and figures | | viii |
| List of acronyms | | xi |
| one | Introduction<br>Hans Skifter Andersen | 1 |
| two | The national context for housing renewal<br>Hans Skifter Andersen | 17 |
| three | National strategies for urban renewal and housing rehabilitation: the case of Sweden<br>Ingemar Elander | 25 |
| four | Housing conditions and housing renewal policy in the UK<br>Philip Leather | 65 |
| five | Strategies for public regulation of urban renewal and housing rehabilitation in Denmark<br>Knud Erik Hansen and Hans Skifter Andersen | 95 |
| six | Urban renewal and housing rehabilitation in Switzerland<br>Roland Haari | 115 |
| seven | Distributing the responsibilities – urban renewal in Vienna<br>Wolfgang Förster | 141 |
| eight | Strategies and policies for urban renewal and housing rehabilitation in France<br>Anne-Marie Fribourg | 155 |
| nine | Urban renewal and housing rehabilitation in The Netherlands<br>René Teule | 175 |
| ten | National strategies for urban renewal and housing rehabilitation in Norway<br>Solveig Aaen | 203 |
| eleven | The renewal of older urban housing in Scotland<br>Nick Bailey and Douglas Robertson | 217 |
| twelve | Housing rehabilitation and urban renewal in Europe: a cross-national analysis of problems and policies<br>Hans Skifter Andersen | 241 |
| References | | 279 |
| Index | | 291 |

# Notes on contributors

**Solveig Aaen** is a consultant at the Norwegian Ministry of Local Government (including housing). She has conducted research on urban renewal and housing rehabilitation in Norway for many years.

**Nick Bailey** is Research Fellow at the Department of Urban Studies, University of Glasgow.

**Ingemar Elander** is a docent at the Centre for Housing and Urban Research, Örebro University.

**Wolfgang Förster** is employed at the Wiener Bodenbereitstellungs- und Stadterneuerungsfonds in Vienna.

**Anne-Marie Fribourg** is a consultant at the Direction de l'Habitat et de la Construction, Ministère du Logement, Paris.

**Roland Haari** is a consultant and researcher at COPLAN, Architektur, Regional- und Ortsplanung und Empirische Sozialforschung in Basel, Switzerland.

**Knud Erik Hansen** is a Senior Researcher at the Department for Housing and Urban Research at the Danish Building Research Institute, Denmark.

**Philip Leather** is Professor of Housing and Urban Renewal at the Centre for Urban and Regional Studies, University of Birmingham.

**Douglas Robertson** is an Assistant Professor at the Housing Policy and Practice Unit, University of Sirling.

**Hans Skifter Andersen** is a Senior Researcher at the Department for Housing and Urban Research at the Danish Building Research Institute, Denmark.

**René Teule** is now employed at the Department of Urban Development, City of the Hague. He was until 1997 a researcher at the OTB Research Institute, Delft University of Technology.

# List of tables and figures

## Tables

| | | |
|---|---|---|
| 2.1 | Characteristics of the nine countries | 18 |
| 2.2 | Composition of the housing market in nine countries | 21 |
| 2.3 | Characterisation of housing policy in nine countries | 22 |
| A3.1 | Capital formulation in permanent housing (1980-91) | 58 |
| A3.2 | Tenure by percentage of housing stock in Sweden (1945-90) | 59 |
| A3.3 | Granted government housing loans for reconstruction (1975/76-1993) | 60 |
| A3.4 | Careful rehabilitation as defined by Swedish housing researchers and experts | 61 |
| 4.1 | The standard of fitness for human habitation and the tolerable standard | 66 |
| 4.2 | Standards of repair used in house condition surveys | 67 |
| 4.3 | Poor housing conditions in the UK | 68 |
| 4.4 | Condensation, mould growth and dampness | 69 |
| 4.5 | Poor conditions by tenure and country (1991) | 73 |
| 4.6 | Mean repair costs by tenure and country (1991) | 74 |
| 4.7 | Poor conditions by dwelling age and country (1991) | 76 |
| 4.8 | Households in the worst conditions by income and tenure, England (1991) | 79 |
| 4.9 | Households in the worst conditions by type and tenure, England (1991) | 82 |
| 4.10 | Households in the worst conditions by ethnic origin and tenure, England (1991) | 84 |
| 4.11 | Resources for private sector renovation, England and Wales | 87 |
| 5.1 | The housing market in Denmark | 97 |
| 5.2 | Housing market indicators in Denmark (1990) | 99 |
| 5.3 | The 1982 Danish Urban Renewal Act (1990) | 111 |
| 6.1 | Population growth since 1950 | 116 |
| 6.2 | Development of the housing stock since 1970 | 119 |
| 6.3 | Occupied dwellings and inhabitants per room | 119 |
| 6.4 | Occupied dwellings with year of construction and renovation | 140 |

| 7.1 | Vienna housing stock: periods of construction | 143 |
|---|---|---|
| 7.2 | Vienna housing stock: technical standards | 143 |
| 8.1 | Housing market indicators, France (1992) | 159 |
| 8.2 | Dwellings by tenure and amenity level, France (1992) | 161 |
| 8.3 | Changes in housing tenure, all households (1984-92) | 161 |
| 8.4 | Amenities in principal residences (1990) | 162 |
| 8.5 | The flow of public subsidies | 168 |
| 8.6 | Number of recipients of personal housing allowance at 31 December 1991 | 171 |
| 8.7 | Distribution of investment in housing (1984-92) | 172 |
| 9.1 | Income distribution of households in decile groups (1991-93) | 177 |
| 9.2 | The development of dwelling stock according to tenure (1947-94) | 177 |
| 9.3 | Housing rehabilitation in the 1980s | 185 |
| 9.4 | Investments and subsidies in Dutch urban renewal in the 1980s | 189 |
| 9.5 | Total investments in the remaining urban renewal (1990-2005) and the relevant cost centres | 197 |
| A9.1 | Monthly housing costs and household incomes of tenants (DGI) with and without housing assistance (IHS) (1 January 1986, 1990 and 1993) | 201 |
| A9.2 | Monthly housing costs and household incomes of owner-occupiers, with and without mortgage (1 January 1986, 1990 and 1993) | 202 |
| 11.1 | The tolerable standard and the standard amenities | 231 |
| 12.1 | Assessment of the extent of urban renewal and housing rehabilitation problems after 1980 | 252 |
| 12.2 | Objectives of urban renewal and housing rehabilitation used in the countries | 255 |
| 12.3 | Characteristics of urban renewal strategies | 264 |

# Figures

| 1.1 | Framework for comparative studies of policies for urban renewal and housing rehabilitation | 3 |
|---|---|---|
| A3.1 | Capital formation in permanent housing (1980-91) | 62 |
| A3.2 | State budget deficit in Sweden (1974/75-1994/95) | 62 |
| A3.3 | Economic growth in Sweden (1975-93) | 63 |
| A3.4 | Unemployment in Sweden (1975-93) | 63 |

*List of tables and figures*

| | | |
|---|---|---|
| 4.1 | Unfit dwellings by tenure, UK (1991/93) | 72 |
| 4.2 | Unfit/BTS dwellings by age, UK (1991/93) | 75 |
| 4.3 | Unfit/BTS dwellings by age and type, UK (1991/93) | 77 |
| 4.4 | Public expenditure on housing renovation, England (1979-95) | 88 |
| 4.5 | Grants by type, England (1969-94) | 89 |
| 4.6 | Dwellings demolished or closed, Great Britain (1969-93) | 90 |
| 5.1 | Percentage of dwellings in older blocks of flats lacking amenities (1990) | 99 |
| 5.2 | Changes in number of dwellings in Denmark lacking amenities | 110 |
| 7.1 | Process of *Sockelsanierung* (overall rehabilitation of inhabited buildings) | 148 |
| 7.2 | Vienna Land Procurement and Urban Renewal Fund | 149 |
| 7.3 | Distribution of renewal responsibilities | 150 |
| 9.1 | Investments in urban renewal according to activities in the 1980s | 187 |
| 9.2 | Investments in urban renewal according to cost centres in the 1980s | 188 |
| 9.3 | Summary of evaluation of urban renewal activities | 190 |
| 12.1 | The historical development of urban renewal and housing rehabilitation in Western Europe | 243 |
| 12.2 | The share of dwellings built before 1945 in nine countries | 247 |
| 12.3 | The share of dwellings without a bathroom | 249 |

# List of acronyms

| | |
|---|---|
| AL | French housing allowance |
| ALF | French family housing assistance |
| ALS | French social assistance |
| ANAH | French National Agency for Housing Improvement |
| ANPE | French National Employment Agency |
| APL | French Personal Housing Aid |
| ASh | Austrian Shilling |
| BPA | Swedish National Building Association |
| BTS | 'below tolerable standard' |
| CBS | Dutch Central Bureau for Statistics |
| CDC | state bank in France which manages national and local community funds |
| CHAC | Central Housing Advisory Committee |
| CHF | Swiss Franc |
| CIV | French Interministerial Committee for Cities and Urban Social Development |
| CNRS | French National Centre for Scientific Research |
| DGl | Dutch Guilders |
| DKr | Danish Krona |
| DoE | UK Department of the Environment |
| ENHR | European Network for Housing Research |
| EU | European Union |
| FAS | French Social Action Funds |
| FAU | French Urban Facilities Fund |
| FF | French Franc |
| FNAH | French National Fund for Housing Improvement |
| GNP | gross national product |
| HAA | Scottish Housing Action Area |
| HEES | UK Home Energy Efficiency Scheme |
| HLM | *Habitation à loyers modéré* (social flat) |

| | |
|---|---|
| HMO | house in multiple occupation |
| HSB | Swedish Housing Association |
| ISR | Dutch Interim Balance Regulation |
| LO | Swedish Trade Union Confederation |
| MUVR | Dutch Memorandum on Urban and Village Renewal |
| NIHE | Northern Ireland Housing Executive |
| OECD | Organisation of Economic Cooperation and Development |
| OPAH | French Planned Projects in Housing Improvement |
| OTB | OTB Research Institute, Delft University |
| PAH | French home improvement grants |
| PALULOS | French home improvement grants |
| PST | French Special Social Programmes |
| SABO | Swedish National Association of Municipal Housing Companies |
| SAF | Swedish Employers' Federation |
| SAP | Swedish Social Democracy |
| SDD | Scottish Development Department |
| SHAC | Scottish Housing Advisory Committee |
| SKr | Swedish Krona |
| SOAB | SABO |
| SOU | White Papers from the Swedish government |
| TADB | French supplementary leasehold tax |
| UN | United Nations |
| UVRA | Dutch Urban and Village Renewal Act |
| WBSF | Vienna Land Procurement and Urban Renewal Fund |

ONE

# Introduction

*Hans Skifter Andersen*

Cities, housing areas and dwellings can be regarded as living creatures that deteriorate, while at the same time they grow, develop and change. Our physical surroundings have to be maintained and adapted to changes in needs and economic conditions. Sometimes, however, market processes of maintenance and renewal do not take place at a satisfactory speed and to a satisfactory extent. In this case, cities decline and housing becomes obsolete. Urban areas and buildings become sick and have to be treated and cured. Governments then often feel inclined to take action.

Most governments in Europe have found it necessary to subsidise and regulate the processes of urban renewal and housing rehabilitation. However, the grounds for public intervention have not been clearly formulated. Why has it not been possible through market processes, supplemented with housing benefits to people with low incomes, to produce a well-maintained and modern housing stock?

Many economists have pointed to government intervention, which has damaged the functioning of the housing market, as the main cause of inadequate maintenance activity. Experience and research from the United States, which has much less regulation, shows, however, that there are strong segregational forces in the housing market which create an accumulation of combined social, economic and physical problems in certain areas of cities. It can be argued that the same urban processes exist in Europe, but that they have in fact been prevented by better welfare systems and by European housing policy, such as large social housing sectors, housing benefits and regulations. As economic conditions, welfare systems and housing policies differ very much from country to country we can also expect problems of urban decay to be very different.

This book examines experiences with problems of urban decay and housing deterioration and looks at measures for solving such problems in different countries in the central and northern part of Western Europe. The main focus is on the older housing stock, while problems of decay in newer social housing estates are only described peripherally. Consequently the individual chapters in the book are mainly concerned with public policies directed towards physical problems in the housing market and less with the more socially-oriented programmes that have emerged in many countries in connection with problems in newer housing estates.

In many countries policies for housing rehabilitation are often intertwined with, and subjugated to, broader policies for urban development and renewal. In such cases these broader urban policies are, to some extent, included in the analysis.

There is no consistent terminology in the different countries to describe these different types of policies. In this book the term 'urban revitalisation' or 'restructuring' is used to denote broader urban policies where physical improvement of housing and the urban infrastructure is only one of several measures used to improve the economic competitiveness of and the conditions of living in a city.

By 'urban renewal' is understood a mostly physical intervention with the purpose of upgrading a whole neighbourhood, where renewal of housing is an important part but is supplemented with improvement of open spaces, traffic regulation and better urban infrastructure.

The last significant main term used is 'housing rehabilitation' which concerns the physical renovation of single properties that are not necessarily located in the same urban area.

We try to expose not only the instruments used by governments for rehabilitation of worn-down buildings and urban areas but also preventative measures that slow down urban decay and housing deterioration.

The main source for the analysis given in this book is the European Network for Housing Research (ENHR), which has formed a special working group on urban renewal and housing rehabilitation. Some of the contributors have also participated in work on this subject in the UN Economic Commission of Europe.

### The framework for comparison of countries

As a basis for the description of each country, a general framework has been developed in the ENHR group, illustrated in Figure 1.1.

Figure 1.1: **Framework for comparative studies of policies for urban renewal and housing rehabilitation**

```
                    ┌─────────────────┐
                    │ General societal│
                    │   conditions    │
                    └─────────────────┘
                             ↓
         Urban renewal problems and policies

  ┌──────────┐  →  ┌─────────────┐  ←  ┌──────────┐
  │          │     │  Objectives │     │          │
  │ Problems │     └─────────────┘     │ Housing  │
  │    of    │           ↕             │  policy  │
  │  decay   │  →  ┌─────────────┐  ←  │          │
  │          │     │ Regulations │     │          │
  │          │     └─────────────┘     │          │
  │          │           ↕             │          │
  │          │  ↔  ┌─────────────┐  ←  │          │
  │          │     │   Effects   │     │          │
  └──────────┘     └─────────────┘     └──────────┘
```

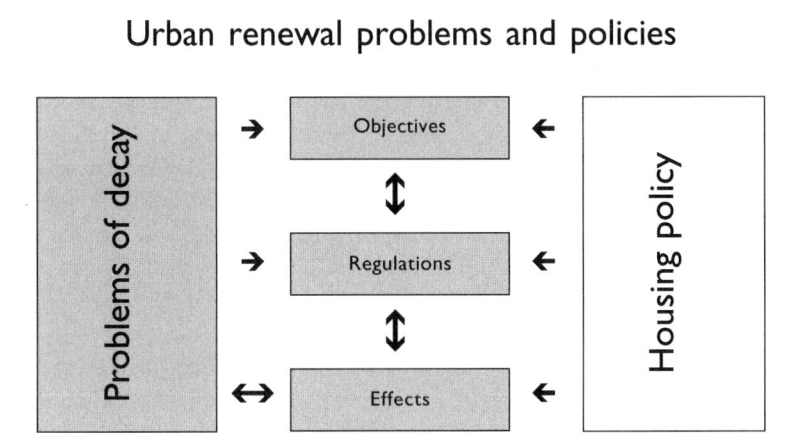

Note: The framework (Skifter Andersen and Hansen, 1994) was discussed in the ENHR Working Group on Urban Renewal and Housing Rehabilitation at a workshop in Bristol in 1994.

The primary purpose of this has been to make it possible to compare the countries in spite of great differences in the societal conditions, in problems of urban decay and in the kind of policies employed. It does not pretend to form a theory capable of explaining problems of decay and the use of policies for urban renewal, but it only ensured that important background information explaining differences between the countries was made available and that the contributors possessed a common understanding of the subject.

As shown in Figure 1.1 the contributors to the book were asked to cover the following subjects:

- general societal conditions for housing in their country;
- housing market conditions and housing policy;
- problems of urban decay and housing deterioration;
- political objectives for urban renewal and housing rehabilitation policies;
- types of public measures used in urban renewal and housing rehabilitation;
- experiences with the effects and efficiency of policies.

The authors were further asked to give a short description of the historic development of urban renewal policies in their country.

The national context for urban renewal and housing rehabilitation is laid down by an examination of some of the societal conditions of decisive importance for housing and urban development. Also, the housing policy and housing market conditions are described as a prerequisite for urban renewal and housing rehabilitation.

The description of urban renewal and housing rehabilitation policies and their effects are divided into four main areas. The first is a discussion of the specific problems of urban decay and deterioration of housing in the countries – the extent of obsolete housing, problems with failing maintenance in parts of the housing stock, and urban decay in the cities. In these descriptions it was thought important to identify the types of problems found in the country, the parts of the housing stock affected by failing maintenance or obsolescence, the population groups affected by the problems and the main causes of these problems.

The second is an analysis of special objectives which are important for working out urban renewal policies. Political objectives are sometimes expressed more or less clearly in official documents or in the political debate. Sometimes they are not expressed explicitly but can be deduced from the way programmes and regulations are formulated. The objectives can include the following:

- the problems that policies are trying to solve;
- what the consequences of the renewal should be (for example, preservation or demolition of buildings and districts);
- what the consequences should be for residents and for the housing market;

- which changes in the functioning of cities and housing areas should take place;
- how renewal processes should be organised, whether by public influence or that of the owners and tenants.

The third area is a description of the character of public regulation – subsidy systems, interventions in the housing market, use of special organisations, and so on. In the framework there are distinctions between three main types of public regulation aimed at increasing housing rehabilitation. The first is called regulation of tenure. In this case the authorities merely establish the general regulatory framework for the properties, their maintenance and improvement, with no direct involvement in the actual renovation work. This form of regulation is, for example, embodied in tax legislation, rent acts, rules relating to loans for improvements and rules relating to owner occupied flats. Any decisions to renovate properties are taken by the individual owner. Where government subsidies are involved these are normally given indirectly in the form of housing allowances or tax deductions.

The second type is called indirect regulation. Here the authorities try to make it attractive for owners to renovate their properties – usually by giving subsidies but also in the form of advice, improvement of open areas, and so on. Although the decision to renovate is taken by the owner, the authorities may demand a specific type of renovation in order to be eligible for a subsidy.

The third type is called direct regulation, where authorities may directly order renovation of a property. With this form of regulation the authorities – normally represented by local government – can compel the owner to renovate, having the following instruments at their disposal: expropriation, orders, restrictions on use, and pre-emptions. Direct regulation often features subsidies that make compulsory action acceptable to the owner. In this form of regulation it is normally the authorities who take the initiative for renovation.

In describing the different implementation programmes, the authors were also asked to discuss the local authorities' powers of control, the public costs, the administrative input required, the number of dwellings and areas covered and the possibility of targeted action by the local authorities, the extent of social considerations and residents' influence, and the nature of the renovation carried out.

The fourth area is a description of the impact of the whole system or of specific regulations. Earlier comparative studies of urban renewal systems have found that it is difficult to get hard data on the effects of a public effort to promote housing rehabilitation. The contributors were asked to examine the following questions:

- the number of dwellings which have been renewed with and without public support;

- the extent of the investment, calculated as the average costs of renewal measures with public support per dwelling or per square metre;

- the efficiency of the subsidies measured as the amount of private investments generated;

- discussion of the extent to which the programmes have been able to solve the essential renewal problems or whether they have been wasted on buildings which the owners should be able to renew by themselves;

- an evaluation of the bureaucratic costs of the systems;

- an evaluation of the economic and social consequences for owners and tenants;

- the importance of the programmes for the fulfilment of other objectives.

This framework has been used to make a comparison between the countries and, in broad outline has also been followed in describing each country. However, differences in national views on the best approach to the subject is sometimes evident.

## The structure of the book

The main body of the book consists of nine chapters which analyse each of the countries concerned, namely Sweden, the UK, Denmark, Norway, Switzerland, Austria, France and The Netherlands. Germany is also included in the comparison of countries. In the UK, different parts of the country have a great deal of autonomy in policy making, on a par with a national level in other countries, and also have their own public administration. This is especially the case in Scotland, even before the introduction of its own parliament due in 1999/2000, where an urban renewal policy has been formulated which differs in some ways from the rest of the UK. Because of this, the book contains a separate chapter on urban renewal policies in Scotland.

The chapters are written by a mixture of contributors from academic and policy-making backgrounds, as is reflected in the differences in style and approach which have emerged. Academic contributors have, as might be expected, set their analysis in the context of references to previous work and broader debates. Policy makers have, in contrast, made little or no references to other work or drawn on untranslated and unpublished work from their own countries which a UK or international readership will find inaccessible. The editors would be pleased to try to facilitate access to further material if any reader should require this.

The final chapter (Chapter Twelve) is concerned with a general overview of the countries and an analysis of the lessons to be learnt from their experiences. Background data on the countries is presented in Chapter Two, including a brief outline of the different housing markets and housing policies and the social and economic conditions of importance to them. There is then a cross-national comparison of the problems and policies of housing renewal and an attempt to explain the differences between the countries. Some conclusions are also reached on the main differences between the strategies chosen.

## Conclusions in brief

The individual chapters appear to show that public policies for housing rehabilitation and urban renewal in European countries come from totally different worlds and that every country has its own way of understanding this policy area and its associated problems. One of the main causes is that involves a great number of different but connected problems and activities. Consequently, the approach taken – and thus the starting-point for programmes and legislation in each case – has been quite different.

Just as the solutions differ, it also appears that the problems of urban decay are very different from country to country. In each case, urban problems occur in a specific geographical, economic and political context. Thus the opportunities for dealing with them are often linked to the current public administration and policies and, in particular, to the general housing policy and characteristics of the housing market. Moreover, it is obvious that even if the nature of the urban problems is similar, divergent political priorities and objectives for urban renewal lead to quite policy solutions.

Some general trends have, however, been clear in most of the countries since the Second World War. In the first period until the start of the 1970s, slum clearance involving the demolition of old buildings and construction of new ones dominated in many countries. This was followed by urban renewal programmes more oriented towards the preservation of existing buildings and urban areas, making it possible for residents to stay after renewal. More general programmes of urban revitalisation and restructuring were also initiated. At the same time, programmes supporting rehabilitation of single properties located inside or across selected areas was started in many countries.

A new and unexpected field of urban renewal emerged in the 1980s in large postwar social housing estates, where increasing problems caused by technical defects and social unrest made it necessary for public authorities to intervene. In some countries this experience brought about change in the understanding of urban renewal from being a finite task to remove or renew old and obsolete housing to that of a continuous effort to solve problems of combined social and physical decay in vulnerable neighbourhoods. Moreover, it has in most countries produced a stronger consciousness that social processes are not the root of urban decay. The interplay between physical and social agendas in relation to renewal has, to an increasing extent, come into focus resulting in new policies which try to develop an integrated approach.

The general trend for housing policy in Europe – in other words, a withdrawal of the state from housing – has also penetrated this area in recent years. Even if the countries have had different starting-points, some of the same general trends are evident. Among the older stock, renewal of housing in whole districts is becoming less important as most of the heaviest slums from last century are being removed. Instead, priority has shifted towards programs directed at single properties. On the other hand renewal of whole districts of postwar social housing has become increasingly common. This mirrors the general change in the focus of housing rehabilitation policies from that directed at physical problems in older housing to social problems in postwar housing. Parallel with this development, direct intervention is decreasing while indirect intervention is becoming the dominant approach with the older housing stock. In most countries this is accompanied by a move towards decentralisation which gives local authorities more influence. There is also a trend towards am emphasis on preventative policies, with regulation of tenure being changed to make it more attractive for private individuals to invest in renewal. Programmes are becoming increasingly selective and means tests more common. The level of subsidies has reduced and it has become more difficult for residents to stay in their dwellings after renewal.

It is quite clear from our study that the problems of housing deterioration vary considerably from country to country. After the Second World War most of the obsolete and deteriorated housing was found in certain older areas in the cities with blocks of flats or rowhouses built before 1920. In some countries most of these problems have been removed. This is especially the case for Sweden and Switzerland and, to some extent in West Germany and Norway. In other countries like Austria, Denmark, the UK, France and The Netherlands, these problems are still very important. Housing built in the period from 1920 to 1950 has also come into focus in recent years because of maintenance problems or the need for improvement.

The most problematic sector in most countries has been private rented housing. This is partly due to some of the fundamental problems with this type of tenure – in other words, the potential conflict between landlords and residents – but also to the inexpedient rent control systems that deprive landlords of the incentive for maintenance and housing rehabilitation.

The problems in social housing vary. In most of the countries a combination of building problems and social problems, caused by a high concentration of people with low incomes, has caused difficulties in high-rise estates of the 1960s and 1970s. Problems in older social housing estates depend on the administrative rules in the housing associations for collection of money saved for maintenance. The conditions for housing rehabilitation in owner-occupied housing used to be quite good. However, in areas with declining demand – such as fringe areas of cities – or with a high concentration of low-income residents, some deterioration has also been observed. Problems with lack of maintenance in owner-occupied flats have also been observed in some countries – especially in the common parts of the buildings outside the individual dwellings. Sometimes residents do not have sufficient incentive to keep the building in good repair or lack a sufficiently good organisation to take care of it.

We have found that five main factors characterise and explain different national policies:

- basic view of problems to solve: city/district/property level;
- function of policies: preventing or curing decay;
- kind of public intervention: direct or indirect intervention, or regulation of tenures;
- role of local authorities: centralised/decentralised control;
- general/selective programmes: priority to certain geographical areas, buildings, tenures, building works or residents (means test).

Important to the design of policies and instruments chosen is the weight attached to broader urban problems compared to housing deterioration and obsolesence in general. Another factor is to what extent these housing problems are seen as part of general social and economic processes in geographically defined urban areas. The main question is whether it is possible to renew single buildings alone, or whether there are combined physical, social and economic problems in urban areas which have to be solved simultaneously. In the latter case, urban renewal projects have to comprise whole urban areas, and housing rehabilitation has to include physical, social and economic measures covering a whole neighbourhood.

In principle the function of chosen policies can be either preventative or curative. Preventative policies aim at supporting market conditions for the maintenance, improvement and renewal of dwellings and urban structures, made by private individuals. Curative policies, on the other hand, come into play when preventative policies have failed, and when problematic deterioration and obsolesence have occurred in certain dwellings and urban areas. It is striking that preventative policies are seldom seen as an integral part of policies against housing deterioration. The actual regulations and programmes implemented have mostly been aimed at curing specific problems of housing deterioration and obsolescence, while few policies exist with the direct purpose of facilitating maintenance and improvement activities.

The first two factors listed to a great extent determine the third – that of the type of intervention chosen to promote housing rehabilitation: whether it should be direct with a strong public involvement; indirect and thus putting more weight on supporting private initiative; or whether it should involve regulation of tenure to facilitate market processes. Direct intervention is mostly used in connection with plans for the renewal of whole urban areas where acute problems have to be cured and it is important to make a simultaneous improvement of the whole area. There are also examples, however, where direct intervention is used against single properties. Indirect regulation is mostly used to promote renewal of single properties. It could have a preventative purpose, but it is mostly used to cure problems which have become or are going to become urgent even if they are not always the most heavy and complex problems of decay. Regulation of tenure has primarily a preventative purpose.

The fourth point refers to the role of local authorities. In some countries both influence on and responsibility for urban renewal has been decentralised to the local level. This implies that local governments have a greater freedom to decide which dwellings should be renewed and how to do it. However, it also often means that they have to pay a greater share of the cost by themselves.

In other countries there is a strong control from central governments. Detailed rules on how to carry out the rehabilitation have been determined by the state and local authorities are much more dependent on central funds.

Finally programmes might be general – meaning that they cover a greater share of dwellings in the stock – or more selective. In the latter case programmes might be restricted to certain geographical areas, or to certain parts of the housing stock, for example, buildings of a certain type or age. There might also be separate programmes for different tenures taking into account the different economic conditions. Furthermore, programmes might specify what type of building works should be supported or give different types of support for different works. Finally, programmes might be selective in terms of the people supported. In many countries there are means tests for housing rehabilitation subsidies so that only people with low incomes or specific needs get support.

Based on these criteria we have identified three different main strategies followed by the countries we have studied.

The first we have called a *strategy of general housing improvement*. This has been followed by Austria, Denmark and Sweden, a typical feature for these countries being that their housing rehabilitation programmes are very general. Nearly all dwellings are covered by a few general programmes involving almost no means testing. There are only few centrally fixed rules about which housing should be renewed and how it should be done. In Denmark and Austria this is mostly left in the hands of local governments; in Sweden in the hands of property owners. In Austria and

Denmark, area renewal has played an important role and the programmes have involved a form of direct intervention. In Sweden the programme is indirect and only includes single properties; such programs are also found in Denmark and Austria. In all three countries tenants' rights and security are important, with rules for participation by tenants and high subsidies to guarantee their stay in the dwellings after renewal.

It is significant that the strategies chosen by these three countries are very much in line with their general housing policy. To a great extent housing is seen as a public good and the state is extensively involved. Denmark and Austria still have severe problems with pre-1920s housing in certain parts of their cities, leading to a continuing need for area renewal and direct intervention. In contrast, Sweden had already solved most of these problems in the early 1970s, partly because they were not so great, but also because of extensive slum clearance activity after the war. The countries all have strong local government and a tradition of decentralised power.

In all three countries the level of subsidies have been quite high. In spite of this, Denmark and Austria have some of the largest housing rehabilitation problems among the countries we compared. One reason for this is that market conditions for private investment – especially in private rented housing – have not been so good. In the case of Denmark, this is partly due to unfavourable general economic conditions for investment in private rental housing, but also that the regulation of tenure has been governed by other objectives than that of encouraging housing rehabilitation. In a way you could say that the preventative policies have been inadequate. Another reason is that direct regulation and high security for residents results in high expenditure per dwelling. This means that only a limited number of dwellings can be renewed within a limited public budget.

The second main strategy we have called a *strategy of strong central priorities*. In particular, the UK and France have followed this strategy, but we have also placed Norway and The Netherlands in this group even though they have some similarities with the first group.

All these countries have developed complex systems with many different programmes directed towards selected parts of the housing stock. In the UK, France and Norway there has been a widespread use of means tests. In each case, local governments are involved in programmes for urban restructuring or area renewal, but their influence is – except for Norway – restricted by detailed rules fixed by the state. The dominant form is indirect intervention, even in area renewal schemes, though in Norway some direct intervention has also been found. Tenants' rights are less important than in the first group of countries but have some attention in the UK and Norway. In earlier years, The Netherlands had emphasised the right of residents to stay in their dwellings but this has been less important recently.

An important explanation of the chosen strategy in some of these countries is that there is a tradition of weak local government and strong central control. This is especially the case in France, the UK and to some extent The Netherlands, although there has been a more recent trend towards decentralisation. In Norway and the UK in particular, housing is regarded as a private rather than a public good. As a consequence the countries have tried to limit public involvement in housing rehabilitation to the most urgent problems and reserve subsidies for people with low incomes.

Some of these countries — especially the UK and France — still have major physical problems in their older housing stock. In Norway and the UK, this is due to the fact that relatively small resources have been used and the level of subsidies has been fairly low. In The Netherlands and parts of the French rental market a strict rent control has hampered private investment in rehabilitation. The use of indirect intervention, selective programmes and means testing has in some way made subsidies more efficient in these countries and this in turn has generated more private investments. Moreover the amount of money spent per dwelling is lower.

However, the disadvantage of a centralised system, especially in France and the UK, has been that it has been more difficult for local authorities to make a coherent renewal of urban areas. It has also been difficult on the local level to give priority to these dwellings and areas most in need, thus making the programmes less effective. The other problem in these countries has been that low-income groups have often been expelled from renewed housing as a consequence of a low level of subsidies.

The last of the three main strategies we have called a *strategy of limited public involvement*. Especially in Switzerland, but also in West Germany, the programmes have been quite limited. Indirect intervention is the rule except for the German urban renewal programme which is more aimed at urban restructuring than at housing rehabilitation. Local authorities have great influence. Germany is the only country with special tax subsidies (depreciations) supporting all investments in housing, thus reducing the need for indirect regulation. There are no special rights for tenants and the amount of direct subsidy is small.

In both countries the state traditionally has a more reduced role than in the other countries we examined, and there is a more liberal housing policy. It is important to note, however, that the general conditions for housing investment in both countries have been very favourable because of low interest rates. This has made it easier for market forces to work and reduced the need for public support of housing. As a result housing rehabilitation problems have been reduced and most of the older stock has been renewed without subsidy. This has been supported by liberal rent control systems. The disadvantage is that poor people have often been expelled from renewed housing, and that housing in general – especially in Switzerland – has become quite expensive.

From this comparison of countries in terms of their urban renewal and housing rehabilitation policies, it can be seen that in spite of different starting-points concerning urbanisation and housing stock there is a connection between the general housing and welfare policies and their application. Countries such as Denmark and Sweden, where housing to some extent is seen as a public good, tend to consider housing rehabilitation in the same light, attaching much importance to the security and rights of sitting residents. In other countries like the UK, Norway and France, where housing policy is mostly regarded as a means of solving housing problems for the poorer sections of the population, housing rehabilitation policies are much more oriented towards selected dwellings and people for which renewal on market terms is not expected to take place without public support. The tendency for complex and selective programmes and strong government control in these countries is also a result of a tradition of weaker influence on the part of local government.

It is also apparent that problems of urban decay and housing deterioration and thus the need for public support for renewal are very much influenced by general conditions in the housing market. In countries like Germany and Switzerland, general economic policies have ensured a low interest rate which has favoured housing investment. Especially in Germany, general tax incentives have been given to support investments in rental housing against a background of liberal regulation of the private rented sector. Together these conditions have made extensive housing renewal possible with or without small government subsidies. In other countries, high interest rates and inexpedient regulation of tenure have to a different degree impeded renewal on market conditions and thus increased the need for public involvement.

The different strategies applied have all had their advantages and disadvantages. The strategy of general housing renewal is very oriented towards the financial security and rights of residents. Moreover the strategy makes it easy to achieve a coherent renewal programme in selected urban areas in order to solve related social, economic and physical problems. The negative consequences are that high subsidies are needed with a smaller share of private investments. With limited public budgets this means that it takes a long time to get through renewal of the poorest part of the housing stock and some of these countries therefore still have considerable renewal needs.

The strategy of central priorities results in a more efficient use of subsidies where only the neediest are supported and more private capital is involved. The price is that it is much more difficult to make coherent renewal of selected urban areas and thus to prevent self-reinforcing slum processes in vulnerable neighbourhoods. Moreover tenants are often not financially secured – an even greater problem with the strategy of limited public involvement which in general has resulted in high rents in Germany and Switzerland. A more detailed comparison of these strategies appears in Chapter Twelve.

TWO

# The national context for housing renewal
*Hans Skifter Andersen*

## Differences in the general societal conditions for housing

Differences in housing and urban renewal problems and policies between the countries are to some extent caused by different geographical, economic and political conditions in the countries. In the following chapter we discuss the importance of differences in population density and scarcity of land, the structure of the public sector, the general economic development and economic policy.

An overview of the conditions in the countries is given in Table 2.1 which looks at the extent of population density and scarcity of land, the position of local governments, population increase, economic growth, economic stability, unemployment, inflation and interest rate, and public expenditure measured as the sum of public consumption, subsidies and income transfers.

Differences in population density and scarcity of land for building purposes have a crucial importance for urban problems. Some of the countries – such as Denmark, Sweden and parts of the UK and France – have a relatively low population density and few problems with providing new sites for urban development. Other countries – such as Norway, Switzerland and Austria – also have a relatively low population density, but at the same time they are mountainous countries and often lack land that is suitable for building purposes. Finally, there are countries with a high population density covering the whole country (The Netherlands) or part of it (Germany, France, the UK), especially in the large urban areas around the big cities.

In countries with high population density or scarcity of land, land prices are high and land use plays a more important role in urban policies. There is a greater need of public assistance and regulation of the processes promoting change and reorganisation of the urban infrastructure and this point of view has had great importance for the elaboration of urban renewal policies. In the countries where land use was of minor importance in the whole or in most of the country, housing rehabilitation has been the main approach to urban renewal, while instruments for public regulation of urban regeneration have mostly been placed in other contexts, as in the general legislation for physical planning.

Differences between the countries concerning the structure of the public sector affects the organisation of urban renewal. The size of municipalities and the political and economic strength of local governments determine to what extent urban renewal can be carried out by the local governments themselves without support or interference from the central or regional governments. The political tradition for central or decentral solutions affects the way urban renewal legislation is worked out and the role local authorities can play in it.

Countries like Sweden, Denmark and Norway have municipalities of a reasonable size which also traditionally have quite high political and economic independence with their own income tax base. Germany, Switzerland and Austria have many small municipalities, but the local governments in the cities have had both power and to some extent

Table 2.1: Characteristics of the nine countries

|  | A | CH | D | DK | F | GB | N | NL | S |
|---|---|---|---|---|---|---|---|---|---|
| Scarcity of land | • | • | • |  | (•) | (•) | • | • |  |
| Strong local governments | • | • | (•) | • |  |  | • |  | • |
| Population increase | • | • |  |  | • |  |  | (•) |  |
| Economic growth 1973-92 (%) | 58 | 25 | 55 | 41 | 53 | 35 | 84 | 46 | 34 |
| Economic instability | • |  |  | • |  |  | • | • | • |
| Unemployment 1992 (%) | 5 | 5 | 6 | 12 | 12 | 10 | 6 | 8 | 8 |
| Inflation, average 1974-93 | 4.3 | 3.4 | 3.4 | 6.5 | 7.1 | 9.0 | 7.2 | 3.9 | 7.8 |
| Interest rate, average 1974-93 | 8.3 | 5.0 | 7.7 | 14.0 | 11.1 | 11.6 | 10.4 | 8.5 | 7.7 |
| Real interest rate, average | 3.9 | 1.5 | 4.2 | 7.0 | 3.7 | 2.4 | 2.9 | 4.5 | 2.9 |
| Public expenditure (% of GNP) | 41 | 23 | 37 | 47 | 43 | 43 | 45 | 44 | 51 |

Source: Statistical Office of Denmark

economic resources to tackle urban renewal on their own. In France, The Netherlands and the UK there has not been a tradition of such an extensive decentralisation of political power to local governments, and these have been more dependent on powers and resources given to them through special legislation and government programmes.

In some of the countries, authorities on the regional level have an extensive influence on housing and urban renewal. This is the case in Germany, Austria and Switzerland. Sometimes regional and local authorities in these countries are the same, which give these local governments especially high independence. This concerns cities like Berlin, Hamburg, Bremen and Vienna. To some extent the different parts of the UK have their own legal systems and public administrations – Scotland, for instance, has its own urban renewal system.

The housing sector is very sensitive to demographic changes that influence housing demand. The general trend in most of the countries is that the population is declining and growing older. France experienced some population increase during the 1980s – among other things caused by immigration from Africa – and West Germany a great influx of people from the former GDR and from Eastern Europe. This has increased the housing shortage in France and Germany.

Compared to the rest of the world the economic level – measured as gross national product or alike – is approximately the same in the countries compared. According to this measure Switzerland and Norway are the most affluent countries. The UK and The Netherlands are found at the other end of the scale, but the differences are so small that they can only have minor importance for housing and urban renewal.

As housing prices and investments are very sensitive to changes in the economy, differences in the fluctuations in economic activity between the countries have had greater importance. The general trend in the European Union has been that the economies slowed down after the first oil crisis in 1973. A new growth period came from 1975 to 1979 followed by a period of long decline until 1984. The new boom period lasted until 1990 when the economies again slowed down. In recent years a new period of growth has begun.

Norway seems to be the only country unaffected by these changes, experiencing a steady economic growth in the whole period (except for a period of stagnation from 1987 to 1991 where real estate prices plunged). In Sweden, Switzerland, the UK and to some extent Denmark, economic growth has been below the average since 1973 (except for a few years) and the ups and downs have been pronounced with severe consequences for the housing market. The economic development has been more steady in The Netherlands, France, Germany and Austria and economic growth has (except for The Netherlands) been above the European average.

Unemployment has often been a good argument for public support for urban renewal and housing rehabilitation. Unemployment is high in Denmark, the UK and France (10-12% in 1992), medium in Sweden and The Netherlands (8%) and relatively low in Switzerland, Austria, Germany and Norway (4-6%).

A fact which is seldom acknowledged in international studies of housing is that the general economic policy in the countries plays a major role in determining the conditions of housing and housing policy (see the discussion in Skifter Andersen and Munk, 1994). In some countries (Germany, Switzerland, The Netherlands and Austria) it has been a primary objective for economic policy to limit inflation. In these countries the average inflation in the last 20 years has been 3-4% per year. In the other countries there has been a considerably higher inflation, between 6½-9% – especially in the period before the last half of the 1980s. The consequence of this high inflation was often a higher interest rate and thus greater capital costs which had a considerable impact on the housing market. In Norway and Sweden the interest rate has been kept down artificially by the use of credit rationing. Denmark, in particular, has allowed quite a high interest rate, which has necessitated a high level of subsidies to make new housing affordable and to keep up housing production.

General tax policies also have a marked influence on housing. In Germany it has been a part of general economic policy not to allow tax deductions on interests on loans for housing. Instead, it is possible in both owner-occupied and rented housing to make depreciations on invested capital. This means an important difference between Germany and the other countries concerning the economic conditions for investments in housing rehabilitation, especially in rented housing. There are no automatic tax advantages in the other countries for rented housing but there are, to various extents, tax deductions for owner-occupiers (see Papa, 1992).

The general political opinion in the countries on the role of the state, which also affects housing policy, is illustrated in Table 2.1 by the total public expenses for public consumption, subsidies and income transfers.

The Nordic countries have the highest public expenses. The next group with medium expenses consists of The Netherlands, UK, France and Austria. The least extensive role of the state in the economy is found in Germany, and especially in Switzerland.

## Differences in housing market and housing policy

Policies for urban renewal and housing rehabilitation are partly contained in the general housing policy of a country and the instruments used for housing rehabilitation are often an extension of measures generally used in the housing policy. Moreover, housing policy has a thorough impact on the problems of housing deterioration and on the ability of owners and landlords to keep up and renovate their buildings.

Housing policy in a country is an answer to housing problems shaped by the special conditions of housing in each country, but it is also marked by differences in political objectives from country to country. The differences in societal conditions and housing policy have led to marked differences in the composition of the housing market in the nine countries (see Table 2.2).

In five countries (Austria, Denmark, France, the UK and Norway) owner-occupied housing constitutes more than half of the dwellings. The UK has close to 70%. Switzerland has the lowest share followed by Germany, The Netherlands and Sweden.

Social rented housing, owned by non-profit housing associations or

Table 2.2: Composition of the housing market in nine countries (%)

|  | A | CH | D | DK | F | GB | N | NL | S |
|---|---|---|---|---|---|---|---|---|---|
| Owner-occupied | 55 | 31 | 38 | 55 | 54 | 68 | 59 | 48 | 42 |
| Private rented | 25 | 64 | 43 | 20 | 23 | 7 | 15 | 12 | 19 |
| Social rented* | 20 | 5 | 15 | 20 | 17 | 25 | 10 | 40 | 22 |
| Other tenures† |  |  | 4 | 5 | 6 |  | 16 |  | 17 |
| All dwellings | 100 | 100 | 100 | 100 | 100 | 100 | 100 | 100 | 100 |

Notes: * Owned by non-profit housing associations or local authorities.
† inclusive cooperatives.

Source: Boverket (1993); Hansen and Skifter Andersen (1993)

by local authorities, has a dominant role in The Netherlands. In most of the countries, social housing constitutes between 15% and 25%, with the UK and Sweden in the upper end and France in the lower. In Germany there is also provisional social housing owned by private owners or landlords, which constitute about 5% of the housing stock, so the total share of dwellings rented or owned under social conditions are 20%. In recent years, many of these dwellings have, however, been transformed to the private rented sector. In Switzerland and Norway there are only a few social rented dwellings; in Norway instead cooperative dwellings are found with some kind of social conditions. Cooperatives also play a major role in Sweden.

The private rented sector is dominant in two countries: Germany and more particularly, Switzerland. It is of least importance in the UK and The Netherlands. In most countries it constitutes between 15 and 25% – the most in Austria and France, least in Norway, Sweden and Denmark.

The composition of the housing market in the countries to some extent mirrors the role attached to housing policy. In some of the countries housing is seen fundamentally as a private good provided by the market while in other countries housing is partly regarded as a common good where it has been an important task for the state to provide reasonable

**Table 2.3: Characterisation of housing policy in nine countries**

|  | A | CH | D | DK | F | GB | N | NL | S |
|---|---|---|---|---|---|---|---|---|---|
| Providing capital | S | M | M | M | S | M | S | S-M | S |
| Level of subsidies | High | Low | Low | High | Med | High | Low | High | High |
| Form of subsidy | S | S(D) | (S)T | T | S,T | D,T | S,T | S(T) | S,T |
| Public housing provision | La | Sma | Med | La | Med | La | Sma | VLa | La |
| Rent control | S | L | L | S | S-M | L | M | S | S |

Notes: *Providing capital*: M=only market institutions; S=state or state-controlled institutions have dominant role.
*Dominant form of subsidy*: S=supply subsidies; D=demand subsidies, housing allowances; T=indirect subsidies through tax deductions or depreciations.
*Public housing provision*: VLa=very large social housing sector; La=large; Med=medium sized; Sma=small.
Rent control: S=strong; M=medium; L=light.

Sources: Papa (1992); Wiktorin (1993); Hansen and Skifter Andersen (1993)

housing for all citizens. In these countries there has been a more extensive government involvement in the financing, production and distribution of housing, which also has been transferred to housing rehabilitation.

In the following we will look at three ingredients of housing and housing policy which demonstrate the degree of state involvement in housing: housing finance (ways of providing capital for housing and the extent and composition of subsidies), provision of housing through public institutions, and regulation of the housing market (especially rent control).

Table 2.3 illustrates the extent of public involvement in housing in the nine countries. Compared with Table 2.1 it can be seen that there is some connection between countries having high public expenditures and countries with high involvement in housing. The countries are now examined in an order of decreasing government involvement.

Sweden has had the most extensive housing policy. The government has controlled housing finance through special financial institutions and there has been a high level of subsidies mostly directed towards the supply of housing, combined with quite a large social housing sector and a reasonably strong rent control in private rented housing.

Austria has had a similar high degree of state involvement in new housing. As strong rent regulations have hampered private investments practically all new housing – except from a very small 'luxury' segment – has been highly subsidised since the Second World War. State subsidies are given to all sorts of social housing as well as for private owned single family housing. Funds are generated from earmarked parts of the general income taxes and from the state taxes. Subsidies are generally high, but vary between the nine *Bundes Länder* (provinces) of Austria.

Denmark does not have state control of housing finance, but capital has been provided through special institutions under government supervision – a system which is now abolished. The level of subsidies is very high, but the major part of subsidies are given through tax deductions for owner-occupied housing. The high level of subsidies has to some extent been necessitated by the high interest rate in Denmark. Rent control is very restrictive.

In The Netherlands a great share of capital for housing was earlier provided by the government, but the system has now been abolished. The state plays a dominant role in housing provision and the level of subsidies is high, mostly given for the supply side of housing. Rent control is quite restrictive.

France provides some of the capital for rented housing through government controlled financial institutions. The subsidies are at a medium level, dominated by tax deductions and supply subsidies. There is a very strong rent control in part of the private rented sector (300,000 dwellings built before 1948) and a more modest one in the rest of the market.

Norway has had a tradition of credit rationing and has, as a part of this economic policy, established a state bank for housing finance which used to dominate the market for housing finance. Beside this strong instrument the Norwegian government has, however, conducted quite a liberal housing policy based on support for owner-occupied housing and cooperatives as a kind of social housing. A stronger rent control is only found in two cities and a weaker one in a few others.

The UK has, especially in the 1980s, gained a reputation of conducting a very liberal housing policy. The level of subsidies is, however, quite high, but the major share is given as housing allowances and tax deductions. Despite the privatisation of council housing this sector still remains one of the biggest social housing sectors in Europe.

It has been a pronounced objective of German housing policy to limit the role of the state and to support owner-occupied housing. The German housing sector has been favoured by a low interest rate which is one of the reasons why subsidies are limited. Another reason is the absence of tax deductions on interests for housing loans. The dominant form of subsidies is tax depreciations on invested capital which is applicable in both rented and owner-occupied dwellings. Direct supply subsidies also play an important role. Germany has had quite a high public involvement in the provision of housing – part of it as provisional privately-owned rented or owner-occupied housing. Rent control is weak.

Finally, it is easy to judge Switzerland to have the most market-oriented housing policy in Europe – helped by a very low interest rate.

THREE

# National strategies for urban renewal and housing rehabilitation: the case of Sweden

Ingemar Elander

## Introduction

As in many other countries, postwar urban and housing renewal in Sweden started as a policy of inner-city slum clearance and demolition. This had the effect of displacing many of the original occupants, who were mostly living in privately owned multi-dwelling houses. However, two thirds of all multi-dwelling housing in Sweden was built *after* the Second World War, and rehabilitation policies have mainly been targeted at this part of the housing stock, which is commonly owned by municipal housing companies. By the end of the 1970s, partially as a result of citizen protests, and partially inspired by the European urban renewal campaign, rehabilitation took a softer direction, and was at the same time spreading to newer estates. The term 'slum clearance' (*sanering*) that had so far been used in the official language was then exchanged for the terms 'housing renewal' and 'urban renewal' (*bostadsförnyelse* and *stadsförnyelse*), still later on to be replaced by the term 'careful rehabilitation' (*varsam ombyggnad*).

With the implementation of the so-called Million Dwellings Programme 1965-74, housing shortage in Sweden had essentially disappeared and investments in the housing sector were reoriented towards rebuilding, renewal and extension. This switch was partly an effect of physical and social needs for renewal, but it was also driven by demands from the construction industry and the construction workers' union to sustain the level of investments obtained in the housing sector. Thus, in 1983 the Swedish parliament approved a 10-year housing renewal programme, and two years later the proportion of restoration in the housing sector exceeded

50% of total construction output. However, in the face of a threatened housing shortage, the subsidies for renewal were diminished in late 1988, the aim being to concentrate resources on new construction. The result of this was a slowdown in the implementation of the renewal programme and new construction again took the larger part of total output in the housing sector (see Table A3.1 and Figure A3.1 in the Appendix to this chapter).

In the mid-1980s a number of measures were initiated to make the public housing stock more attractive to present and future residents. The formal influence of tenants on the management of public housing was strengthened through legislation, and a number of socially targeted loans and grants were offered for rehabilitation. A broad set of policy goals were formulated that were not, however, always compatible with each other. The most obvious tension, for example, was that renewal should be sensitive to the needs of both buildings and residents, as well as fostering extensive use of capital and manpower.

Thus, policies for urban housing regeneration in Sweden have always been formulated and implemented within various programmes, partly supporting, partly contradicting each other, and giving the municipalities and the landlords fairly wide scope for discretionary action. While the need for renewal in the older public housing stock (built before 1965) has been mainly physical, the estates built later have been rehabilitated for social reasons. Despite the latter concern, during the 1980s rehabilitation was strongly criticised as being too comprehensive and insensitive towards the buildings as well as the residents. This is a reflection of the fact that public support for regeneration has in practice been very pliable to state financial needs. Not surprisingly, at the moment when the housing sector at large, including regeneration, is subordinated to the overriding goal of desubsidisation, the slogans of the day are 'rehabilitation with care', 'rehabilitation in bits and pieces', 'rehabilitation on terms of the residents', and 'rehabilitation governed by management', all within the framework of the concept of 'sustainability'. However, in the face of an unprecedented drop in the construction of new housing[1], echoes of a view regarding state-subsidised, massive renewal as a vehicle of economic growth reappear, and in spring 1993 the parliament decided upon a revival of the 10-year programme, involving a number of state subsidies. The main motive for reintroducing a number of such subsidies was to stimulate employment in the building sector, but the effect in this respect seems to have been modest (*Planera, Bygga, Bo* [Journal of the National Board of Housing, Building and Planning], 1995, no 3, p 9).

The aim of this chapter is to review the postwar national strategies for urban renewal and housing rehabilitation in Sweden. Firstly, a context is given, highlighting some important economic and political determinants of urban renewal and housing rehabilitation, that is, those that are commonly, in the literature, connected with the Swedish welfare state model. Secondly, the official policy objectives of multi-family housing renewal are reviewed, including brief descriptions of two main renewal policy programmes. Finally, some issues concerning the evaluation of the results and effects of these policies are discussed, including a review of policy objectives, instruments and outcomes.

## Context

### The Swedish welfare state model

The development of the Swedish welfare state gave birth to the widely-held image of a society successfully finding a middle way between unfettered capitalism and state-controlled communism. There were at least four elements that were commonly regarded as crucial when it came to defining this 'Swedish model' (Johansson, 1994).

Firstly, the Swedish model was based on an 'historical compromise' between the labour movement and its counterparts among conservatives and the employers' organisations. This means that in the 1930s the labour movement officially recognised the rights of private property ownership in exchange for an assurance that the property owners and their allies among the political parties would remain loyal to democratic procedure and accept social-democratic reforms. More specifically, this has been described as a compromise in the labour market between LO (the Swedish Trade Union Confederation) and SAF (the Swedish Employers' Federation), formed in the famous Sâltsjöbaden Agreement in 1938. This Agreement created a spirit of compromise and a willingness to solve different labour market conflicts by negotiation. LO and SAF proved that they could deal with these conflicts without any intervention by the cabinet or parliament.

Secondly, the Swedish model refers to the fact that Swedish politics has been dominated by consensus, that is, there has been a low level of conflict regarding the procedures for decision making, and conflicts have been minimised during the legislative process. In addition, the party system has been very stable. Thus, between 1922 and 1988 only five parties were represented in parliament: Conservatives, Liberals, Agrarian/ Centre Party, Social Democrats and Communists. What has been exceptional is the fact that in this consensual political climate, Swedish Social Democracy (SAP) has occupied a position of parliamentary power 'without parallel in the history of modern democracy'. Measuring political power in terms of government leadership, majority rule and number of votes, no other party has even approached success in all these aspects. "Thus the SAP has occupied a unique position not only in Sweden, not only in comparison with other labour parties, but also within the framework of international parliamentary democracy" (Therborn, 1992, pp 1-3).

Thirdly, the public sector has been large. Rapidly expanding during the 1960s and 1970s, it was developed according to the following principles: (i) the welfare state principle, meaning that central and local government provided people with social welfare reforms in education, health and elderly care, child allowances, housing, etc; (ii) a universalistic strategy, meaning that social reforms were largely general, and not dependent on level of income – thus, everyone, rich as well as poor, enjoyed the same basic security net; (iii) a local welfare state, meaning that the main part of the welfare state was the responsibility of municipalities and county councils.

Fourthly, the Swedish model incorporated an active labour market policy, including the principle of 'solidaristic' wage policy, which meant that the enterprises that could not pay wages at the agreed level were thrown out of the market, while enterprises with a high productivity made even larger profits and thus could expand so as to create new jobs. To support this policy, a number of selective means were invented aiming at re-education, relief-work projects, relocation of workforce, local job creation, and so on. The state responsibility in this full employment strategy was to manage the business cycle by allowing the release of capital during slumps and withholding capital as the economy became overheated.

Finally, one should keep in mind one thing that was crucial to the success of the Swedish model: "the single most important factor that accounts for Swedish welfare" is the fact that, once industrialism got started, economic growth in Sweden was more rapid and more constant than in all other countries except for Japan. When in the 1970s the

Swedish economy began to perform less well, the model began to crumble" (Lewin, 1994, p 70).

## The Swedish model on the wane

At the beginning of the 1990s, Sweden was still a country with increasing production, marginal unemployment and a comparatively high degree of equality between classes, social groups and the sexes. The situation has since become radically different. Production was on the decline, unemployment had risen to an unprecedented 8%, and growing social and regional inequalities were reported by researchers and the media. Neoliberal economists and non-socialist politicians commonly described Sweden as a nation on the verge of bankruptcy, symbolised by a state budget deficit, amounting to one third of total state expenditure (see Figures A3.2, A3.3 and A3.4 in the Appendix to this chapter).

Looking at *the liberal diagnosis* of the Swedish crisis, four themes stand out clearly: (i) high taxes have eroded people's willingness to work; (ii) policies geared towards equality have been an impediment to people further educating themselves, thus causing a loss of human capital; (iii) too many regulations have caused inefficient policy sectors; and (iv) the public sector has grown out of proportion[2]. The main political strategy chosen by the non-socialist government should be seen against this background: for example, giving high priority to such goals as lowering the general tax level, increasing the span between people with low and high incomes, deregulating housing and other policy sectors, and becoming more restrictive as regards grants to the municipalities. The rationale behind these and related measures undertaken by the former government was a firm conviction that dismantling the state in favour of the market would turn the wheels in the direction of economic recovery. According to this analysis, the crisis is mainly a product of Social Democratic postwar misgoverning and thus can only be resolved by liberal economic policy.

Representing a contrary view, economic historian Lennart Schön and his colleagues at the University of Lund have carried out longitudinal studies of the Swedish economy ever since the end of the 1970s (Schön, 1993). Drawing upon detailed investigations of the development of Swedish industry at large, as well as its components, Schön concludes that this development is parallel to the international economic crises that have occurred about every 40 years ever since the 1840s. Thus, in the 1890s, the 1930s and the 1970s structural crises hit the international economy hard, with repercussions for Sweden. Very crudely, these crises were the effects of sharpened competition on the world market. To overcome them it was necessary to invent new 'development blocks' that could trigger a new phase of economic growth. From the 1850s onwards such a block was created around the building of railways. The following 40-year cycles gave birth to similar blocks around the electric engine and the combustion engine industries (the 1890s), the car industry (the 1930s) and the electronics industry (the 1970s). In the processes of creating these blocks the role of the state and other institutions (banks, financial corporations, etc) was crucial.

Following from this analysis is a conclusion radically different from that of the liberal economists and politicians:

> **Today, again there is great need for real integration built upon accelerated renewal and modernisation of lagging parts. In the transformation process of history, where large investments have been made simultaneously in several areas, the giving of credits has not been hampered by the current supply of savings. Now as before there is need for strong and competent financial and political institutions which can bridge imbalances in time and space – until savings within 5-10 years will tend to grow faster than investments, when income and competition will increase within a wider Europe and a wider world economy.** (Schön, 1993, p 17)

Returning to the four elements used to define the Swedish model, one firstly has to conclude that there is not much of a compromise left in Swedish politics in the 1990s (Johansson, 1994; see also Lewin, 1994). Thus, citizens' distrust of parties and politicians has grown considerably during the last 20 years, the level of dissent in parliamentary committees has risen substantially ever since the mid-1980s, and the parliament has experienced three new actors: the Christian Democrats (1985-), the Green Party (1988-91; 1994-) and New Democracy (1991-94). The public sector is facing great financial problems, which has triggered debates about the costs of welfare state programmes, the possibilities of municipalities going bankrupt, and both feasible and unfeasible solutions to these financial problems. Commonly these solutions have meant reorientation from the state to the market, including the selling of nationalised companies, the adoption of market-oriented criteria of operation and the deregulation of state rules. Finally, the unprecedented growth of unemployment during the first years of the 1990s may be regarded as the definitive nail in the coffin of the Swedish model.

## Swedish housing in a comparative perspective

According to a number of international housing experts, Swedish housing policy has been among the best in the world at producing good quality dwellings for everyone. Following the Swedish Constitution adopted in 1974, all citizens have a right to a dwelling, just as they have a right to employment and education. The official housing policy developed by the Social Democrats after the war requires policy to be generic and not biased in favour of any one tenure or group. In practice, this means that even low-income, working-class and unemployed people have been able to rent dwellings satisfying decent requirements of size, quality and costs. Thus, public as well as private rented housing in Sweden has been able to meet broadly defined social needs and demands. To give just a few crude measures: every individual in Sweden has a dwelling area averaging 47 square metres; only 1% of the dwellings are non-modern; only 2% of the households are overcrowded. Of course, however, these statistical measures hide a more complex reality. To take one example, one- and two-person households generally have much more space per person than most families with children at home (Hedman, 1992, p 87).

Although the image of success has by now been painted by so many observers that there is little reason to deny its validity (see the references given in Lundqvist et al, 1990; see also Ambrose, 1992; Cars and Hårsman, 1991; Duncan and Barlow, 1991), there is no general agreement about the underlying mechanisms. Among the factors behind the success have been mentioned Social Democratic welfare policy (Headey, 1978), the absence of notable land speculation (Dickens et al, 1985) and the unitary rental system (Kemeny, 1993). In addition to these views, Nesslein (1988) argues that general economic growth and rising living standards of the population at large are more important factors than any specific policy measures. All of these approaches may touch upon factors that are crucial when it comes to understanding the mechanisms behind housing success, although it remains to construct a comprehensive explanation.

However, in Sweden all the factors just mentioned are either no longer at hand or called into question. For three years (1991-94) the Social Democrats were out of power in favour of a government that wanted to roll back the welfare state, the instruments of municipal land control have been weakened, the State Housing Loans system has been taken away, rent-setting has become more or less subject to the market and the Swedish economy is stagnating, although since 1995 signs of recovery have been emerging. No wonder then that it is rather the other side of the success coin that has increasingly attracted attention. Thus according to a view shared by all political parties, the cost of housing has become a burden on today's taxpayers to an extent that has become unacceptable (see Elander [1994a] for analyses of the currently planned, and partly implemented, restructuring of the Swedish housing system).

Before using housing as an example of the waning Swedish welfare model, however, one should not forget the strong interest basis traditionally backing up this policy sector. Historically there has been a close linkage between the Social Democratic Party and several important interest organisations in the sector. Often referred to as the 'Popular Movements Coalition' (Gustavsson, 1980), this group comprises the national housing cooperatives (HSB and Svenska Riksbyggen), the Construction Workers Union, the union-owned Swedish National Building Association (BPA) and, last but not least, the National Federation of Tenants' Associations and the National Association of Municipal Housing Companies (SABO). The last two have been key instruments for the 'corporatist implementation' of social housing policy (see Lundqvist, 1988; Adams, 1987, p 131; Heclo and Madsen, 1987, especially 220ff). The close relationship between these organisations and the Social Democratic governments has favoured state intervention to put a check on speculation in land and housing property. On the other hand, government has guaranteed a market for the large building companies through the state-housing loan system and through allowances to those occupants not able to pay for their housing out of their own income.

On the other side of the housing policy arena there has been a non-socialist coalition including the builders, the private landlords and the homeowners. Thus both labour and capital have been represented politically by a number of interest groups leaning towards the Social Democratic and the non-socialist bloc respectively. According to the Swedish model, conflicts between the two blocs are normally resolved within a framework of mutual trust. Thus, even if construction workers and builders oppose each other in wage negotiations they normally go hand in hand demanding more capital for the housing and building sector. In a broad sense one could speak of a tripartite arrangement between the two interest blocs and a Social Democratic state. One should note that the local authorities and their housing companies have a strong position in the state corner of this triangle. In addition, taking the crucial role of housing professionals into account, one may analyse the network of actors in housing policy in terms of a housing policy community (Elander, 1995).

So what about the electoral support for 'social' housing as conceived by the Social Democratic party?[3] Before 1975 social housing was supported by a large majority of electoral groups, represented by the Social Democrats, the Communists, the Centre Party and the Liberals. In the 1990s, however, social housing is called into question not only by the latter two, but even by the Social Democrats, with a trend towards favouring desubsidisation and a market rental system (Elander and Strömberg, 1992, pp 114-15; Elander, 1994a). Nevertheless, the success of Swedish housing policy, and the strong interest basis of this policy, still constitutes a stronghold against the radical privatisation urged by the Conservative Party (*Moderata Samlingspartiet*), the leading party within the non-socialist coalition government.

Indeed, the goals of the non-socialist government as regards housing were formulated clearly enough by Birgit Friggebo, the Liberal Party's Minister of Housing until 1 December 1991, when the Ministry was partitioned:

> **Partitioning the Ministry of Housing is one step towards the abandonment of the special treatment given to the housing market. The liquidation is one stage in the development of the market economy also as regards housing.**
> (*Planera, Bygga, Bo*, 1991, no 6, pp 10-11)

Returning to power after the September 1994 parliamentary election, the Social Democrats reappointed a Minister of Housing and Energy who was not, however, given a separate department. Instead the issues of housing were incorporated into the Ministry of Business Affairs (*näringsdepartementet*). In practice, the road towards desubsidisation and deregulation of housing that was initiated by the former Social Democratic government, and followed by the non-socialist government, continued, although at a slower pace than that urged by the Liberal Party and the Conservative Party.

## Urban renewal and housing rehabilitation strategies

Reviewing urban renewal policies in a number of European countries, Priemus and Metselaar (1992) found that many governments define the concept of urban renewal very broadly. Thus they include not only the classic fields of physical planning, housing policy and building policy, but increasingly other fields of policy, in the process making urban renewal policy something like 'an endless task'. This observation gains further strength from the fact that urban renewal policy above all is municipal policy with all its local variations. Sweden was one of the countries that the two authors found to be lacking an explicit, comprehensive urban renewal policy. Bearing this in mind it is nevertheless possible to sketch government's approach to urban renewal during the postwar period. This will be done in three steps: firstly by looking at the politics of inner-city slum clearance; secondly by highlighting the policies aimed at renewing the public housing, multi-family estates; and thirdly by offering a brief review of the government's housing and urban renewal approach in the 1990s.

### The politics of inner-city slum clearance

The Social Housing Commission, set up as early as 1933, came to have great importance with regard to postwar housing policy. According to its terms of reference, the principal task was to propose measures for dealing with the large stock of slum housing in densely built-up areas. The Commission's first report was also in line with this although by that time the government had got other housing policy problems that it thought were more urgent. The priority was to settle 'the population crisis' by stimulating the production of new, more spacious family dwellings. Consequently almost every housing reform initiated by the Commission during the latter part of the 1930s was geared to the construction of new dwellings. During the war, however, housing production sharply declined at the same time as population figures rose, thanks to exceptional birth rates.

Thus, when the Social Housing Commission presented its two principal reports at the end of the 1940s, the problem of slum housing in densely populated areas would hardly have seemed less acute than 15 years before. To the overcrowding and the bad sanitary conditions there had in fact been added a rapid increase in the volume of traffic requiring a widening of the streets. *Soon the old to the dust shall topple* (*Störtas skall det gamla snart i gruset*) is the apt title of Gärd Folkesdotter's book about the Labour Movement's view of slum clearance just after the war (Folkesdotter, 1981). Quoting from the Swedish version of 'The Internationale', the English translation might be: 'the earth shall rise on new foundations'.

To topple the old proved to be easier said than done, however. In contrast to the radical proposals of the first report (SOU, 1945:63), which were directed towards new production, the proposals of the slum clearance report (SOU, 1947:26) did not lead to any government bill. This was in spite of the fact that the latter proposals were by no means as revolutionary as had been anticipated in the postwar programme of the Labour Movement, or as had been desired by such important referral bodies (*remissorgan*) as the National Housing Loan Office, the Swedish Agency for Administrative Development, the Tenants' National Association and the National Association of Swedish Architects (Hatje, 1978, pp 8-11). In the light of the prevailing housing shortage, and in order to bridge the housing gap, it seemed much easier and much more efficient to build new than to demolish the old.

The reforms resulting from the Social Housing Commission's proposals on new production stimulated in the first instance municipal housing construction in integrated areas on the outskirts of population centres. The idea was that in the future, first and foremost, municipal foundations and companies should build rental flats on municipally owned land in accordance with the plans laid down by the council and its committees. However, there was a broad variation in the way things turned out from one municipality to another – stemming not least from large differences in the land ownership structure. It became apparent that a really powerful expansion of municipal construction presupposed that the municipality owned the 'raw' – that is, undeveloped – land (see for example, Johansson and Ödmann, 1974; Strömberg, 1984).

Nor is it likely that the problem of private ownership of land could have seemed less acute to those who wanted to wipe out inner-city slums. Here there were many separate owners, at the same time as radical solutions called for large coordinated projects. Not that the problem was a new one; it had attracted attention as long ago as the beginning of the century, and over the years the municipalities had been equipped with increasingly sharpened legal weapons to combat the private interests represented by individual landlords. Yet only by way of exception was the municipal planning monopoly, the site leasehold right or the pre-emption and strengthened expropriation legislation brought into play to enforce coordinated, municipally planned slum clearance. In 1969 the National Board of Housing (*bostadsstyrelsen*) was forced to make the following acknowledgement:

> Experience has shown, however, that the municipalities cannot purposefully direct housing development merely with the aid of the planning monopoly. Whether there exists any real possibility of such direction depends to a large extent on the land ownership situation. (Author's translation from Bostadsstyrelsen, 1969, p 12)

With a few interesting exceptions – for example, in the town of Örebro, where the local politicians made use of their housing foundation to extensively reshape the inner city as early as the 1950s – the local authorities left redevelopment to private interests. The great wave of redevelopment was not set in motion until private building contractors, acting in accordance with the rules of the market, had succeeded in buying up sufficiently large and attractive areas for commercially profitable projects to be carried out (Egerö, 1979; Folkesdotter and Vidén, 1974; Strömberg, 1984). As summarised by Vidén:

> Right up to and into the 1970s housing renewal in the case of the old buildings in the centre of the town involved as a rule what was at the time referred to as total slum clearance (*totalsanering*), in other words, demolition and new construction – usually with increased exploitation and often for purposes not concerned with housing. Ordinary older housing was not regarded as having much value by those pursuing the renewal, nor was it regarded as preservable from the techno-economic point of view. This was especially true in the case of the old low wooden type of building, and in many town centres the majority of such buildings were obliterated during the period in question. Taller stone buildings were largely turned into office buildings and thereby escaped the threat of being demolished when real-estate economics dictated the time was ripe for slum-clearance. (Author's translation from Vidén, 1994, pp 38-9)

During the 1970s, however, *sanering* as a concept was wiped out altogether in favour of the terms 'urban renewal' and 'housing renewal', and, soon enough, 'careful rehabilitation' (*varsam ombyggnad*) became the slogan of the day. In 1973 the Housing Renovation Act was put into force, including the first specific renovation norms (*ombyggnadsnormer*). Now it even became permissible to deviate from the 'lowest acceptable standard' concept that had so far set the norms for housing renovation (Vidén, 1994, pp 38-9).

## Renewal of public housing estates

By the mid-1970s, home ownership was expanding rapidly in Western Europe,

> promoted and aided by governments of many political complexions. While large-scale urban renewal continued, increasing emphasis was placed on the rehabilitation of private housing (and some older social housing) rather than clearance and replacement. (Harloe, 1994, p 45)

The political support for social housing eroded and some sections of this tenure tended to become residual housing for a marginalised population. In some areas physical deterioration of the stock and social conflict were rapidly increasing.

In Sweden, with the implementation of the so-called Million Dwellings Programme 1965-74, the "near perennial problem of a housing shortage essentially had disappeared" (Heclo and Madsen, 1987, p 217) and investments in the housing sector were reoriented towards rebuilding, renewal and extension. In 1985 the latter kind of investments exceeded the former (Table A3.1 and Figure A3.1 in the Appendix to this chapter). The bulk of the housing stock built before 1961 was privately owned and often in obvious need of renewal for purely physical reasons. On the other hand, the greater part of the public housing stock was built after 1961, but was in many cases in need of rehabilitation anyway. This was partly because of rather considerable wear and tear in conjunction with the effects of having been somewhat hurriedly built during a period of rapid urbanisation. More important was perhaps the political and social need for rehabilitation of public housing areas. Many of these areas seemed to run the risk of becoming resorts for immigrants and people with low incomes and social problems (Lundqvist, 1988).

The political support for social rented housing was increasingly called into question by the non-socialist parties, and even by some Social

Democrats. However, the official standpoint taken by the Social Democratic Party was to defend social rented housing from privatisation, and the 1980s witnessed an optimistic strategy to improve its quality. Attempts by municipal housing companies to sell off part of their stocks were promptly stifled by new legislation enforced by the Social Democrat and Communist majority in parliament. Diversification of the housing stock, decentralisation of management, increasing the influence of tenants and ambitious renewal programmes were among the elements of this strategy (Elander, 1991). To a certain extent this strategy was successful, although in the long run residualisation will almost inevitably put its mark on many of the public housing estates (Öresjö, 1994).

In 1983 the Swedish parliament approved a 10-year Housing Improvement Programme based on the following principles and goals:

- everyone has a right to modern, well-equipped housing;
- everyone has a right to sufficiently maintained housing;
- improved accessibility to flats for the disabled;
- intensified energy conservation coordinated with other housing improvements;
- more equal and more integrated housing;
- more efficient use of construction capacity.

The first two items are just an echo of the concept of housing as a social right included in the Swedish Constitution. The second item also postulates the need for maintenance, while the third and the fourth earmark this need in two respects, that is, with regard to disabled people and energy conservation. The fifth item brings the social dimension explicitly into renewal, while the sixth item highlights production and employment. Indeed, it is as if everyone would get their slice of the cake, as is often the case at the level of policy formulation.

Although initially only houses over 30 years old were included, the programme was soon extended to cover the younger housing stock as well. To stimulate public, private and cooperative landlords, very favourable loans were offered. These were targeted at periodically required maintenance measures in the common parts of the buildings and specific problems caused by rot, mould, dampness, corrosion, radon and other defects that affect health and safety, as well as more comprehensive rehabilitation. Generally speaking, the more comprehensive the measures, the more favourable were the available subsidies and loans (Carlén and Cars, 1991, p 134; Vidén, 1994, p 46).

Although goals, ambitions and measures varied much among municipalities, it is possible to point out some common features in many of the projects that were implemented under the Housing Improvement Programme. Thus, new management policies were developed, including a broader service responsibility on the part of the landlords as well as a tougher stance towards disruptive households; schools, day care facilities and other public services were improved in many areas; repair of leaking roofs, and of rotting window frames, improvements in thermal and noise insulation, and other technical improvements, were also carried out. The technical improvements to the buildings took the greater part of the rehabilitation costs, while social and management measures were relatively inexpensive, as were outdoor improvement measures (Carlén and Cars, 1991, p 134-5).

The reasons for renewal varied a lot from one area to another. In the older housing areas there were usually technical and functional needs to be met, while in the younger areas the high cost of management, due to unlet dwellings, social disorder and a great need for social upgrading and maintenance, was the strongest motivating force for renewal. As aptly summarised by the Swedish architect and researcher Sonja Vidén on the basis of a study of 16 renewal projects carried out in the 1980s:

> The *housing areas built in the 1940s–1950s and older* were socially steady, important social networks had been built up in them, and they had many environmental qualities, in the buildings and outdoors, appreciated by people living there – all severely threatened by a conventional extensive renovation. Still, a real and growing need for renewal existed. The time had come for several expensive and extensive measures to be taken, such as new plumbing, improvement of electrical installations, renovation and sometimes better insulation of facades, roofs, etc. Many dwellings, especially in the oldest areas, were in need of renovation, and at least in the longer term there was also a need for adaption to new living patterns, other, more varied types of household etc., and to new demands – for instance better accessibility for old and disabled persons.

On the other hand, in *the younger areas, built during the Million Homes Programme*, the direct or indirect reasons for renewal were social instability and environmental shortcomings, in the common parts of the buildings as well as the outdoor spaces. Those shortcomings were combined with a great need for maintenance and repairs of structures in bad shape: facades, flat roofs, windows, balconies, etc. The distribution of dwelling sizes was often too narrow, and not even in those young areas was accessibility for the disabled achieved to any greater extent (Vidén, 1993, pp 81-2).

Sometimes the contradiction between needs and proposed measures became appalling:

> The oldest housing area, and the only privately owned one (Lindholmen, 1870-1890) was completely non-modern and would have been abolished were it not for the engagement and support from the researchers involved. The project was characterized by strong tenant participation, in planning and in practical work. (Vidén, 1993, p 83)

However, in the face of a threatened housing shortage the generous loans and interest subsidies for renewal suddenly deteriorated in late 1988. The aim of this policy switch was to concentrate resources on new construction. Consequently there was an immediate slowdown in the implementation of the renewal programme and an increase in new construction (see Table A3.1 and Figure A3.1 in the Appendix to this chapter). Whether the rapid switch was devastating to long-term planning and implementation of housing rehabilitation, as argued by some critics, may be disputed. Indeed, the slowdown was welcomed by many experts, arguing that rehabilitation had become too comprehensive and insensitive in respect both of the buildings and of the residents. As summarised by one of the critics:

> Although this was not the intention of the rules, practice showed that the easy way to get projects through the authority's application process, to get the biggest subsidies, and to reach the highest increases of rent, was to go for extensive renovation. Limited actions adjusted to the needs

of the present tenants, the actual buildings, or neighbourhoods, could cause delays and give poor financial return. (Vidén, 1993, p 83)

Another critic summarised the experience of the Housing Improvement Programme after its first five or six years in five points:

1. the users are still inferior;
2. utility, defined in measurable units, is given the highest priority, while beauty, comfort etc, are secondary – these values are not included in the use value concept;
3. on interpreting loan and building rules secure alternatives are given the highest priority – a little too much is regarded as better than too little;
4. the consequences for buildings and the environment have been mainly negative in the case of estates built in the 1940s and the 1950s – these areas often had very fine qualities;
5. social problems are often treated as if they can be handled by technical means. (Troedson, 1989)

Thus, the 10-year Housing Improvement Programme of the 1980s included a broad set of policy goals that were only more or less compatible with each other (see Schéele et al, 1990). Renewal should be careful in respect of the buildings and their residents and at the same time foster extensive use of capital and manpower. The initiative for implementing this programme was left to the landlords, dependent on the regional boards of housing for financial support and on the municipal housing committees for building control. This was well in accordance with the general Swedish model of housing, giving a fairly large degree of discretion to the owners of the dwellings, albeit within a general legal and financial framework.

In 1985, two years after the inauguration of the 10-year Housing Improvement Programme, the Ministry of Housing established a special delegation concerned with services for tenants, or more exactly to make it possible for elderly, sick and disabled people to live on their own, outside hospitals and other public institutions. During the period 1985-90 this delegation was given SKr100 million to foster the development of coordinated services to enable the members of these groups to live on their own. Although this was only a small fraction of the amount of money offered to the landlords as loans and subsidies for rehabilitation according to the 10-year programme, it gave an opportunity for landlords and municipalities to apply for money to support projects designed to coordinate services and to mobilise tenants, associations and relatives for the achievement of a richer everyday life and greater sense of community on the estates. Subsidies were given to 105 local projects in more than 70 municipalities. The programme was officially declared finished in 1994 and has now been integrated into the ordinary governmental administration. With no special funds at their disposal, the National Board of Housing, Building and Planning, cooperating with the National Board of Health and Welfare, will thus continue fostering coordinated services for the tenants, through education, information, research and other forms of knowledge accumulation and distribution (*Samordnad boendeservice*, no 3 [Newsletter published jointly by the National Board of Housing, Building and Planning, and the National Board of Health and Welfare], 1994).

The official goals behind the programme for Coordinated Housing Services can be summarised in three main points: (i) to develop the renewal of housing in a way geared to giving tenants the opportunity of staying on and with special consideration for various people's needs of nursing, care, support and service in their housing environment; (ii) to coordinate the intentions of different parties and categories regarding, and instruments for, nursing/care/support; and (iii) to try out different forms of influence for the consumers. Taken literally, this meant that no policy should be executed without prior investigation of people's needs and without input by the users, especially those who were disabled. One could even say that the authorities themselves adopted a grassroots perspective as a basis for their renewal policy. An ambitious evaluation programme was linked to the implementation of the area improvement programme, the results of which have been published in several reports and newsletters. Some of the results of these are presented in the concluding section of this chapter.

The housing renewal goals as defined by the central government are reflected at the municipal level either through national programmes like the two exemplified above, or through locally defined priorities. Thus, in a study of three large municipalities it was found that a number of physical, financial, organisational, social and ecological goals were intertwined in various local policy documents. Most common were the physical goals, while the ecological ones had the lowest priority (Rehn, 1990). However, the ecological goals have become much more prominent during the 1990s, as is aptly illustrated by the municipal activities around the local Agendas 21 (see Khakée et al, 1995).

## Housing and urban renewal in the 1990s

The late 1980s seemed to offer confirmation of the advantages of a softer approach both to housing renewal and to urban renewal in a wider sense. Experiences gained from the rehabilitation of large public housing estates and from the large-scale renewal of inner cities argued in favour of small-scale redevelopment that was more sensitive to the needs and demands of the residents. In terms of quantity, the housing needs of the population were largely met, and there was a growing competition among landlords to get all their dwellings let out. This was also well in line with an increasing market orientation of Swedish society at large. Thus, careful rehabilitation became a seller's argument.

In addition, the fact that environmentalism invaded the national and the local policy agendas gave further strength to the softer approach. Careful rehabilitation and sustainable development were demands that seemed to go hand in hand. Researchers and experts with experience from several research and development projects argued that the demand for careful rehabilitation derived from "social purposes, the interest in preservation and the need to reduce costs". According to them, careful rehabilitation was "a method, a way of approaching a task, which is always applicable when something is to be done to an existing building". They continued:

> Carefulness is a question of ascertaining what prior conditions and qualities exist, and of respecting and utilising them to the maximum possible extent when goals and needs are to be met. Careful rehabilitation is in other words a question of accomplishing the maximum utility and comfort with the minimum of intervention and disturbance. This means that the rehabilitation must be based on an overall view of what one starts from – the building, the

neighbourhood and the residents – and of what one wishes to achieve – restored and new functions. (Blomberg et al, 1985, p 45; see further Table A3.4 in the Appendix to this chapter)

Thus, the concept of careful rehabilitation took a prominent position on the housing policy agenda at a time when investment in housing seemed to have reached its peak, when economic growth in Sweden was waning, and when desubsidisation of housing became a goal common to the Social Democrats and the non-socialist parties. It was incorporated into building legislation and became a guideline when distributing state loans for rehabilitation. However, it is a matter of dispute to what extent careful rehabilitation really is a characteristic of renewal in practice. 'My home is my castle. Rehabilitation with rehousing causes hard feelings' is a telling headline of an article published by a Swedish daily. Interviews with researchers display criticism echoing that put forward by many researchers during the 1980s (*Dagens Nyheter*, 13 November 1995).

Considering the current problems facing the Swedish economy, one should not be astonished to find, in parallel with the pleas for careful rehabilitation and sustainable development, a number of spectacular projects like the Swedish–Danish Öresund bridge and the Dennis Highway Project in Stockholm[4]. Expressing a national strategy to boost Swedish economic growth in the current crisis, these two and other infrastructural projects obviously do not satisfy the demands raised by most environmentalists, and the final outcome of these issues will have a great significance, both symbolically and in terms of tangible results. In other words, the overall picture of Swedish environmentalism is complicated, and despite the 'boostered' growth projects, one can also find many bold attempts at realising the visions of radical environmentalism, perfectly in line with the softer approach to urban renewal. Thus, sustainable urban development has become a commonplace in the set of policy goals given high priority by the political élites in Sweden as in other countries (Khakée et al, 1995).

The 1988 cutback in the interest subsidies aimed at renewal had almost caused a halt to the ambitious 10-year improvement programme decided upon in 1982. However, facing a drop in building investments and a drastic increase in unemployment among construction workers, measures to stimulate investments in renewal were again decided by the parliament. In presenting a list of state subsidies for maintenance, repair and rebuilding, the National Board of Housing, Building and Planning (*boverket*) in the autumn of 1993 announced that it is

> now exceptionally favourable to maintain, repair and rebuild dwellings and other buildings. Building costs are being pressed down, the interests are relatively low and there are state subsidies that could be used in order to improve the houses and create employment in the locality. This newsletter briefly describes the various subsides and where to get further information about them. (Author's translation from *Boverket Information* [Newsletter from the National Board of Housing, Building and Planning], 11 December 1993, pp 11-12)

The following list gives an idea of the subsidies that were available:

1. Interest subsidy for repair/maintenance of rented and co-op houses.
2. Subsidy according to the 1993 year rules for rebuilding multi-family houses.
3. Special rebuilding subsidy for dwellings occupied by elderly people.
4. Creating dwellings for various categories of disabled people.
5. Rebuilding of nursing homes, etc.
6. Rebuilding of dwellings which are considered of particular value from a cultural point of view.
7. Special subsidy for repair and maintenance of certain municipal estates (schools, day care centres, libraries, etc).
8. Subsidy for adjusting public meeting-places to meet the requirements of handicapped people.
9. Repair and rebuilding of public meeting-places.
10. Subsidy for artistic ornamentation on housing estates.
11. Subsidy for installing solar heating in dwellings and offices.
12. Subsidy for investments causing lower levels of radon in one/two-dwelling homes.
13. Tax reduction for job costs relating to repair and maintenance ('Repair

your house 1993-1994 and lower your tax', as per the title of a leaflet published by the National Board of Taxation [*riksskatteverket*]).

Although the chairman of the parliament's housing committee (*bostadsutskottet*) optimistically calculated that the programme would create 30,000 new jobs, the decision did not pass uncontested. One representative of the Conservative Party said that unemployment can never be solved by massive state subsidies, characterising the new programme as an expression of "rehabilitation hysteria" (*Från riksdag och department* [News from the parliament and the ministries], 1993, no 8). Indeed, the programme includes a number of subsidies, and during 1993/94 the regional units of the County Boards (*länsstyrelserna*) were extensively scanning potential targets for rehabilitation in housing and building. However, except for a few months in late 1993/early 1994, interest rates were frozen at too high a level to stimulate investments in housing rehabilitation on a broad scale, and the banks were much more reluctant to give loans than during the building boom in the late 1980s. In addition, taken one by one, each item was too small to attract any greater interest on the part of the landlords.

In spring 1994, the National Board of Labour Market (*arbetsmarknadsstyrelsen*) announced an unexploited budget surplus as of SKr4 billion. The parliament in consensus took a firm decision to earmark SKr1.5 billion of this surplus for repair and rehabilitation, not only of housing but also of public buildings. The initiative for this decision was taken jointly by the Left Party, New Democracy and the Social Democrats, but the National Board of Labour Market and the National Board of Housing, Building and Planning had also raised the issue as early as November 1993.

Further support for housing renewal was decided by the parliament in December 1994. Following the economic programme of the new Social Democratic government, subsidies amounting to SKr1.8 billion were then earmarked for general housing rehabilitation, improvement of the climate in dwellings damaged by damp and mould, and renovation of dwellings for elderly and handicapped people. The main motive for reintroducing a number of renewal subsidies at this precise moment was to stimulate employment in the building sector, but so far the effect in this respect seems to have been modest (*Planera, Bygga, Bo*, 1995, no 3, p 9). Thus, during the first quarter of 1994, only 1,700 dwellings began to be restored, as compared to 2,173 dwellings the first quarter of 1993 and

11,063 dwellings the corresponding quarter of 1992. On the other hand, as many as 275,000 dwellings in multi-dwelling buildings built before 1951 have not so far experienced any extensive improvement. Arguably, these dwellings are already or will soon be in great need of rehabilitation (*Planera, Bygga, Bo*, 1994, no 1).

## Objectives, instruments and outcomes

In view of the fact that, as already stated, the concept of urban renewal is commonly defined very broadly, this is something that also pertains to its evaluation. Thus, as in all kinds of evaluation studies, a number of questions should be considered right at the outset. Should research start from a top-down or a bottom-up perspective? Should it relate to stated goals or to theoretical, goal-independent criteria? Should it concentrate on process or on results? Should it be internal or external? Different schools of evaluation research give different answers to questions like these, and any type of study should at least give some basic arguments in favour of the chosen approach (see Elander and Schéele, 1989). This concluding section starts by briefly touching upon three methodological questions to be addressed when evaluating the effects and results of housing and urban renewal policies.

### Methodological considerations

Firstly, there are a lot of case studies upon which to reflect. However, the general given is that the wave of rehabilitation has included a number of different approaches, each of them characterised by more or less specific strategies and results as regards number and type of actors and interests involved, financial and other measures used, and consequences for all involved. Thus, one should be careful not to try to generalise from one or a few cases. The dilemma facing any attempt at comprehensive evaluation of housing rehabilitation can be illustrated by reference to a recently published thesis entitled *Residential relocation, urban renewal and the well-being of elderly people: Towards a realist approach* (Ekström, 1994).

Combining an extensive register study, involving a population consisting of 22,579 people over the age of 64, with participatory observation and in-depth interviews, Ekström found that: (i) the intrusion in people's homes caused by rehabilitation sometimes leads to severe health problems; (ii) because of the variations in implementation, and the various ways people react to the intrusion, no general conclusions can be drawn; (iii) it is possible, though, to explain why certain people suffer but not others – power and control are the crucial concepts for understanding this; (iv) strikingly, many rehabilitation projects are characterised by the fact that the residents have been forced into subordination by authorities and landlords, which also means that they have lost influence and respect.

A central postulate in the dissertation is that the development of knowledge in this area does not, in the first place, call for more quantitative data but for the elaboration of theory and for methodological reorientation. Owing to the dominance of empirical quantitative studies, our knowledge of the causal mechanisms which underlie observed correlations is severely limited, just as is our knowledge of how a complex of contextual circumstances affect the meaning of relocation. Thus, a wider lesson to be learnt from Ekström's study is that, when studying housing rehabilitation in any of its aspects, it is always important to scrutinise the differences in local implementation and be careful not to generalise from one case or group of cases that might be very divergent.

Secondly, any purpose, object or situation related to renewal may be evaluated from different perspectives (Elander and Schéele, 1989). Changes in the housing environment involve a range of aspects and interests. For instance, a physical change in the built environment has not merely architectural, functional and technical consequences but also economic, social and cultural ones. These are seen differently depending on whether one is young or old, man or woman, owner or tenant. The variety of aspects and interests is also reflected in the public organisation. If we limit ourselves to a local authority, it can, through its housing company, be both owner and administrator of housing while being at the same time, through the social welfare board and administration, an advocate for users' interests. On top of this, the authority must see that the public interests are served. Furthermore, the local authority, this time through the housing committee, has to weigh general interests against special interests. In addition, of course, housing and urban renewal could also be evaluated in terms of its relationship to macroeconomic growth and the state finances.

Thirdly, as we need to look at the renewal process from different perspectives certain methodological consequences will also follow. From a macroeconomic point of view, financial and other quantitative data are crucial, as is an analysis of official documents, when it comes to scanning the goals and outputs of national policies. Looking at the local implementation of renewal policies, one should try to map the policy networks, or implementation structures, through which policy is created. This should be done independently of any official version, thus involving knowledge gathered from residents, service workers, etc, in the neighbourhoods affected by renewal. Indeed, what is needed is a flexible use of various qualitative methods such as participant observation, spectator observation, in-depth interviewing and document analysis (Patton, 1984).

Keeping these considerations well in mind it is, of course, still possible to list a number of findings about objectives, instruments and outcomes that can be useful when it comes to the comprehensive evaluation of housing and urban renewal. Largely following the comparative framework stipulated by Hansen and Skifter Andersen in Chapter Five of this volume, let me briefly characterise the renewal programmes and the kind of public interventions that have been implemented in housing rehabilitation since the 1980s, the instruments that were used and the outcomes that could be observed.

## Objectives

- Renewal has been mainly area-based: in the 1950s and 1960s targeted at older inner-city blocks of houses; later on at younger, more or less peripheral multi-dwelling estates.

- Renewal has not been explicitly targeted at special groups of the population, although in practice it has sometimes resulted in gentrification (with regard to inner-city blocks), or 'turn-around' on parts of the more peripheral estates, mostly owned by the municipal housing companies (Vidén and Lundahl, 1992, p 186). Conversely, other estates have at the same time experienced a tendency towards residualisation, ie, qualitative deterioration and an increasing proportion of low-income, unemployed, disabled and elderly tenants in the public housing stock. Concentration of immigrants on certain estates has been shocking to many politicians, housing managers and researchers, and expressions such as 'ghettoisation' and 'Liverpoolisation', earlier unheard of in the Swedish debate, have entered the arena (Öresjö, 1994).

- Since the mid-1980s priority has often been given to renewal of multi-dwelling estates owned by municipal housing companies and facing a concentration of social problems.

- Originally, renewal was overwhelmingly physical in character, resulting in radical changes in the affected buildings and their environments, while in the 1980s a softer approach became more common, taking into account not only physical but also social and cultural aspects, and also giving the residents more of a say in the renewal process.
- Although some of the measures were earmarked for better energy use or accessibility (eg, installation of lifts), comprehensive renewal was favoured through comparatively more generous subsidies given to larger projects.
- Of course, the rising building costs, the high interest rate, and the generally worsened economic situation in Sweden are factors that have strongly contributed to cooling down the demand for investments in the building sector. Thus, recent government programmes to boost renewal initiatives are planted in a much harsher climate than similar programmes 10 years earlier.

## Instruments

- Carrot rather than stick has been used by the central government when it comes to stimulating housing rehabilitation, although loans and subsidies have been accompanied by quite detailed building norms and rules. However, the tendency has been to simplify the support system, offering fewer and more general kinds of loans and subsidies.
- Public support for renewal has been given mainly as direct subsidies to pay some of the costs, as subsidised loans and as information and advice. Although public subsidies for rehabilitation are still quite generous, they will gradually disappear as a result of the government's desubsidisation policy.
- The role of local authorities has been both to provide a general framework for renewal through plans and to give building permits according to rules laid down by the National Board of Housing, Building and Planning (*boverket*, earlier *planverket* and *bostadsstyrelsen*).
- Although requirements concerning the housing standard to be obtained after renewal have been quite high, the power of tenants to keep the

amount of measures within limits has gradually increased. However, through a recent change in legislation, landlords may now start renewing without prior approval by a tenants' association — the 'consultation certificate' (*hyresgästintyget*) has been taken away[5].

- In formal terms as well as in practice, coordination of various kinds of actors has been a precondition for rehabilitation to be implemented. Thus, private, cooperative and public landlords have commonly worked with local government professionals in specific rehabilitation projects that have also included local tenants' committees or groups of tenants organised on an ad hoc basis.

- Renewal of one- and two-dwelling homes has mostly been carried out by the owners themselves, often without state support. The amount of work put into such renewal is probably underestimated as a lot of it falls outside the official statistics.

- The amount of capital put into renewal of multi-dwelling buildings may often have been a little exaggerated as many landlords have probably redefined part of their maintenance as equal to renewal in order to be eligible for state support.

Compared to many other countries, Sweden has had a very comprehensive system of loans and subsidies. Thus more than 90% of all housing produced in Sweden from 1946 to 1985 involved state loans (Niva, 1989, p 112), and there have been very few cases of housing renewal that have not attained state support (Hansen and Skifter Andersen, 1993). Even the non-socialist government in power from September 1991 to October 1994 offered quite an impressive list of subsidy forms (see above), and this despite its firm intention to deregulate and desubsidise the housing market.

## Outcomes

In 1985, due to the renovation activities during the 1970s and early 1980s, only 5% of all dwellings in Sweden fell below a basic modern standard. For example, the number of dwellings lacking toilet, bath and central heating was marginal. Thus, the purely physical reasons for renewal during the 1980s and 1990s have been quite minor. On the other hand, the level of ambition in national and local policies has risen, as indicated by such goals as adaptation of flats for the disabled, installation of lifts, energy conservation, improvement of the climate in dwellings and minimisation of the degree of radon. In brief, common *physical outcomes* of restoration have been: fusion of smaller dwellings, increasing number of rooms per dwelling, installation of lifts, installation of district heating, exchange of equipment in kitchen and bathroom and installation of three-glass windows. Although it has for about 20 years been permissible to deviate from the concept 'lowest acceptable standard', in practice renovation has often followed the norms to be applied in new construction, thus causing physical change that has neither been necessary for technical reasons, nor in line with the demands of the residents (Blomberg et al, 1985, pp 34-5). To be honest, however, in the 1990s careful rehabilitation obviously takes a stronger position in the housing policy debate and sometimes also in practice than ever before during the postwar era, as illustrated by a number of rewards given to showpiece cases (*Planera, Bygga, Bo*, 1994, no 4, pp 26-8).

When it comes to evaluating the *social dimension* of housing renewal, the programme for Coordinated Housing Services mentioned above is a case in point. The programme was intensively scrutinised project by project even during its official lifetime from 1985 to 1990, and recently the National Board of Housing, Building and Planning (*boverket*) jointly with the National Board of Health and Welfare (*socialstyrelsen*) published their final evaluation in one main report and four sub-reports. To exemplify the kind of conclusions drawn by the authors, the following positive effects, pertaining to the organisation of work, are enumerated in a newsletter (*Samordnad boendeservice*, 1994, no 3): everyday life education (*vardagsutbildning*), community of interests (*intressegemenskap*), voluntary work (*frivilliga insatser*), joint use of premises (*lokalsamnyttjande*), coordination of personnel (*personalsamordning*), division of work (*arbetsfördelning*) and flexibility. Taken together, these have contributed to making it possible for elderly people to stay on in their present dwellings and environments. Negative items noted are high development costs, dependency on strong project leaders, investment costs, evaluation costs and loss of autonomy (as compared to rehabilitation carried out by the ordinary organisation). The newsletter concludes that coordination of actors and activities in the local community makes it possible to improve services, to increase the residents' sense of community and influence, and to improve social life through physical rehabilitation within an acceptable financial framework. One example highlighted to illustrate these conclusions is the improved opportunities for elderly people to stay on in their ordinary dwellings and neighbourhoods.

Of course, these conclusions taken from an official newsletter should not be taken entirely at face value. However, they undeniably illustrate the social character of the programme. Notably, the reports are planned to be used as a body of experience and a point of reference in future development work. Despite the high ambitions of this single programme, one should keep in mind, of course, that the social consequences of rehabilitation on a broader scale might be less encouraging, as illustrated by a growing number of marginalised or residualised estates that have been the targets of such programmes and projects (Öresjö, 1994).

As for the *political outcomes* of the housing rehabilitation programmes in Sweden in the 1980s and 1990s, they could be discussed within the framework of the concept 'policy network'. This concept has lately been extensively used to characterise and analyse the way public policy is implemented in various sectors. Broadly speaking, the term has been mainly used as "a generic label embracing different types of network relationship", such as "competitive and corporate pluralism; state and societal, sectoral and meso-corporatism; group sub-government; iron triangles; clientalism; issue networks; policy community; negotiated economy" (Schubert and Jordan, 1992, p 1). Rhodes (1986), for example, distinguishes between five types of networks ranging along a continuum from highly integrated *policy communities* to loosely integrated *issue networks*. Using this framework, I have tried to analyse the networks through which a specific programme of housing renewal in Sweden was carried out in the 1980s (Elander, 1994b), and tried to demonstrate its potential as an instrument for comparative analysis (Elander, 1995).

In housing rehabilitation in Sweden one may identify the contours of a policy community at the national policy level. Integrated into this policy community are three groups of actors represented by the landlords, the tenants and the public authorities respectively. In the first category we find interest organisations representing the residents of various kinds of housing tenures, eg, SABO, the Swedish Association of Private Landlords (*Fastighetsägareförbundet*), the national federations of cooperative associations (HSB, Riksbyggen and SBC), and the associations of homeowners. In the second category, the tenants are at the national level represented by the National Federation of Tenants' Associations, while in the third category we find the National Board of Housing, Building and Planning (*boverket*) and the 24 county boards (*länsstyrelser*).

Until November 1991 the leading role in this policy community was taken by the Ministry of Housing. However, on 1 December that year the non-socialist government decided to dissolve the ministry altogether. The new Social Democratic government which took power in September 1994 appointed a minister of Housing and Energy, though without an independent ministry. Issues of physical planning are handled by the Ministry of the Environment and Natural Resources, while social and financial aspects of housing belong to the domain of the Ministry of Health and Social Affairs and the Ministry of Finance respectively.

Within each of these three groups (landlords, tenants, public authorities) and especially the first and the third, technicians, architects and other professionals have played a crucial role in defining the problems, objectives and instruments of housing rehabilitation. However, when programmes have been converted into local projects the implementing networks have not been as streamlined as might be expected taking the national umbrella policy community into account: the membership of the networks has often been fluid, different municipal boards and offices have been involved, and sometimes a particular enthusiast (*eldsjäl*) has played a crucial role as a project leader. Thus the broader, socially orientated programmes in particular have come closer to the ad hoc-like issue networks than to policy communities, using the terminology proposed by Rhodes.

Looking at the outcomes of the renewal programmes from a state financial point of view, they have, of course, contributed to the burden of a budget deficit the reduction of which ranks number one among the priorities of the former non-socialist government as well as of the Social Democratic government now in power. Nevertheless, rehabilitation programmes are still being used by the government as instruments for stimulating production and decreasing employment, although on a much smaller scale and in a much more fragmentary fashion than before. Despite this, such programmes may have a symbolic value that could be used by the political parties in the parliament to show their supporters that they really do care for employment among the construction workers as well as for housing quality. However, investments in roads, railways and other infrastructural amenities are more typical than investments in housing when it comes to describing current urban renewal trends in Sweden.

## Rehabilitation in the future

Reflecting on the future of housing rehabilitation, one may firstly highlight the trend towards social polarisation in Swedish housing. Despite the official political ambitions, it is obvious that housing segregation in Sweden is increasing, and now also includes the phenomenon of marginalisation or residualisation (Öresjö, 1994)[6]. Although this is fundamentally a problem of class, gender (low income, single mothers) and ethnicity, and not a housing problem in itself, housing rehabilitation programmes are increasingly being designed to create environments that should be attractive to anyone regardless of income, class, gender and ethnicity. However, one may have good reason to doubt the efficiency of such programmes. They may be successful in particular cases, but are unlikely to affect the broad contours of social composition on housing estates. If you don't have the money you can't buy the dwelling you desire, and wealthy people just do not rent a flat on one of the problem estates:

> **Last but not least, the social problems remain. They have not arisen on the estates but have been put there by the housing market and the local housing authority. Therefore comprehensive rehabilitation often means that the problems are merely moved – to similar estates which have not yet undergone renewal and which risk landing in an even more difficult position. (Author's translation from Vidén and Lundahl, 1992, p 187)**

Secondly, considering the fact that desubsidisation is a goal shared by most political parties in Sweden, the amount of subsidies for rehabilitation is unlikely to increase. In addition, there are few signs that interest rates will drop to a level that would create any substantial degree of rehabilitation activity among landlords. This, in turn, will be an impetus to give a higher priority to management and maintenance, thus decreasing the immediate need for large-scale renovation. In that respect multi-dwelling estates will be more like one- and two-dwelling homes, where continuous maintenance reduces the need for extensive renovation.

Thirdly, the housing stock irrevocably gets older, and there will always appear physical problems that have to be met by substantial renovation. Thus as many as 275,000 dwellings in multi-dwelling buildings built before 1951 have not so far experienced any extensive improvement. Arguably these dwellings are already or will soon be in great need of rehabilitation (*Planera, Bygga, Bo*, 1994, no 1).

Finally, parts of the housing stock will always face specific problems. At the moment, the interior climate of dwellings is an issue that attracts special attention among experts and policy makers. Thus moist, mould and high levels of radon in many dwellings constitute a problem requiring rapid action. In one municipality, Halmstad in the south of Sweden, owners of one-dwelling homes with an unacceptably high level of radon have to make the necessary renovations, otherwise they will be charged a fine of SKr500 per month. As compared to earlier practice that was largely based on indirect regulations, this kind of compulsory action taken by a municipality is an extraordinary case within the framework of the housing rehabilitation system in Sweden. However, it is up to each municipality whether it will take the advantage of this measure or not, and it is also not quite clear whether the municipalities really have the constitutional right to charge such a fine (*Nerikes Allehanda* [daily newspaper], 3 January 1995). Thus the government is considering the enactment of a new law to strengthen the responsibility of the municipalities with regard to the radon problem (*Dagens Nyheter*, 20 November, 1995).

## Acknowledgements

This chapter is based on research carried out under the auspices of a research project on 'Postwar urban and housing renewal in Sweden' conducted by Thord Strömberg at the Centre for Housing and Urban Research in Örebro, and sponsored by the Swedish Council for Building Research. I am grateful to Hans Skifter Andersen, Thord Strömberg, Annika Schéele, Lars Ilshammar and Gunnar Persson for valuable comments on earlier versions, and to Malcolm Forbes for having checked the language. Special thanks to Lars for constructing the tables and figures.

## Notes

[1] In 1994 no more than 1,836 new dwellings were started. According to Gösta Blücher, Head of the National Board of Housing, Planning and Building, this figure is the lowest for more than 100 years (as interviewed in *Planera, Bygga, Bo*, 1994, no 4, p 5).

[2] See, for example, the 113 proposals to combat the crises presented by the Lindbeck Commission that was created by the government in the early spring of 1993. The list of proposals was published at length in *Från riksdag och department*, 1993, no 10.

[3] Tenure diversity and tenure neutrality are two crucial components often ascribed to 'social housing' in Sweden. As shown by Table A3.2 in

the Appendix of this chapter, the relative strength of each different type of tenure has remained the same since the implementation of the Million Dwellings Programme that was accomplished by 1975. Of course, this does not exclude the presence of qualitative differences between different types of tenure, for example, with regard to cost, influence and standard. Social housing in a non-Swedish context has commonly been targeted at specific groups with special needs (see Elander, 1994a; Harloe, 1994).

[4] After a lot of hesitation in June 1994 the Swedish government affirmed the building of the bridge.

[5] Further, the following conclusion is based on empirical research on many pre-1990 renewal practices: "In Sweden it is self-evident that the tenants, and the social welfare organisations, should have an influence on renewal. In spite of this, many renewal processes make the tenants feel powerless and brushed aside" (Vidén, 1993, p 84). Thus, it is no wonder that the tenants' associations strongly oppose the recent change of legislation (see, for example, the editorial of *Vår Bostad* [Journal of the National Federation of Tenants' Associations], 1994, no 5).

[6] Thus, a leading Swedish daily reported on the Råslätt Estate, located about 10 minutes by bus from the town centre of Jönköping:

> **About 2,500 out of 4,200 inhabitants are first and second generation immigrants.... The young generation grown up there calls their immigrant ghetto 'little America'. There is a risk that it will develop into a minimum case of an American slum, where invisible borders are passed, ending up in China, the Middle East or India.** (*Dagens Nyheter*, 5 February, 1995, Sunday supplement)

# Appendix to Chapter Three

Table A3.1: Capital formulation in permanent housing (1980-91) (SKr million, 1985 prices)

| Year | New construction | | | | Reconstruction | | | |
|---|---|---|---|---|---|---|---|---|
| | Total | Multi-dwelling buildings | One-/two-dwelling buildings | Total | Multi-dwelling buildings | One-/two-dwelling buildings | Total |
| 1980 | 27,900 | 7,428 | 20,472 | 7,736 | 4,434 | 3,393 | 35,636 |
| 1981 | 25,078 | 7,993 | 17,085 | 8,826 | 5,797 | 3,029 | 33,904 |
| 1982 | 22,854 | 8,779 | 14,055 | 10,404 | 7,671 | 2,733 | 33,258 |
| 1983 | 20,619 | 8,675 | 11,944 | 12,159 | 9,174 | 2,985 | 32,778 |
| 1984 | 17,919 | 7,972 | 9,947 | 17,139 | 12,486 | 4,653 | 35,058 |
| 1985 | 15,913 | 7,477 | 8,436 | 22,232 | 15,949 | 6,283 | 38,145 |
| 1986 | 14,046 | 6,782 | 7,263 | 23,256 | 16,241 | 7,015 | 37,302 |
| 1987 | 17,592 | 8,759 | 8,833 | 22,981 | 17,557 | 5,424 | 40,573 |
| 1988 | 24,041 | 12,278 | 11,763 | 19,940 | 14,556 | 5,384 | 43,981 |
| 1989 | 28,704 | 15,163 | 13,541 | 17,370 | 12,262 | 5,108 | 46,074 |
| 1990 | 32,809 | 17,891 | 14,918 | 16,586 | 10,514 | 6,072 | 49,395 |
| 1991 | 33,217 | 19,299 | 13,918 | 15,529 | 9,612 | 5,917 | 48,746 |

Source: Bostads- och bebyggelsestatistisk årsbok (Yearbook of Housing and Building Statistics) (1994, p 111)

*Urban renewal and housing rehabilitation in Sweden*

Table A3.2: Tenure by percentage of housing stock in Sweden (1945-90)

|  | 1945 | 1960 | 1970 | 1980 | 1985 | 1990 |
|---|---|---|---|---|---|---|
| **Rented** | | | | | | |
| Private | 51 | 40 | 30 | 21 | 21 | 20 |
| Public | 2 | 9 | 17 | 20 | 21 | 21 |
| Cooperative | 4 | 11 | 14 | 14 | 16 | 18 |
| Owner-occupied | 38 | 36 | 35 | 41 | 40 | 40 |
| Other | 5 | 4 | 4 | 4 | 2 | 1 |
| **Total** | 100 | 100 | 100 | 100 | 100 | 100 |

Note for Table A3.3: According to the main rules a building loan is granted for rehabilitation provided that the building is more than 30 years old and has not undergone a more comprehensive rehabilitation during the last 30 years, reckoned from the time of submission of the application for a loan, that the measures are not merely of limited scope, that the cost of these measures is reasonable in the light of the nature and extent of the work and the remaining period of utilisation of the building, and that the building's qualities are preserved to a reasonable extent. If the loan is for measures for improving flats, there is the further provision that the standard of the flats after completion of the measures shall not exceed the normal standard of new-built flats.

Exceptions from the main rules occur in certain cases. The calculation of the housing loan derives from a so-called loan basis, which corresponds to the reasonable rehabilitation cost. This loan basis must not exceed the calculated loan basis for a corresponding new building or the calculated value of the building once it has been rehabilitated. If the building is of cultural/historical value or its preservation is of importance for a culturally/historically valuable environment, the loan basis can be a higher amount.

Table A3.3: Granted government housing loans for reconstruction (1975/76-1993)

| | Number of dwellings | | | Granted loans in SKr 000s | | |
|---|---|---|---|---|---|---|
| Fiscal year | Individually built one/two- dwelling buildings | Collectively built one/two- dwelling buildings | Multi- dwelling buildings | Individually built one/two- dwelling buildings | Collectively built one/two- dwelling buildings | Multi- dwelling buildings |
| 1975/76 | 117 | 7,245 | 11,908 | 2,352 | 189,041 | 127,908 |
| 1976/77 | 176 | 8,277 | 8,222 | 6,305 | 259,430 | 116,528 |
| 1977/78 | 222 | 10,795 | 9,891 | 7,900 | 352,181 | 234,752 |
| 1978/79 | 434 | 11,854 | 11,216 | 13,679 | 425,038 | 330,223 |
| 1979/80 | 237 | 11,797 | 11,979 | 11,829 | 447,815 | 473,991 |
| 1980/81 | 583 | 9,304 | 11,943 | 16,334 | 387,616 | 649,057 |
| 1981/82 | 521 | 8,515 | 16,833 | 27,404 | 343,004 | 977,725 |
| 1982/83 | 370 | 6,961 | 20,997 | 16,705 | 300,767 | 1,110,522 |
| 1983/84 | 513 | 5,628 | 22,976 | 26,682 | 281,374 | 1,389,644 |
| 1984/85 | 595 | 5,156 | 35,469 | 44,701 | 270,515 | 2,547,686 |
| 1985/86 | 490 | 4,841 | 34,214 | 44,200 | 260,859 | 2,805,278 |
| 1986/87 | 442 | 4,452 | 40,331 | 38,294 | 271,932 | 3,463,100 |
| 1987/88 | 953 | 4,928 | 37,563 | 70,590 | 337,252 | 3,227,305 |
| 1988/89 | 874 | 4,068 | 28,778 | 93,245 | 309,704 | 3,275,998 |
| 1989/90 | 434 | 3,574 | 23,650 | 45,733 | 286,650 | 2,708,216 |
| 1989 | 738 | 3,047 | 26,190 | 72,133 | 229,389 | 3,131,077 |
| 1990 | 400 | 4,689 | 23,862 | 42,151 | 393,791 | 2,603,078 |
| 1991 | 547 | 3,714 | 64,596 | 80,412 | 337,577 | 8,160,413 |
| 1992 | 910 | 9,772 | 36,483 | 193,210 | 2,216,676 | 6,983,389 |
| 1993 | 2,803 | 16,579 | 60,104 | 314,320 | 2,841,230 | 12,440,449 |

Source: *Bostads- och bebyggelsestatistisk årsbok* (Yearbook of Housing and Building Statistics) (1994, p 111)

## Table A3.4: Careful rehabilitation as defined by Swedish housing researchers and experts

Careful rehabilitation is a frequently employed concept and has, in recent years, been indicated as the goal of reconstruction. The demand for careful rehabilitation derives from social purposes, the interest in preservation and the need to reduce costs. Though the motivation for carefulness is not the same on the part of all concerned, a common denominator is the desire to economise on resources. A great deal of money can be saved by avoiding major intervention and demolition. It is possible to calculate how much is saved by, for instance, keeping a wall instead of demolishing it and building a new one. But a part of economising on resources is the preservation and utilisation of often irreplaceable qualities. Such qualities are not always easy to measure but on a more or less conscious plane they enrich our experiences of space, light, colour and form, and tell us of the history of the buildings and the lives that have been lived in them.

Carefulness has seldom to do with the choice of standard. A lift can be installed with greater or less care, a bathroom can be newly installed or made to function better in a careful or uncareful way, etc. Or a simple piece of repair work, involving no raising of the standard, can be done with the most hair-raising lack of care. Carefulness is a method, a way of approaching a task, which is always applicable when something is to be done to an existent building.

Carefulness is a question of ascertaining what prior conditions and qualities exist, and of respecting and utilising them to the maximum possible extent when goals and needs are to be met. Careful rehabilitation is, in other words, a question of accomplishing the maximum utility and comfort with the minimum of intervention and disturbance. This means that the rehabilitation must be based on an overall view of what one starts from – the building, the neighbourhood and the residents – and of what one wishes to achieve – restored and new functions.

*Careful rehabilitation is:*
- to regard the existent buildings as a resource, whose features are to be accepted provided that they do not clearly impede intended functions for residents and workers;
- to utilise the natural possibilities that the building and the neighbourhood possess regarding good, well-balanced function with a good standard;
- to accomplish alterations and additions in such a way that they are in harmony with the character of the building in design and material;
- to make further carefulness possible – to alter in such a way as not to impede maintenance and future alteration;
- to respect the fact the housing being altered is people's homes.

*On the other hand, careful rehabilitation is not:*
- to preserve at any price – it must be possible to replace worn-out parts and to introduce new functions;
- to be content to fulfil the lowest rehabilitation requirements, where higher requirements are desirable and can be fulfilled, or to neglect to remove manifest defects not covered by regulations.

Source: Blomberg et al (1985, p 45)

*Housing renewal in Europe*

**Figure A3.1: Capital formation in permanent housing (1980-91) (SKr million, 1985 prices)**

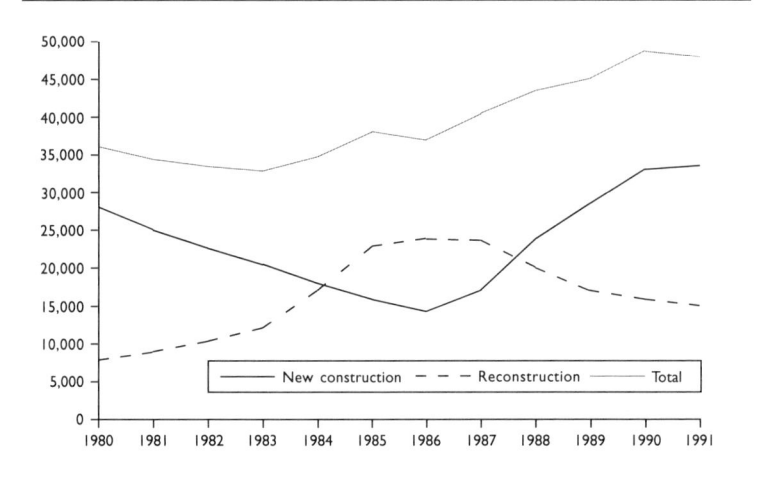

Source: *Bostads- och bebyggelsestatistisk årsbok* (Yearbook of Housing and Building Statistics) (1994, p 111)

**Figure A3.2: State budget deficit in Sweden (1974/75-1994/95) (SKr billion)**

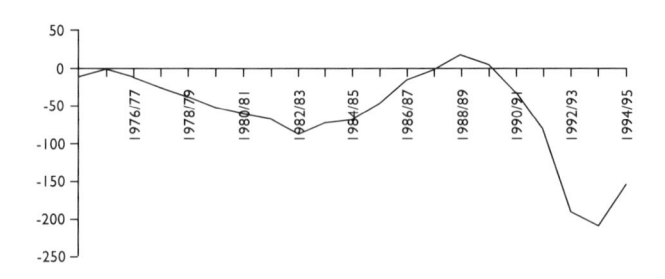

Source: *Statistisk årsbok* (Statistical Yearbook) (1980, 1985, 1990, 1992, 1995)

**Figure A3.3: Economic growth in Sweden (1975-93) (GDP in purchasers' prices by percentage)**

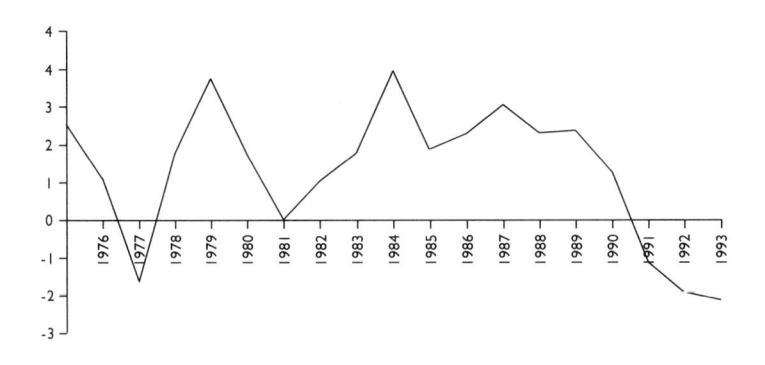

Source: *Statistisk årsbok* (Statistical Yearbook) (1980, 1985, 1990, 1992, 1995)

**Figure A3.4: Unemployment in Sweden (1975-93) (by percentage)**

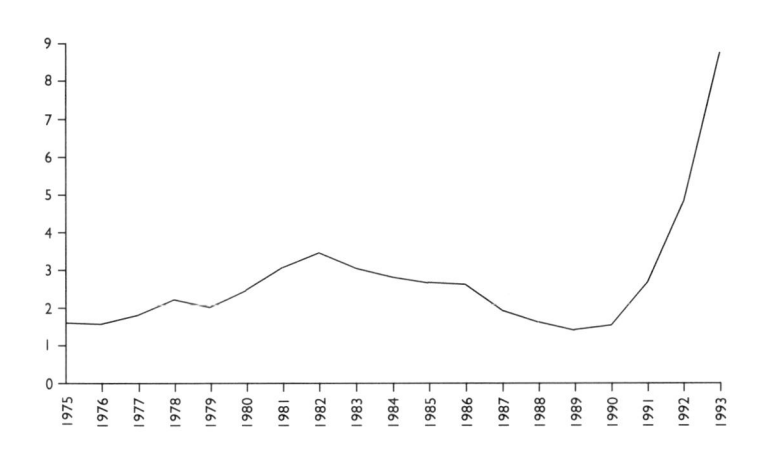

Source: *Statistisk årsbok* (Statistical Yearbook) (1980, 1985, 1990, 1992, 1995)

FOUR

# Housing conditions and housing renewal policy in the UK

*Philip Leather*

The aims of this chapter are, firstly, to provide a comprehensive review of evidence on the nature and scale of housing conditions in England and the characteristics of those experiencing these conditions and, secondly, to examine policies to tackle poor housing conditions and their effectiveness.

## House condition problems in England

The *standard of fitness for human habitation* is the minimum standard for housing conditions in England, Wales and Northern Ireland. In Scotland the most comparable measure is the *tolerable standard*, which differs from the fitness standard in a number of ways, but most significantly by excluding disrepair.

The standard of fitness for human habitation is of great importance in housing renewal policy as it determines the extent of remedial work which is eligible for mandatory grant aid from the state. A brief summary of the fitness and tolerable standards are set out in Table 4.1. Since a dwelling is only unfit if it both *fails to meet one or more of the requirements* and by reason of that failure *is not reasonably suitable for occupation*, it can be seen that judgements about fitness are complex.

Estimates of repair costs are also widely used to measure poor housing conditions in England. These are more easy to grasp than the fitness standard but still pose two major problems. The most important is the *standard of repair* against which costs are measured. The 1991 English House Condition Survey, the most authoritative source of data on poor conditions, used four separate measures of disrepair (see Table 4.2).

Table 4.1: The standard of fitness for human habitation and the tolerable standard

| The standard of fitness for human habitation in England, Wales and Northern Ireland | The tolerable standard for Scotland |
|---|---|
| The fitness standard is defined in Section 83 of Schedule 9 to the 1989 Local Government and Housing Act and the 1992 Housing (Northern Ireland) Order. A dwelling house is fit for human habitation unless, in the opinion of the local housing authority, it fails to meet one or more of the requirements above and, by reason of that failure, is not reasonably suitable for occupation | The tolerable standard for Scotland is defined in Section 86(1) of the 1987 Housing (Scotland) Act |

**Common elements**

| | |
|---|---|
| The dwelling should: | The dwelling should: |
| • be structurally stable | • be structurally stable |
| • be free from dampness prejudicial to the health of the occupants | • be substantially free from rising or penetrating damp |
| • have satisfactory facilities for preparing and cooking food including a sink with a satisfactory supply of hot and cold water | • have satisfactory facilities for the cooking of food within the house<br>• have a sink provided with a satisfactory supply of both hot and cold water within the house |
| • have an adequate piped supply of wholesome water | • have an adequate piped supply of water within the house |
| • have adequate provision for lighting, heating and ventilation | • have satisfactory provision for natural and artificial lighting, for ventilation, and for heating |
| • have a suitably located WC exclusively for the use of the occupants | • have a WC available for the exclusive use of the occupants of the house and suitably located within the house |
| • have an effective system for the drainage of foul, waste and surface water | • have an effective system for the drainage and disposal of foul and surface water |

**Different elements**

| | |
|---|---|
| • have a suitably located bath or shower and wash hand basin, each provided with a supply of hot and cold water<br>• be free from serious disrepair | • have satisfactory access to all external doors and outbuildings |

Sources: DoE (1993a); Scottish Homes (1993)

**Table 4.2: Standards of repair used in house condition surveys**

**Urgent repair** is all repairs needing urgent action to eliminate threats to the health, safety, security and comfort of the occupants and whose neglect would result in further rapid deterioration.

**General repair** is all works needed within five years, including repairs to services and amenities as well as the fabric of the dwelling.

**Comprehensive repair** covers all repairs needed, together with replacement work to items which have less than 10 years remaining life.

**Standardised repair** is general repair costs per square metre of floor space.

Source: DoE (1993a)

The second problem is the costing of repair work. Actual costs charged to householders for repair works vary substantially from place to place and from builder to builder. National surveys use standard schedules of cost and as a result generally underestimate real repair costs. Nevertheless repair costs provide the most understandable indicator of house condition problems available.

## Unfitness

Table 4.3 shows details of poor housing conditions in England, Wales, Northern Ireland and Scotland across all tenures. Accepting problems of comparability, the table shows that almost 1.8 million dwellings were *unfit for human habitation or below the tolerable standard* in 1991. Levels of unfitness are highest in Wales (although this figure relates to 1986 since when conditions may have improved) and Northern Ireland. In Scotland the proportion of dwellings below the tolerable standard in 1991 was substantially lower than the proportion of unfit dwellings elsewhere, but differences between the two standards make it difficult to compare conditions in Scotland with those in the rest of the UK. Information on the average cost of making dwellings fit is only available in England and Northern Ireland and, as Table 4.3 shows, this cost was more than twice as high in Northern Ireland in 1991.

The classification of a dwelling as unfit does not mean that it is unoccupied. In England in 1991 it was estimated that 1,354,000 or 89%

Table 4.3: Poor housing conditions in the UK

|  | England (1991) | Wales (1986)† | NI (1991) | Scotland (1991) |
|---|---|---|---|---|
| **Number of dwellings:** | | | | |
| *Unfit or BTS\** | | | | |
| Number | 1,498,000 | 131,000 | 50,360 | 95,000 |
| % | 7.6 | 11.8 | 8.8 | 4.7 |
| *Needing urgent repairs over £1,000* | | | | |
| Number | 3,510,000 | 117,000 | 91,770 | 109,500 |
| % | 17.8 | 10.9 | 15.9 | 5.4 |
| **Average cost per dwelling (£) for:** | | | | |
| Making fit | 3,301 | na | na | 6,922 |
| Urgent repairs | 680 | 641 | 222 | 899 |
| General repairs | 1,130 | na | 1,185 | 1,219 |
| Comprehensive repairs | 2,100 | 1,581 | 1,256 | 4,806 |

Notes: * Figures for Scotland are for dwellings 'below the tolerable standard' (BTS) which excludes disrepair and may thus omit some dwellings which would be judged unfit elsewhere.

† Published figures for unfitness in Wales are not comparable to those for England, Northern Ireland (NI) and Scotland because they relate to unfitness in 1986 measured by the pre-1989 standard. The figure in the table has been adjusted to reflect the new standard on the basis of data from the 1991 English House Condition Survey. Banded data on urgent repairs is also unavailable for Wales and the level of urgent repair has been assumed to be equivalent to the proportion of dwellings requiring comprehensive repairs greater than £4,200 at 1991 prices.

Sources: 1991 English House Condition Survey, 1991 Scottish House Condition Survey, 1991 Northern Ireland House Condition Survey: special tabulations; Welsh Office (1988)

of all unfit dwellings were occupied. However, the severity of unfitness varies. Over half of the unfit dwellings in England in 1991 failed the fitness standard on only one criterion. Similarly, it was estimated that while the cost of making dwellings fit averaged £3,300, this figure was less than £500 in nearly one third of cases. At the other end of the scale, 5% of unfit dwellings required more than £15,000 to make them fit.

Table 4.4: Condensation, mould growth and dampness

|  | England | | Scotland | |
|---|---|---|---|---|
|  | No of dwellings | % of stock | No of dwellings | % of stock |
| Condensation and mould growth | 247 | 13.4 | 44 | 22.8 |
| Penetrating and rising damp | 231 | 12.0 | 37 | 18.5 |
| Both of these | 187 | 5.5 | 25 | 12.0 |
| Any problem | 3,921 | 19.9 | 584 | 28.7 |

Sources: DoE (1993); Scottish Homes (1993)

## Reasons for unfitness

Unfitness is a legal concept which requires professional interpretation. It does not convey much to the lay person about the actual problems which households living in unfit housing experience. In England, serious disrepair and inadequate facilities for food preparation were the most common reasons for unfitness (39% of unfit dwellings in each case), followed by inadequate provision of a bath/shower or washbasin. In Northern Ireland, serious disrepair was also the most common problem (64% of unfit dwellings), followed by dampness prejudicial to health (51%) and inadequate food preparation facilities (44%). Comparable details are not available for Wales.

## Dampness, condensation and mould growth

The problem of dampness is sufficiently serious to merit further examination (Table 4.4). This is more prevalent in western and northern areas of the UK because they receive more rainfall than the south and east. In Northern Ireland, 51% of unfit dwellings experienced dampness prejudicial to health, compared to only 22% in England. In Scotland, 49% of dwellings below the tolerable standard were not substantially free from damp. Comparable figures are not available for Wales. But dampness problems are more widespread than these figures suggest. A special analysis of dampness and condensation in the 1991 Scottish House Condition Survey revealed that 29% of the whole dwelling stock showed evidence of dampness, condensation or mould growth (Scottish Homes, 1993). Even in England, where problems were less serious, about one in five dwellings suffered similar problems. Older dwellings are more likely to experience dampness, but condensation and mould growth are more prevalent in the post-1945 stock, largely because they are associated with non-traditional construction techniques.

## Disrepair

Data on repair costs is easier to interpret and there are fewer inconsistencies between surveys. Table 4.3 shows that about 3.8 million properties across all tenures in the UK needed urgent repairs costing more than £1,000 in 1991. This is equivalent to one in every six dwellings. Urgent repairs are matters such as water leaks, serious dampness or dangerous wiring which would, if not tackled immediately, lead to further substantial damage to the fabric of affected dwellings. As with unfitness, the level of urgent disrepair in Scotland is significantly lower than elsewhere in the UK, but there are fewer differences between England, Wales and Northern Ireland in the proportions of dwellings with high urgent repair costs. The bulk of disrepair arises in external dwelling elements, with roof coverings and external doors or windows each accounting for 13% of outstanding repair costs in England in 1991 and chimneys accounting for a further 10%. Other significant elements were amenities and services (8% of costs), wall structures (7%), exterior wall finishes (6%) and internal ceilings (6%). The frequency with which repairs were needed showed a similar pattern, with repairs to windows or doors (required by 40% of dwellings), interior walls (37% of dwellings), and wall finishes (31%) the most common problems.

## Amenities and services

A further measure of poor conditions is the absence of basic amenities such as an internal WC, hot and cold water supplies, a fixed bath or shower, a wash hand basin, and a sink with draining board. In England, some 205,000 dwellings (1% of the stock) lacked one or more basic amenities in 1991. The equivalent figures in Northern Ireland were 19,100 dwellings (3%), and in Wales 42,200 (4%). In Scotland, with slightly less stringent definitions, only 13,000 dwellings (0.6%) lacked at least one standard amenity. These numbers have declined steadily in recent years.

Heating systems are also an important aspect of housing conditions. While the availability of central heating has increased in recent years, some 3.2 million dwellings in England (16% of the stock) lacked some form of central heating in 1991, with a further 109,000 (19%) in Northern Ireland, 499,000 (22%) in Scotland, and 213,000 (18%) in Wales.

In terms of thermal insulation, 91% of dwellings in England had some form of loft insulation in 1991 but only 8% had insulation 150mm or more deep. Some 57% of dwellings had some double glazing. In Northern Ireland, only 22% had some double glazing. In Scotland, 78% of dwellings had loft insulation more than 100mm deep, while 46% had some double glazing. In Wales, 79% of households had some form of loft insulation in 1986, 81% had an insulated hot water tank, and 28% had partial or full double glazing.

*Houses in multiple occupation*

Estimates of unfitness and disrepair include both dwellings occupied by a single household, and those shared by persons who do not form a single household, often termed houses in multiple occupation (HMOs). Shared housing plays an important role in the housing market for certain groups but conditions are often poor and recent proposals for housing homeless households in the private rented sector make it important to begin to raise standards in this sector.

The wide variety of different sharing arrangements makes it difficult to arrive at a comprehensive definition of a house in multiple occupation and there are no up-to-date estimates of the numbers involved. A 1985 survey found that there were some 334,000 HMOs in England and Wales (Thomas and Hedges, 1986). But numbers may subsequently have increased as a result of both the growth in private renting which has occurred during the current recession in the housing market, and the increased demand from students arising from the expansion of further and higher education.

A follow-up to the 1985 survey (Kirby and Sopp, 1986) looked at conditions in HMOs in more detail, although self-contained units with shared hallways were excluded. This found that four fifths of HMOs were unsatisfactory in terms of either management, level of occupancy, or provision of amenities. Over a fifth of all HMOs had inadequate facilities for preparation and storage of food, and between 10% and 15% lacked adequate ventilation, space heating, water supply, and access to a WC, bath or shower, and a sink or basin. More than four out of five lacked a satisfactory means of escape from fire. One third had repair costs of more than £15,000 at 1985 price levels, and a further 46% had repair costs of between £5,000 and £15,000. On average, just over a quarter of the costs of repair related to the external parts of the dwellings concerned, with a further third for the repair of internal private areas. Common parts such as stairs or landings accounted for 15% of the total repair bill, while some 16% was accounted for in meeting standards such as the need for an adequate means of escape from fire. Subsequent efforts to tackle poor conditions in HMOs will have reduced these numbers but significant problems still remain in this sector.

## Poor conditions and tenure

The picture of poor housing conditions described above relates to all tenures, although there are substantial differences in housing conditions between tenures, and between the occupied and vacant housing stock. Figure 4.1 shows differences in levels of unfitness by tenure in 1991 and

**Figure 4.1: Unfit dwellings by tenure, UK (1991/93)**

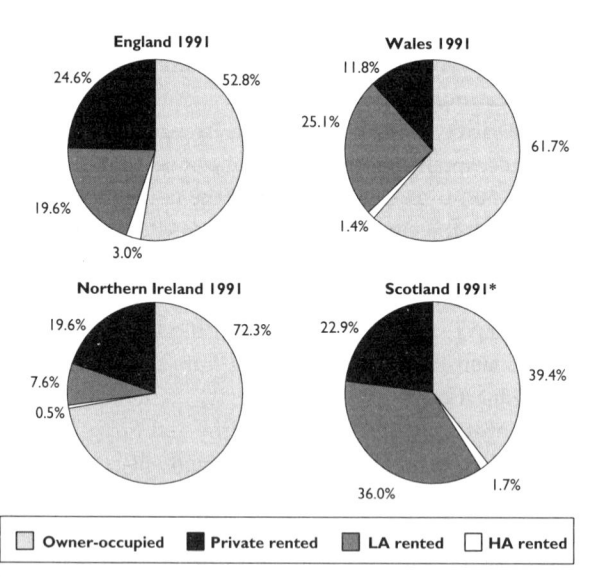

England 1991: 52.8% / 24.6% / 19.6% / 3.0%
Wales 1991: 61.7% / 11.8% / 25.1% / 1.4%
Northern Ireland 1991: 72.3% / 19.6% / 7.6% / 0.5%
Scotland 1991*: 39.4% / 22.9% / 36.0% / 1.7%

☐ Owner-occupied  ■ Private rented  ▨ LA rented  ☐ HA rented

Note: * Scottish data for dwellings below tolerable standard.

Source: 1991 English House Condition Survey, 1991 Scottish House Condition Survey, 1991 Northern Ireland House Condition Survey: analysis of data; 1993 Welsh House Condition Survey: special tabulations

Table 4.5 shows the numbers of dwellings affected. In each country the pattern is similar. In the occupied stock, by far the worst conditions are found in the private rented sector, where unfitness levels are typically three or four times greater than the average. Except in Northern Ireland, where unfitness in the owner-occupied sector is also comparatively high, there is little difference between the other tenures. But because the majority of dwellings are owner-occupied, the greatest number of unfit dwellings is found in this sector. In England, for example, there are 713,000 unfit owner-occupied dwellings compared to only 333,000 in the private rented sector.

Table 4.5: Poor conditions by tenure and country (1991)

| | Number of dwellings (000s) | | | | | |
|---|---|---|---|---|---|---|
| | Owner-occupied | Private rented | HA | LA* | Vacant | All dwellings |
| **Unfit/BTS** | | | | | | |
| England (1991) | 715 | 333 | 41 | 265 | 145 | 1,499 |
| Wales (1986) | 49 | 14 | na | 9 | na | 61 |
| Northern Ireland (1991) | 29 | 8 | 2 | 3 | 9 | 51 |
| Scotland (1991) | 37 | 22 | 2 | 34 | na | 95 |
| **Total** | **830** | **377** | **45** | **311** | **154** | **1,706** |
| **In need of urgent repairs over £1,000** | | | | | | |
| England (1991) | 2,108 | 565 | 70 | 539 | 228 | 3,510 |
| Wales (1986)† | 82 | 19 | na | 11 | na | 112 |
| Northern Ireland (1991) | 54 | 11 | 0 | 9 | 18 | 92 |
| Scotland (1991) | 56 | 21 | 1 | 31 | na | 109 |
| **Total** | **2,300** | **616** | **71** | **590** | **246** | **3,823** |

Notes: * Housing association (HA) dwellings in Wales are included with local authority dwellings.
† Data for Wales relates to all repairs and is closer to the comprehensive repair standard. Repair costs for Wales have been updated to 1991 prices using an inflation factor of 1.4.

Sources: 1991 English House Condition Survey, 1991 Scottish House Condition Survey, 1991 Northern Ireland House Condition Survey: special tabulations; Welsh Office (1988)

Unfitness levels are also extremely high among vacant dwellings. This is not surprising as poor condition is a major reason for dwellings remaining unlet or unsold. But in addition vacant dwellings are more likely to deteriorate than occupied dwellings because they are vulnerable to vandalism and because there are no occupants to report repair problems to landlords or to tackle problems for themselves.

Disrepair also differs between tenures (Table 4.6). As with unfitness, the private rented sector has by far the highest mean disrepair costs among occupied dwellings, while local authority and housing association dwellings have the lowest costs. Vacant dwellings have very high repair costs.

### Dwelling age and condition

These overall figures give a clear picture of the scale of house condition problems but they do not give an indication of the types of dwelling

**Table 4.6: Mean repair costs by tenure and country (1991) (£)**

|  | Owner occupied | Private rented | HA | LA* | Vacant | All dwellings |
|---|---|---|---|---|---|---|
| **Urgent repairs** | | | | | | |
| England (1991) | 580 | 1,290 | 460 | 510 | 2,960 | 680 |
| Wales (1986) | 496 | 960 | na | 244 | 641 | na |
| Northern Ireland (1991) | 878 | 2,141 | 131 | 248 | 3,609 | 899 |
| Scotland (1991) | 230 | 694 | 61 | 149 | na | 222 |
| **General repairs** | | | | | | |
| England (1991) | 1,050 | 1,940 | 710 | 820 | 3,040 | 1,130 |
| Wales (1986)† | 1,658 | 3,484 | na | 938 | na | 1,581 |
| Northern Ireland (1991) | 1,187 | 2,846 | 189 | 393 | 4,698 | 1,219 |
| Scotland (1991) | 1,209 | 2,892 | 617 | 910 | na | 1,185 |

Notes: * Housing association (HA) dwellings in Wales are included with local authority dwellings.

† Data for Wales relates to all repairs and is closer to the comprehensive repair standard. Repair costs for Wales have been updated to 1991 prices using an inflation factor of 1.4.

Sources: 1991 English House Condition Survey, 1991 Scottish House Condition Survey, 1991 Northern Ireland House Condition Survey: special tabulations; Welsh Office (1988)

which are most likely to be unfit or in poor repair. Some variations in levels of unfitness and disrepair costs by tenure stem from differences in investment. Consistent neglect of investment in repair and maintenance by private landlords has contributed to poor housing conditions in this sector, while the provision of repairs services and planned maintenance in the local authority and housing association sectors have improved standards. Within the owner-occupied sector, the picture is more varied with some households investing substantial amounts in repair, improvement and maintenance and others being able to invest relatively little.

But variations in the age and dwelling type profile of dwellings in each tenure are the main influence on housing conditions. Age is the most important factor influencing dwelling condition, as Figure 4.2 shows in relation to unfitness. Rates of unfitness increase steeply for dwellings over 80 years of age. Repair costs also increase with dwelling age.

**Figure 4.2: Unfit/BTS dwellings by age, UK (1991/93)**

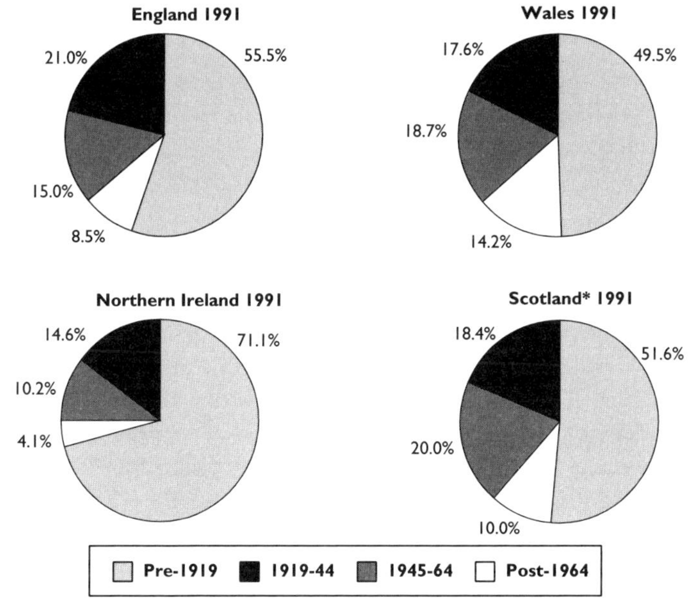

England 1991: 21.0%, 55.5%, 15.0%, 8.5%

Wales 1991: 17.6%, 49.5%, 18.7%, 14.2%

Northern Ireland 1991: 14.6%, 71.1%, 10.2%, 4.1%

Scotland* 1991: 18.4%, 51.6%, 10.0%, 20.0%

☐ Pre-1919  ■ 1919-44  ■ 1945-64  ☐ Post-1964

Note: * Scottish data for dwellings below tolerable standard.

Source: 1991 English House Condition Survey, 1991 Scottish House Condition Survey, 1991 Northern Ireland House Condition Survey: analysis of data; 1993 Welsh House Condition Survey: special tabulations

Table 4.7: Poor conditions by dwelling age and country (1991)

| | % of dwellings by age | | | | |
|---|---|---|---|---|---|
| | Pre-1919 | 1919-44 | 1945-64 | Post-1964 | All dwellings |
| **Unfit/BTS** | | | | | |
| England (1991) | 15.5 | 8.4 | 5.3 | 2.2 | 7.6 |
| Wales (1986) | 19.1 | 8.5 | 2.2 | 0.7 | 8.7 |
| Northern Ireland (1991) | 29.5 | 11.3 | 4.0 | 0.8 | 8.8 |
| Scotland (1991) | 11.8 | 4.5 | 3.7 | 1.2 | 4.7 |
| **In need of urgent repairs over £1,000** | | | | | |
| England (1991) | 35.3 | 23.0 | 11.8 | 4.4 | 17.8 |
| Wales (1986)* | 24.3 | 9.1 | 3.7 | 0.3 | 10.9 |
| Northern Ireland (1991) | 45.7 | 25.4 | 10.6 | 2.3 | 16.0 |
| Scotland (1991) | 14.0 | 6.6 | 3.3 | 1.2 | 5.4 |

Notes: * Banded data on urgent repairs is unavailable for Wales and the level of urgent repair has been assumed to be equivalent to the proportion of dwellings requiring comprehensive repairs greater than £4,200 at 1991 prices.

Sources: 1991 English House Condition Survey, 1991 Scottish House Condition Survey, 1991 Northern Ireland House Condition Survey: special tabulations; Welsh Office (1988)

## Dwelling type and condition

In combination with age, dwelling type is also important, with particular categories such as pre-1919 terraced houses in England and Wales, pre-1919 tenements in Scotland, older rural properties in Northern Ireland, and converted flats or purpose-built high rise flats throughout the UK being examples of dwellings types strongly associated with poor conditions. To illustrate this in more detail, Figure 4.3 shows the proportion of all unfit dwellings in the owner-occupied sector accounted for by various dwelling age/type categories in England in 1991. Pre-1919 terraced houses formed by far the largest individual category of unfit dwelling, and pre-1919 dwellings in total accounted for 55% of all unfit units. But there were also significant numbers of unfit inter-war and postwar houses. In the owner-occupied sector, unfitness was therefore a problem among a diverse range of dwelling types. In the private rented sector, problems were more concentrated in the older housing stock with pre-1919 dwellings accounting for over three quarters of all unfitness problems.

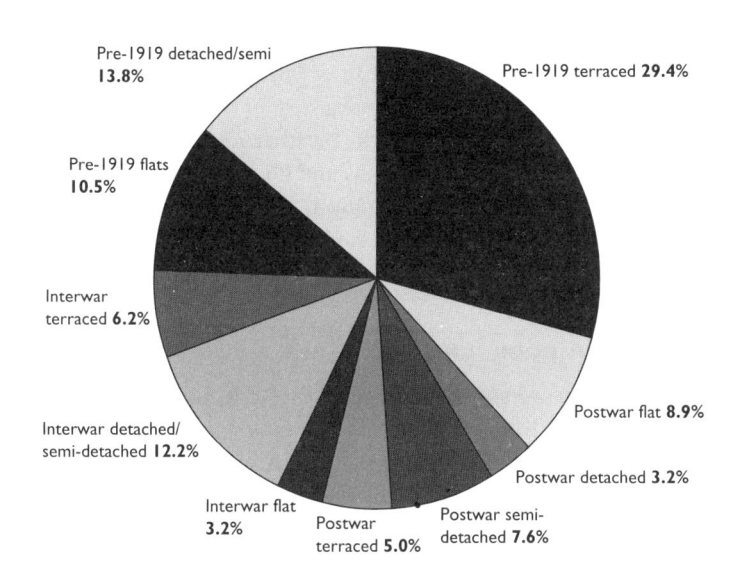

Figure 4.3: Unfit/BTS dwellings by age and type, UK (1991/93)

- Pre-1919 detached/semi **13.8%**
- Pre-1919 terraced **29.4%**
- Pre-1919 flats **10.5%**
- Interwar terraced **6.2%**
- Interwar detached/semi-detached **12.2%**
- Interwar flat **3.2%**
- Postwar terraced **5.0%**
- Postwar semi-detached **7.6%**
- Postwar detached **3.2%**
- Postwar flat **8.9%**

Source: 1991 English House Condition Survey, 1991 Scottish House Condition Survey, 1991 Northern Ireland House Condition Survey: analysis of data; 1993 Welsh House Condition Survey: special tabulations

## Location of poor condition housing

Poor condition houses are not evenly distributed throughout the country. Northern Ireland and Wales have more severe problems than England and Scotland. Within England, there are strong regional differences in unfitness and disrepair, which reflect the age of the housing stock. Inner London has the highest levels of poor housing conditions, with almost twice as many unfit dwellings (14%) as England as a whole and some 16% of dwellings in poor condition compared with 10% for England. The north west has the next highest rate of unfitness, followed by the East Midlands and, surprisingly, Outer London. The West Midlands, the South West and the South East have the lowest levels of unfitness.

Accurate data on local levels of unfitness is not available for England, as the national house condition survey is based on too small a sample to provide local data, while district-level surveys differ in approach and do not provide full coverage. However, DoE estimates suggest that there are notable concentrations of poor condition private sector housing in Inner London, the South Wales valleys, the districts of North East Lancashire, rural areas in the North and North East of England and in West Wales, in the East Midlands, and in a scattered group of larger cities including Manchester, Leicester and Bristol. In Northern Ireland and Scotland, the larger cities such as Belfast, Glasgow and Edinburgh continue to have concentrations of poor housing conditions but, as we have already seen, there are also high proportions of substandard housing in the more isolated rural areas.

## Who lives in poor housing?

Although it is important to understand the scale and nature of poor housing conditions in the UK and the factors such as dwelling type and age which influence these conditions, it is also important to give consideration to the households which experience these conditions. As we have seen, the majority of substandard houses are occupied. But who lives in such dwellings? Are particular types of household more likely to experience bad housing conditions? And do certain household characteristics compound the problems by making it difficult for households to move or to deal with condition problems in situ? Social surveys linked to the national house condition surveys provide a wealth of evidence on the characteristics of those who live in poor conditions.

### Low incomes

Above all else, the most obvious characteristic of households living in poor condition housing is that more of them tend to have low incomes than those living in better conditions. Some two thirds of households living in the worst condition housing in England in 1991 were on below average incomes, and those in the lowest income band were one and a half times more likely to live in poor conditions than the population as a whole.

This relationship holds true across all tenures (Table 4.8) but the link between poor conditions and low income is strongest in the owner-occupied sector and weakest in the local authority sector. These results are not unexpected. In the owner-occupied sector, house prices are

Table 4.8: Households in the worst conditions by income and tenure, England (1991)

| Annual income band | Owner-occupied | Private rented | Housing association | Local authority | All households |
|---|---|---|---|---|---|
| **No of households in worst condition dwellings (000s)** | | | | | |
| Up to £5,000 | 223 | 254 | 42 | 171 | 690 |
| £5,000-£10,000 | 253 | 141 | 20 | 112 | 526 |
| £10,000-£16,000 | 275 | 75 | 4 | 40 | 394 |
| Over £16,000 | 203 | 65 | 1 | 2 | 271 |
| **All households** | **955** | **536** | **68** | **326** | **1,881** |
| **% of households in worst condition dwellings** | | | | | |
| Up to £5,000 | 11.3 | 43.7 | 12.0 | 9.1 | 14.4 |
| £5,000-£10,000 | 9.3 | 28.9 | 9.3 | 8.4 | 11.0 |
| £10,000-£16,000 | 7.3 | 19.0 | * | 7.3 | 8.3 |
| Over £16,000 | 4.6 | 28.0 | * | * | 5.7 |
| **All households** | **7.4** | **31.5** | **10.2** | **8.4** | **10.0** |

Notes: The table refers to households living in the worst conditions. These are defined in the 1991 English House Condition Survey as the 10% of dwellings with the highest repair costs per square metre. The overall number of households experiencing poor conditions is therefore predefined. The table shows variations in the extent to which households in different income and tenure groups are represented within the group living in the worst conditions.
* Indicates numbers in category too small to produce percentages.

Source: DoE (1993a)

influenced by the quality of the accommodation and as a result those on lower incomes can only afford to buy poor condition housing. In addition, households on low incomes are least likely to be able to invest in repair and maintenance, further strengthening the association between low incomes and poor conditions. The picture in the private rented sector is similar, but the link between income and conditions may be distorted by a number of factors. Local shortages may permit some landlords to charge higher rents than the condition of their properties might suggest. Housing benefit payments may allow some low income households to occupy better housing than their incomes would suggest. Finally, lingering controls on rents may provide an incentive for some higher income households to remain in poor rented accommodation.

In the housing association and local authority rented sectors the link between income and poor conditions is weaker but nevertheless still present. A range of indirect factors have been held responsible for the concentration of certain groups in the poorest condition local authority housing. Homeless people, for example, are likely to have low incomes, to be offered the most readily available accommodation, and to be forced to accept whatever they are offered. This combination of factors inevitably channels this group into poorer quality housing. More generally, lower income households may be less able to wait for offers of better quality accommodation than those on higher income levels.

Although low income households as a whole are significantly more likely to live in poor condition housing than owners on higher incomes, Table 4.8 also shows that a substantial number of more affluent owners occupy substandard housing. The one million homeowners in poor condition housing are roughly split equally between the four income bands in the table, with almost a quarter of a million owner-occupier households in substandard housing in the highest income band.

Information from the Scottish House Condition Survey supports this picture of the relationship between poor housing conditions and low incomes. In 1991 the average repair cost for owner-occupiers ranged from £1,542 for those with an income of less than £3,000 per annum to £1,137 for those with an income of £24,000 or more. As a result, outstanding repair costs in Scotland were equivalent on average to almost a quarter of the annual income of the poorest group of homeowners, while accounting for less than 1% of the income of the most affluent group.

*Economic activity*

A range of other factors linked to low income also differentiate households living in poor housing conditions. Unemployed people are more likely to live in poor condition housing than those in employment. Retired people and those who are permanently sick or disabled fall somewhere between these two groups. Semi-skilled and unskilled manual workers are also much more likely to live in substandard housing than professional and managerial staff, with junior non-manual and skilled manual workers falling between.

## Age and household type

Successive national house condition surveys have shown that both young and older single people are, in general, the most likely household age/type groups to experience poor housing conditions. Table 4.9, which shows the household type composition of households living in the poorest conditions by tenure in England in 1991, confirms this finding. The 1991 Scottish House Condition Survey found a similar picture.

In the owner-occupied sector, single adults and single older people are the most likely groups to experience poor conditions, while larger adult households are the least likely. Young people starting out on their housing careers often choose or are obliged to purchase poor condition dwellings which they then renovate, often with the aid of a local authority grant. Older people often experience poor housing conditions as a result of declining incomes in retirement, which make it difficult to afford to carry out work. Increasing frailty also makes it more difficult for older people to carry out smaller maintenance jobs. Widowed women whose partners had previously taken responsibility for repair and maintenance are particularly vulnerable.

Poor conditions are spread more evenly in the private rented sector, albeit at a much higher level. Single older people are far more likely to experience poor conditions in this sector than any other group. In local authority accommodation, lone parent and large family households are more likely to live in substandard housing, with older people faring relatively better. The concentration of lone parent and large family households among groups such as homeless households who are more likely to obtain lower quality local authority accommodation explains this in part. In housing association accommodation, younger single households and two adult households experience the worst conditions.

Variations in house conditions by the age of household confirm this picture. In Scotland, the 1991 House Condition Survey found that households aged 65 or more became progressively more likely to occupy below tolerable standard housing with age. The 1991 English House Condition Survey found that among homeowners, households where the head was aged under 34 or over 75 were most likely to experience the worst housing conditions. A similar picture was found in the private rented sector, where almost half of all households with a head aged 65 or over lived in poor conditions.

Table 4.9: Households in the worst conditions by type and tenure, England (1991)

| Household type | Owner-occupied | Private rented | Housing association | Local authority | All households |
|---|---|---|---|---|---|
| No of households by type in worst condition dwellings (000s) | | | | | |
| Single adult | 127 | 95 | 21 | 39 | 282 |
| Small adult | 156 | 103 | 9 | 24 | 292 |
| Single parent | 17 | 23 | 5 | 42 | 87 |
| Small family | 185 | 58 | 8 | 48 | 299 |
| Large family | 102 | 25 | 1 | 39 | 167 |
| Large adult | 84 | 57 | 1 | 31 | 173 |
| Older couple | 131 | 57 | 6 | 40 | 234 |
| Older single | 153 | 118 | 19 | 62 | 352 |
| All households | 955 | 536 | 68 | 326 | 1,886 |
| % of households by type in worst condition dwellings | | | | | |
| Single adult | 15.3 | 29.0 | 30.8 | 11.6 | 17.5 |
| Small adult | 6.3 | 27.8 | 22.0 | 7.7 | 9.1 |
| Single parent | 6.4 | 32.3 | * | 11.6 | 11.2 |
| Small family | 7.4 | 25.7 | 11.1 | 10.0 | 9.1 |
| Large family | 6.8 | 24.3 | * | 10.6 | 8.3 |
| Large adult | 4.9 | 33.7 | * | 8.5 | 7.6 |
| Older couple | 6.1 | 31.7 | 7.0 | 5.8 | 7.6 |
| Older single | 10.6 | 46.3 | 9.7 | 6.5 | 12.4 |
| All households | 7.4 | 31.5 | 10.2 | 8.4 | 10.0 |

Notes: The table refers to households living in the worst conditions. These are defined in the 1991 English House Condition Survey as the 10% of dwellings with the highest repair costs per square metre. The overall number of households experiencing poor conditions is therefore predefined. The table shows variations in the extent to which households in different type and tenure groups are represented within the group living in the worst conditions.
* Indicates numbers in category too small to produce percentages.

Source: DoE (1993a)

## Length of residence

It is also known that there is a relationship between the propensity to live in substandard housing and length of residence, with those who have lived for a long period in the same house more likely to experience poor conditions. For owner-occupiers, the 1991 English House Condition Survey revealed a more polarised pattern, with those resident for under two years and those resident for more than 20 years experiencing most problems. Almost one third of homeowners who had lived in the same dwelling for more than 20 years experienced poor conditions, making them over four times more likely to have problems than homeowners as a whole. This polarised pattern adds support to the picture of young and older single person households as being the most likely type of owner-occupier household to live in substandard housing. In the local authority sector, the likelihood of experiencing poor housing conditions increases with length of residence, but the extent of variation between short and longer term residents is minor. This of course reflects local authority repair and maintenance practices, which are unlikely to be influenced by the length of residence of individual households. Surprisingly, however, housing association tenants show a polarised pattern similar to that of homeowners. The presence of short-term residents in poor conditions in this sector could be partly explained by short-life housing provision, but the increase in the proportion of households experiencing poor conditions with length of residence is more difficult to account for.

*Ethnic origin*

The propensity of households to experience poor housing conditions is also dependent upon their ethnic origin. Table 4.10 shows the proportion of households from four aggregated ethnic groups living in poor housing conditions in 1991 in England. The Scottish, Northern Irish and Welsh surveys do not includes tables on ethnic origin and poor condition in their published reports.

Across all tenures, households of Asian or Other minority ethnic origin are about 1.5 times as likely to experience poor conditions as White households, with Black households also more likely than average to live in substandard housing. Small numbers make it difficult to draw firm conclusions for all tenures. In the owner-occupied sector, both Black and Asian households experience markedly poorer conditions than White households, with Black households the most likely to suffer. In the private rented sector, Asian households experience the worst conditions

Table 4.10: Households in the worst conditions by ethnic origin and tenure, England (1991)

| Household type | Owner-occupied | Private rented | Housing association | Local authority | All households |
|---|---|---|---|---|---|
| No of households by ethnic group in worst condition dwellings (000s) | | | | | |
| White | 880 | 516 | 64 | 317 | 1,777 |
| Black | 22 | 5 | 0 | 2 | 29 |
| Asian | 47 | 7 | 0 | 1 | 55 |
| Other | 4 | 9 | 3 | 5 | 21 |
| All households | 953 | 536 | 68 | 326 | 1,882 |
| % of households by ethnic group in worst condition dwellings | | | | | |
| White | 7.1 | 31.4 | 10.7 | 8.5 | 9.7 |
| Black | 18.0 | * | | * | 11.0 |
| Asian | 15.7 | 48.9 | | * | 15.6 |
| Other | * | 28.7 | | * | 10.2 | 14.2 |
| All households | 7.4 | 31.5 | 10.2 | 8.4 | 10.0 |

Notes: The table refers to households living in *the worst conditions*. These are defined in the 1991 English House Condition Survey as the 10% of dwellings with the highest repair costs per square metre. The overall number of households experiencing poor conditions is therefore predefined. The table shows variations in the extent to which households in different ethnic and tenure groups are represented within the group living in the worst conditions.
* Indicates numbers in category too small to produce percentages.

Source: DoE (1993a)

with almost half living in the worst housing. Numbers of households sampled in the local authority and housing association sectors were too small to allow conclusions to be drawn.

## People living in HMOs

The DoE survey of HMOs also looked at the characteristics of the occupants, although the survey excluded self-contained flats and thus over-estimated the predominance of single people. People living in HMOs tended to be relatively young, and four out of five live alone. There were very few families with young children in this form of accommodation.

Nearly a quarter of HMO tenants were unemployed and a high proportion were on a low income.

## The framework of renewal policies

Public intervention to deal with poor housing conditions has been a key element of housing policy for more than a century. During this period a complex framework of measures has been built up by legislation and the interpretation by the courts of the powers and duties provided. The 1989 Local Government and Housing Act introduced a radical revision of these powers. In brief, the main features of the policy framework for private sector housing renewal are now as follows:

- **Local authorities** (or the Housing Executive Northern Ireland) **are the main agents for the implementation of renewal policies** in their areas, with housing associations playing a supporting role.

- **Local authorities have a duty to consider housing conditions in their district** on an annual basis and to decide what action to take.

- The **standard of fitness for human habitation** (in Scotland the tolerable standard) forms the trigger for public intervention to deal with poor housing conditions. In dwellings occupied by more than one household, additional standards apply.

- **Different policies are used in each tenure** to deal with houses which are identified as unfit.

- **Renovation grants are available as of right to owner-occupiers living in unfit dwellings** for work required to make the property fit, but the amount of grant is determined by a test of resources (or means test) and is subject to an upper limit of £20,000. In theory, owners who do not act to remedy unfitness can be compelled to do so, or have their dwelling closed, that is made subject to an order preventing occupation.

- **Private landlords can be compelled to make their properties fit**, or to close them. Grant aid is available as of right, subject to a test of the landlord's resources.

- In dwellings which are occupied by more than one household (HMOs), local authorities have powers to require the **provision of adequate amenities** and of **means of escape from fire**.

- In some circumstances, **local authorities can carry out work in default** to remedy poor housing conditions in HMOs, and charge the costs to the owner, while in extreme cases, they can take over the management of the property.

- Local authorities have **discretionary powers to provide grants for work to a higher level** than the fitness standard, and to provide minor works assistance, mainly to help older people to stay put.

- Local authorities also have **powers to compulsorily acquire and demolish individual dwellings** or groups of dwellings where they can show that this is the best way to deal with poor housing conditions.

- They also have powers to **declare renewal areas where there is a concentration of low income households in substandard houses**. Renewal areas provide a focus for efforts to improve conditions through a variety of mechanisms including renovation grants, group repair schemes and redevelopment. They replaced older powers to declare housing action areas and general improvement areas. However, area renewal does not form a major component of renewal activity in most areas.

- **Housing associations, Staying Put and Care and Repair agencies**, and the Energy Action Grants Agency also play a role in housing renewal. Housing associations can acquire and improve poor condition dwellings for rent or resale, while Staying Put and Care and Repair agencies provide practical help to homeowners with the execution of building works. Both housing associations and home improvement agencies usually work closely with local authorities. The Energy Action Grants Agency administers the Home Energy Efficiency Scheme (HEES) via a network of approved contractors or installers. Resources for this latter programme come from the Department of Energy.

- **The DoE** is the government department with responsibility for housing renewal. The DoE does not implement policy but sets and reviews the policy framework, provides advice on implementation, allocates capital resources to local authorities for renewal policies and carries out research into the effectiveness of policies. The Housing Corporation, a notionally independent agency, allocates resources to housing associations for the acquisition and renovation of poor condition dwellings.

## Levels of activity

Table 4.11, and Figures 4.4, 4.5 and 4.6 show levels of investment in renovation, the number of grants provided and the level of demolition of housing in recent years. As a result of resource cutbacks, levels of activity have declined sharply. Since 1992, the amount of subsidy for renovation grants and related activity in England has been substantially reduced. The overall level of resources invested in grants in England over the 1983/84 to 1991/92 period has declined from £1.5 billion to less than £0.5 billion at constant 1990/91 prices (Figure 4.4). In 1992, only 34,928 mandatory renovation grants were provided in England compared with 214,000 improvement, repair and intermediate grants when the grant system was at its peak in 1984 (Figure 4.5). Clearance has fallen from almost 100,000 dwellings per annum in the UK in 1971 to about 4,000 in 1991 (Figure 4.6).

## Problems with renewal policy

The framework for renewal policy introduced in England and Wales in 1990 is not working effectively, largely as a result of the shortage of resources. At present the government is undertaking a major review of policy. In brief the main problems with the present system are as follows:

- Underlying most problems is the shortage of capital resources. Local

Table 4.11: Resources for private sector renovation, England and Wales (£m)

| | 1991/92 outturn | 1992/93 outturn | 1993/94 estimate | 1994/95 plans | 1995/96 plans |
|---|---|---|---|---|---|
| Government funding to local authorities for renovation of private housing in England | 57 | 251.7 | 335.3 | 324.4 | 225.8 |
| Amount available after local authority contribution | 335.6 | 447.1 | 540.7 | 376.3 | 358.5 |
| Capital expenditure on renovation of private housing in Wales | 131.2 | 191.9 | 193.2 | 197.2 | na |

Source: DoE (1994); Welsh Office (1994)

**Figure 4.4: Public expenditure on housing renovation, England (1979-95)**

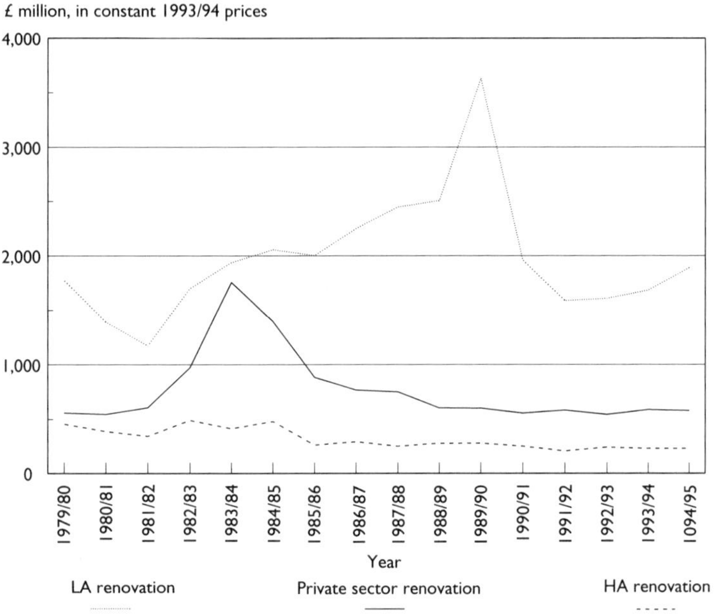


Source: Wilcox (1995)

Housing renewal policy in the UK

**Figure 4.5: Grants by type, England (1969-94)**

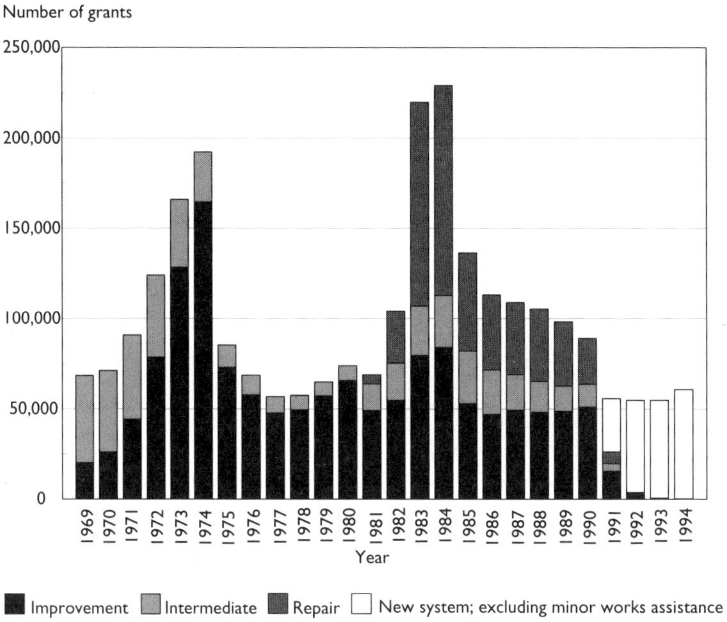

Number of grants

[Bar chart showing number of grants from 1969 to 1994, with categories: Improvement, Intermediate, Repair, New system; excluding minor works assistance]

Source: DoE, SDD and Welsh Office (various years)

**Figure 4.6: Dwellings demolished or closed, Britain (1969-93)**

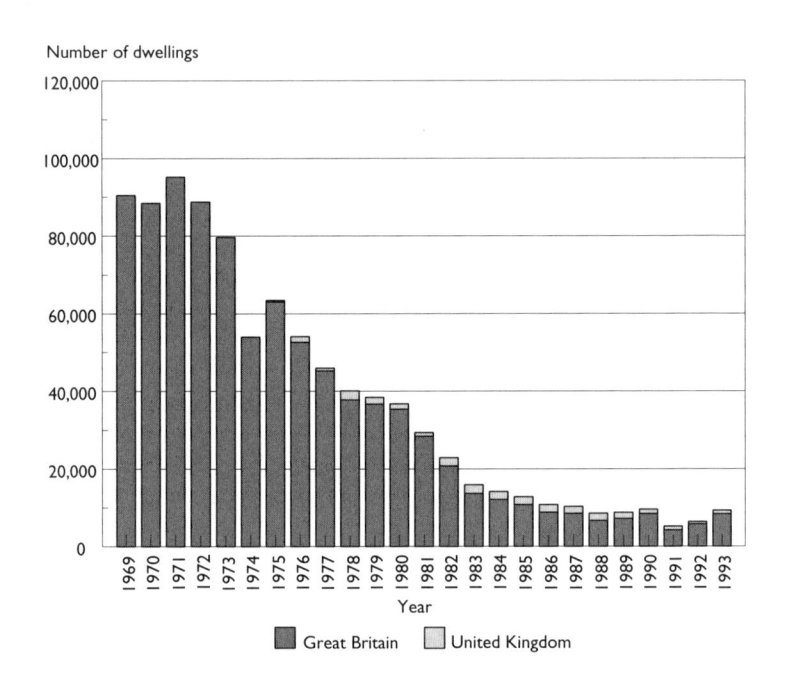

Number of dwellings

[Bar chart showing dwellings demolished or closed in Great Britain and United Kingdom from 1969 to 1993. Values decline from approximately 90,000 in 1969 to under 10,000 by the early 1990s.]

Great Britain □ United Kingdom

Source: DoE, SDD and Welsh Office (various years)

authorities determine the level of investment which they devote to private sector housing renewal within their overall capital programme, but the government has a strong influence on this through its controls on local authority capital expenditure and more directly through the subsidy it provides for housing renewal investment. Allocations of subsidy on private sector renewal activity in England have fallen by an average of 23% between 1993/94 and 1994/95.

- In Wales the picture is less serious. The Welsh Office has made private sector renovation high priority, and there is a separate budget for mandatory renovation grants expenditure for individual local authorities. Additional resources have been made available for local authorities adopting area-based renewal policies. Expenditure on renewal has been maintained at about £200 million for the last three years (Table 4.11). Although the number of grants provided has fallen since the peak of activity in 1984 the decline has been much less than in England. Some 11,543 renovation grants were provided in Wales in 1992 compared to almost 30,000 in 1984. The maximum ceiling for individual grants has also been set higher than in England at £24,000 rather than £20,000.

- Many local authorities cannot meet the demand for mandatory renovation and disabled facilities grants. In most areas, there is little or no publicity. In some cases local authorities are attempting to limit demand by placing enquirers on waiting lists for surveys or the test of resources. Other authorities have developed systems to prioritise mandatory grant applications, including policies to restrict entitlement to particular areas. All of these measures are open to legal challenge as they restrict the right of those living in unfit housing to a grant.

- Few local authorities are actively surveying their areas to identify unfit dwellings, despite the obligation placed on them to do so by the 1989 Local Government and Housing Act. In order to cope with the shortage of grant resources, many authorities have found it expedient to avoid surveying properties unless they are forced to or unless this fits into a planned renewal programme.

- There are a number of weaknesses in the test of resources which mean that many applicants cannot afford to make the contribution which the test indicates. The most serious problem is that the test of resources compares income to a notional set of allowances rather than to actual outgoings. One important cost which is not taken directly into account is mortgage repayments. These can not only make it difficult for a household to afford to meet its share of building costs, but can also make it impossible for the household to raise a secured loan to meet these costs. As a result, some households are forced to consider unsecured loans, which are much more expensive to service.

- Relatively few privately rented properties now receive grants. In 1991/92 only 1,540 mandatory renovation grants (7% of the total) went to private landlords in England. In many areas, local authorities are holding back from taking action against poor conditions in the private rented sector because they are concerned about the cost of the grants which this action might oblige them to provide, or because with the virtual elimination of controls on rent levels they are opposed to the provision of grant aid to private landlords on principle. As some of the poorest housing conditions are found in private rented dwellings, this is a serious cause for concern.

- Area renewal policies are progressing slowly and there have been fewer declarations than expected. Many local authorities are being cautious in declaring renewal areas because they are uncertain about the availability of finance implementation. Where renewal areas have begun to succeed, this is because authorities have taken firm measures to restrict demand from elsewhere or where resources have come from other programmes such as City Challenge.

- Group repair schemes enable local authorities to simultaneously improve a number of adjacent dwellings. Through the use of a single contract, the local authority can secure a greater degree of control over materials and workmanship and thus achieve higher standards and some economies of scale. However group repair is inconsistent with means-tested grants. If some households in a block are ineligible for grant or entitled to less grant than others, it may be difficult to persuade them to take part in a group repair scheme and thus problematic to get projects off the ground.

- Most practitioners take the view that the current level of dwellings clearance is too low but to achieve a substantial increase would be difficult. Owner-occupation levels are now high in the areas where conditions are poorest and there would be considerable opposition to clearance from owners unless compensation terms were sufficient to allow them to purchase a similar home nearby or to secure some improvement in housing conditions. The costs of clearance and the provision of compensation and disturbance payments are also extremely high in comparison with the amounts of government subsidy which individual local authorities receive. Demolition programmes can also generate demands for rehousing in the local authority or housing association sectors which cannot be met because of the shrinking pool of relets and the growing numbers of homeless people.

- Housing association rehabilitation activity has fallen to less than 15% of the Housing Corporation's current programme. In the late 1970s, housing associations played a vital role in the rehabilitation of older housing by buying poor condition properties and rehabilitating them for rent or for sale, especially in general improvement areas and housing action areas. The level of renovation peaked at 18,500 in 1984 before falling rapidly to only 7,000 in 1992. Although research has suggested that the causes of this change in the role of associations are complex, the shift to mixed funding arrangements and fixed levels of housing association grant have made rehabilitation unviable in many areas.

## Conclusion

As we have seen, although housing conditions are proportionately worst in the private rented sector, the majority of privately owned poor condition properties in England are now owner-occupied. Successive governments have promoted home ownership among lower income households and over the postwar period a substantial proportion of poor condition pre-1919 dwellings formerly rented out by private landlords have become owner occupied. Not surprisingly, the poorest condition properties have commanded the lowest prices in most cases and attracted those least able to afford house purchase, despite the higher ongoing repair and maintenance costs associated with such properties. In addition, an increasing proportion of homeowners are older people whose incomes have fallen after retirement. As a result, home ownership is no longer associated exclusively with affluence. The UK may differ from most European countries in having a relatively high level of home ownership in the older housing stock and among low income households.

Many low income homeowners find it difficult to meet the costs of repairs and improvements because they cannot afford the costs of a new loan or a top-up to their existing mortgage. The traditional approach to renovation in the owner-occupied sector in the UK is through the provision of capital grants with eligibility determined primarily on the basis of dwelling condition. But with a large pre-1919 stock still remaining, and with problems emerging in the 1919-45 stock, it is no longer realistic to expect this approach to continue. The government has already taken the step of targeting grants on the basis of household income in an attempt to reduce demand/entitlement. The first attempt has not succeeded but the grant system will be recast to match demand more closely to resources and a number of options are available to meet this objective.

The problem with this approach is that it does nothing to ensure, encourage or facilitate renovation in the bulk of the stock where grants are not available (Leather and Mackintosh, 1994). The challenge in the UK in coming years is to find alternative mechanisms which will generate investment in the older housing stock to replace the resources previously invested by the state. The search for such mechanisms has only just begun.

FIVE

# Strategies for public regulation of urban renewal and housing rehabilitation in Denmark

*Knud Erik Hansen and Hans Skifter Andersen*

## The historical development of urban renewal in Denmark

Until the end of the 1960s, unhealthy housing conditions were the main reason for public involvement in housing rehabilitation in Denmark. The authorities were entitled to prevent the use of unhealthy housing. They also had the powers to require dwellings in poor condition to be modernised or demolished and replaced with new housing. The local authorities did not make full use of these powers, however.

After 1969 the grounds for public involvement in housing rehabilitation were extended beyond unhealthy housing conditions. The authorities could now also demand that a property be rehabilitated, if it did not meet up-to-date standards or was in a bad state of repair. This was made possible through a slum clearance act which resulted in a growing public involvement in urban renewal, with local authorities managing the activity.

The policy was still mainly to demolish blocks of properties and build new housing estates in the renewal areas. This caused massive protests from residents who demanded a say in the process, often preferring to preserve properties instead of demolishing them.

In the mid-1970s regulations were changed. The authorities now had to inform the residents and involve them in the planning of renewal activities. Later, the policy was further changed with fewer dwellings being demolished and more being renovated. This type of activity was mostly concentrated in the bigger cities.

By the 1980s most dwellings in the urban renewal areas were preserved with only very few being demolished. By then, the policy aimed more at creating additional open space for recreation and seldom involved new construction. A new law was passed, *byfornyelseslove* (Urban Renewal Act). This was aimed at rehabilitation, with demolition being the exception. The rights of the residents were further strengthened by allowing them to veto certain elements of a renovation scheme.

Until the 1980s, public housing rehabilitation schemes were mostly dealing with the late-19th century housing stock. But in the 1980s problems requiring public intervention emerged in housing estates from the 1960s and 1970s.

The regulations in the Urban Renewal Act are complex and the legislation can be complicated to use. Renewal activities are subsidised by the public and therefore expensive for both state and local authorities. As a result, in the late 1980s there was a growing interest in less expensive and less extensive public involvement in housing renewal. Following this, in the early 1990s new laws were passed with this in mind, also aimed at housing requiring less comprehensive renovation.

## Economic conditions

Denmark is a small country with about 5.1 million inhabitants and 2.4 million dwellings. The population stagnated in the 1980s and is expected to fall in the future. The overall need for housing is therefore expected to decline. With one of the highest gross national products (GNP) per capita in Europe (about $26,000 per inhabitant in 1993), it is a rich country. There was rapid economic growth from 1960 to 1973, but the economy stagnated in the 1980s. These problems were a result of a period of high inflation and interest rates, coupled with a large fiscal deficit in the 1970s. This led to a decline in private housing investment in the 1980s, which also had a negative effect on housing rehabilitation.

The economic situation changed at the beginning of the 1990s, and Denmark now has low inflation and low interest rates. Economic growth has returned. Real interest rates are still quite high, which can pose problems for housing investment.

Denmark is a welfare state and a large share of the economy is public consumption, with a correspondingly high tax burden and relatively low private consumption. This also effects housing consumption. There are, however, relatively few people with incomes so low that they cannot meet the costs of a dwelling in good condition.

## Housing policy and the housing market

Housing in Denmark is an important part of the welfare state, and public involvement in housing is comprehensive. It is not seen as a public good, but it is an important political objective that adequate housing should be available for all citizens. Housing policy aims to influence both public and private sectors using both direct and indirect instruments.

Since the 1950s, housing finance has been based on a limited number of private mortgage institutions, which were authorised to give loans based on the security on fixed property. Finance was raised by the sale of bonds on the capital market and interest rates followed the market.

Table 5.1 shows the pattern of housing tenure in Denmark in 1993. Just over 50% of the stock is owner-occupied, mostly in the form of single family dwellings. About 20% of the stock is rented from local authorities or non-profit-making corporations.

With high interest rates in the 1970s, Denmark introduced generous subsidies to make housing affordable, especially for new building. New social housing and cooperative housing also received interest payment subsidies. There were extensive tax subsidies for all owner-occupied housing, at probably the highest level in Europe. Housing allowances were also quite favourable. The total amount of housing subsidies amounted to more than $1,000 per inhabitant per year at the beginning of the 1990s, of which about 70% were given as tax subsidies for owner-occupied housing.

Table 5.1: The housing market in Denmark

|  | % of all dwellings |
|---|---|
| Owner-occupied | 54 |
| Single family houses | 50 |
| Owner-occupied flats | 4 |
| Cooperatives | 4 |
| Rented dwellings | 42 |
| Private persons | 11 |
| Private corporations | 11 |
| Non-profit corporations | 17 |
| State and local authorities | 3 |

Source: Skifter Andersen (1992)

Social housing in Denmark is owned by non-profit-making housing associations, who are authorised by local authorities and subject to detailed legislation. Every estate or section is a separate financial unit, so there is no cross-subsidy or pooling of costs or rents between and high low cost estates. There is extensive involvement of tenants who often constitute the majority of members of the boards of directors for the associations. There is a special board for each housing estate elected directly by the tenants, and these boards can decide on how to use some of the budget earmarked for maintenance.

Table 5.2 shows some key indicators of the housing market in Denmark in 1990.

Private rented housing in Danish towns and cities is subject to strict rent control which covers 90% of the private rented stock. In principle rents are determined by the costs associated with the running of the property. The rent includes an amount per square metre transferred to a maintenance account and a fixed, so-called capital yield for the owner (see Skifter Andersen, 1992). The remaining rent is based on a budget for other costs including payments on mortgages. There is also a price control system for cooperative housing.

## Deterioration

Some sections of the Danish housing stock have not been adequately maintained and improved over the years and consequently the dwellings have deteriorated. This mainly applied to tenements dating from before 1950, and in particular to those built before 1920. There are also problems in some newer social housing estates.

The degree of deterioration and lack of improvement varies with tenure (Figure 5.1), with those that are, or have been, subject to controls on rents more likely to lack amenities. There are no available figures for the state of repair of housing in Denmark, but figures on amenities usually reflect this.

There are several causes of deterioration, a major one being the regulation of private rented housing. This is a complicated process which does not give landlords enough economic incentive to maintain the properties. Moreover, private rented housing is mostly found in the older housing stock, where there is a greater potential for deterioration.

A high proportion of the tenants in private rented housing are relatively worse off because of being unemployed and/or on a low income. There

Table 5.2: Housing market indicators in Denmark (1990)

| | |
|---|---|
| New dwellings per year per 1,000 inhabitants (1980-89) | 5 |
| Number of dwellings in stock per 1,000 inhabitants | 450 |
| Average dwelling size per square metre* | 86 |
| Dwellings without bath, % of stock | 11 |
| Dwellings built before 1950, % | 46 |
| Average rent per year ($) | 4,100 |
| Rent/disposable household income % | 16 |
| Average house prices in ($) | 90,000 |

Note: * Net floor area.

Figure 5.1: Percentage of dwellings in older blocks of flats lacking amenities (1990)

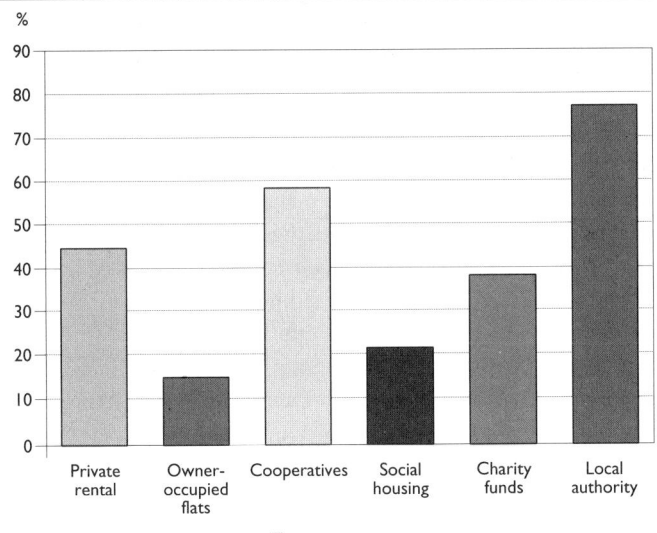

are twice as many single households as the national average and less than a third of the average level of families with children. This tenure also has a higher than average proportion of both young and older people. Of all privately owned rental housing 86% is located in the bigger towns and cities, with some 50% in Copenhagen.

The figures on dwellings lacking amenities are also high for private cooperatives in tenements. However, in practice the figure is probably a great deal lower, as many improvements in cooperatives are not registered.

Most cooperatives are former privately owned rental housing, purchased in poor condition.

Owner-occupied flats, which form only 4% of the total stock, seldom lack amenities. These flats were previously rented housing, and most have a WC, a bathroom and central heating. This has been a precondition for change in tenure to owner-occupation in recent years. Most owners keep their dwellings well maintained, although in some of the estates there might be some problems with maintenance of other parts of the buildings. The owners are organised in an association of homeowners that should take care of common maintenance, but often too small a budget allocation is made. This is because residents want housing costs to look small when selling. As a consequence costs for larger maintenance works have to be collected directly in every case and some are not able to pay, causing financial difficulties for the association.

Most older social housing has been well maintained, but there have been problems in some social estates dating from the 1960s and 1970s. These are usually unattractive concrete estates with structural defects. Low income groups and residents with social problems have often been concentrated in flats in these estates, increasing the range of problems.

Pre-1950s private rented tenements represent the largest need for renovation. An estimate from 1989 suggests that there is a need for DKr22 billion to be invested in private rented dwellings to bring them up to modern standards. Public rented housing requires investment of DKr8 billion and the social rented sector needs DKr2 billion.

Owner-occupied single family houses have so far seldom reached a state of problematic deterioration in Denmark. Where they do, this is because older owners have failed to keep up with repair and maintenance, and this is normally reflected in the price upon sale. Problematic deterioration has mostly been found in two areas:

- Dwellings in old inner-city areas, consisting largely of properties of historical value. The deterioration in these districts is often closely linked with the industrial and commercial development of the area.

- Housing and residential areas dating from the onset of industrialisation at the end of the 19th century and the beginning of the 20th century. These are mainly high-density tenement blocks. In the bigger cities tenements will be four- or five-storey buildings, in the smaller towns two- or three-storey. There is often a lack of open space, poor light and sub-standard sanitation. These properties often are or have been seriously run down. Deterioration is largely attributable to the age of the buildings. However, these areas have also suffered because a large proportion of the buildings are privately rented with insufficient regulation to ensure regular repair and maintenance.

## Political objectives

The main objective for public involvement in housing rehabilitation and urban renewal at the *national* level has been to preserve older poor standard housing and to upgrade to modern standards. In addition, there has been a social objective of improving housing conditions for poor people, as the worst dwellings usually have a high proportion of low income residents. The aim is to make it possible for the existing residents with low incomes to stay in the area or alternatively to choose a similar but modernised dwelling in another area. Involvement and consultation with residents in the renewal process has been an important goal.

It has also been seen as a major benefit that urban renewal creates jobs. Unemployment in the building sector has been a decisive factor in the establishment of some of the most recent renovation programmes. Energy-saving and broader environmental concerns have also been of growing importance over the past 10 years.

The national objectives have been very much reflected at the *local* authority level. In most areas up-to-date housing has been the main goal. Most local authorities have given high priority to poor condition housing areas with low income groups. In other municipalities, often smaller ones, high priority has been given to the upgrading of city centres to make the town more attractive for business and tourism.

## Regulation of tenure

A number of factors can have an influence on private sector activity in the maintenance and rehabilitation of the housing stock. These include regulation through rent controls and the taxation of property. One of the most important causes of inadequate maintenance and improvement of dwellings in Denmark is the inexpedient regulation of private rented housing. In general, legislation has aimed to achieve other objectives than to promote housing maintenance and rehabilitation. However, there are some exceptions.

## Financing of housing rehabilitation

In comparison with many other European countries, it is easy to get a loan for housing rehabilitation in Denmark. From the Danish mortgage institutions it is possible to obtain a loan with security on the property covering up to 90% of renovation expenses, as long as the overall debt on the property remains below 80% of its value. Interest rates are low in comparison to personal loans from banks. However, until the mid-1980s interest rates were generally so high in Denmark that investment in housing rehabilitation became expensive for ordinary households, especially where it was not possible to get tax deductions on interest charges.

## Tax benefits

Owner-occupiers have also been able to obtain favourable treatment over tax relief on loan interest payments. This has had a considerable effect on rehabilitation in the owner-occupied sector, especially single family housing. In recent years, however, the government has begun to reduce the tax benefits from up to 70% of interest to around 40%. Rented housing and cooperatives have not enjoyed tax benefits for investment in housing renovation although residents in cooperatives have sometimes been able to obtain these benefits when financing improvements with personal loans from banks. But it should be noted that these loans have high interest rates.

## Regulation of private rented housing

The Danish private rented sector has been subject to strict rent control (see Skifter Andersen, 1992). In principle, rents should mirror the costs of running the property. Regulated rents (covering 90% of the stock) are calculated as the sum of budgeted running costs plus a 'capital yield' calculated as a percentage of the property's 1973 value.

Rents can be raised above this through a maintenance levy charged on a per square metre basis (about $10 per square metre per annum in 1994). This money does not have to be spent in the year collected. Each year landlords are obliged to account to tenants for expenditure and reserves accumulated. Some of the money is paid to a central fund for the private rented sector which can only be used when all other money has been allocated. Money from the central fund is lent at low interest rates for housing rehabilitation in the sector. Rents can also be raised after improvements have been made to cover loan interest and repayments plus yield on the owners' invested capital.

In principle, Danish regulations should give reasonable incentives to maintain and improve private rented dwellings. The system forces landlords to earmark money for maintenance from their rental income with the central fund having a positive impact. The main problem has been that the money collected for maintenance has been insufficient and most properties' maintenance accounts have been in deficit. Moreover rental income to cover the capital yield has not been increased for many years so it seldom covers the real capital costs. Many properties are being run at a loss, with landlords trying to minimise this by saving on maintenance costs, resulting in deterioration.

In recent years the government has started to take action to solve these problems. Rents have been increased to allow more money to be set aside for maintenance and changes in legislation are being considered to provide better incentives for landlords and tenants to renovate. One important initiative is an experimental pilot project which allows landlords and tenants to agree to suspend some rent control rules thus allowing higher rent increases which fund an increased level of rehabilitation. To encourage this, the government gives subsidies which cover part of the rent increase.

## Regulation of cooperatives

The cooperative sector is relatively small, but has increased rapidly since the 1980s following government encouragement of the transfer of private rented dwellings to cooperatives. Many transferred properties were in poor condition, and lacked a bathroom or central heating.

Residents have a share of the cooperative which collectively owns the property. Principal regulation is through control of share prices. Shares are allocated to properties according to their size, the price based on the difference between the value of the property and its debts. The price can increase to reflect individual residents' improvements with depreciation taken into account.

The main problem for cooperatives is that they do not receive interest rate tax relief for rehabilitation loans, making improvements expensive. Moreover prices of shares often fall because of rehabilitation, as the taxable value of the property is not increased in line with the debts.

However the Danish experience points to cooperatives being a better functioning tenure than private rented housing, mainly due to residents being motivated to maintain and improve their properties. Cooperatives have made greater investment in rehabilitation in recent years and been more active in utilising new subsidies introduced by the government for rehabilitation.

There are two main reasons for this. One is that it has been relatively inexpensive to buy and live in cooperatives, so that residents have been able to build up reserves for renovation. The other is that cooperatives tend to be well organised and have a good community spirit. Some have problems with poor management and may in future have fewer reserves as the price for shares gets closer to the market price.

## Owner-occupied flats

Several factors contribute to the deterioration of tenements of owner-occupied flats. One is a lack of measures to ensure that all owners contribute to common expenditure. This has been a particular problem in the last few years as values have declined. For many owners, it has not been possible to finance renovation costs through new mortgages.

Tenements with smaller owner-occupied flats often have problems with building management. The residents are often younger people who live in the flats for a only few years, and lack both long-term commitment and experience of collective property management. In comparison to the cooperatives, community spirit can be weak.

A general problem is that the poor state of a building is not always reflected in the price when a flat is sold. Most buyers look only at the internal condition of their part of the dwelling. Future building renovation costs are thus often insufficiently accounted for.

## Regulation of social housing

Social housing has the best maintenance record within the Danish housing stock. This is partly because most of these dwellings were built after 1940, but is also due to the well-functioning regulation of the sector.

There are strict rules about how much money can be charged for maintenance and put aside for future replacement. Housing associations are supervised by local authorities who can demand that rents be increased to raise funding for maintenance.

As part of a policy to diminish differences in rents between newer and older dwellings, the government has introduced a system where some rental income from older dwellings is paid into a central fund, from which the associations can get funding through cheap loans for rehabilitation.

## Urban renewal and housing rehabilitation programmes

As indicated in Chapter One, public regulation of urban renewal and housing rehabilitation for different programmes can be divided into 'direct' and 'indirect' approaches. In the case of direct regulation, local authorities have the power to compel private owners to renovate their dwellings in accordance with certain rules. In the case of indirect regulation the authorities do not have such powers, but instead try to motivate private owners to renovate through subsidies or other incentives. Conditions for support can include requirements relating to the kinds of renovation undertaken and limits on expenditure.

The form of public intervention has been influenced by the problems of deterioration, the objectives of the policies and the characteristics of the tenures involved. There have been three programmes since the late 1960s: one from the 1960s and 1970s, one for the 1980s and one for the first part of the 1990s.

### Programmes with direct regulation

#### Slum clearance programme

The target for public programmes in the 1960s was the tenement districts made up of buildings constructed during the onset of industrialism in the latter half of the 19th century. These were often made up of closely built four- or five-storey buildings. In Copenhagen and the larger towns one street could have two, sometimes three, rows of tenements. Often there were buildings for small craft and trade industries in the yards. Many buildings lacked toilets and almost all were without baths and central heating.

There were two main programmes to deal with these problems, the sanitation law (*boligtilsynsloven*) and the slum clearance law (*saneringsloven*). Both gave the local authorities the leading role. They were based on direct regulation, giving public authorities the power to enforce implementation of a renewal plan even if opposed by the owners.

According to the sanitation law, all municipalities with more than 25,000 inhabitants had to form a sanitation commission (*boligkommision*) to deal with unhealthy dwellings. This could forbid occupation of insanitary dwellings (ie, condemnation). The owner could modernise, but only if the modernisation could be implemented at sufficiently low cost. The authorities could not require the building to be demolished, nor could they compulsorily purchase the building and have it demolished.

This law had a relatively minor effect, being mostly used for single buildings. There were, however, examples of blocks of buildings being condemned and then left empty for a builder to redevelop the property.

The main programme was based on the slum clearance law in force from 1969 to 1982. During this period, significant changes were made. At the start slum clearance was at the fore, but by the end of the 1970s policy had changed to favour renovation rather than demolition.

Authorised urban renewal companies were empowered to develop renewal plans. Local authorities commented on these plans and passed them to the Ministry of Housing. The Ministry then considered the plan, and then approved or rejected it. Approval gave access to subsidies for implementation.

In practice, local authorities were the lead agents in urban renewal. They had considerable influence over the urban renewal company, and approval from the Ministry of Housing implied that the local authority had accepted the plan.

By the mid-1970s residents had gained influence. Urban renewal companies were required to inform residents and to invite their comments on proposals. Only after considering these comments could they advance the plan. Residents also had an opportunity to influence the plan through councillors on the local authority.

A plan normally covered one block of tenements, and local authorities often combined plans to cover selected areas. An approved plan gave the authorities (or the urban renewal companies) powers to expropriate (acquire property under compulsory powers) for demolition and large scale renovation. They could order owners to carry out maintenance and improvements and expropriate the property if the order was not implemented.

The local authorities paid the cost of planning, demolition, and so on, and subsidised the renovation. To calculate the subsidy the costs of renovation were divided in two main parts. The first was covered by an increase in the value of the property resulting from the renovation work.

The subsidy for this was provided through cheap loans or by subsidy on private loans. The other costs, those that exceeded the increased value, were covered by a grant. Residents had the right to individual housing allowances which covered the first year's rent increase and were gradually withdrawn over five or ten years. There were no fixed rules for the standard of the renovation. In practice the local authorities required full renovation and repair as well as measures to bring the dwelling up to date (with WC, bath, central heating, insulation, double glazing, and a new kitchen).

**Renovation programme**

In 1982 the Urban Renewal Law signalled a new policy towards renovation. Since the slum clearance law was already being used for renovation in most areas, the new law did not represent a completely changed policy.

The law included powers similar to those in the slum clearance act, with one main exception. Both the owner and the resident could reject specific parts of a renovation scheme. Local authorities could still demand that the building be fully repaired with energy efficiency measures plus basic installations. However, the residents and the owner could refuse improvements, such as a bath and new kitchen.

Urban renewal companies were given a new role. Their rights to take decisions on plans were transferred to local authorities, with the companies becoming consultants to or agents of the authorities. This change was not significant, as renewal had functioned this way in practice under the previous law. However, after 1991, urban renewal companies no longer had to be authorised, allowing local authorities to choose any consultant.

The Urban Renewal Law included one major new procedure. It was previously only possible to implement a scheme that included at least one block of properties. Now procedures for the renovation of single properties were included. Money allocated for these procedures was initially restricted, but local authorities were now free to choose between procedures for single properties and housing areas.

Public subsidies also changed slightly. Residents still had the same right to individual benefits. There was no formal cost limit for a renovation project. This was considered unproblematic if renovation costs were less than 75% of the rebuilding costs, but it is not unusual for renovation costs to be equal to, or greater than the costs of replacement.

The programme allowed local authorities to make plans within a yearly investment limit of about DKr1 billion, the precise amount being set annually. At the end of the 1980s it was about DKr1.5 billion increasing to about DKr3 billion by the 1990s.

## Programmes with indirect regulation

Until 1990 the public strategy for urban renewal and housing rehabilitation was based almost exclusively on the Urban Renewal Law and involved direct regulation. This changed in the early 1990s. Two new main programmes have been passed along with some smaller ones.

One programme is the private renewal programme based on the Private Urban Renewal Act (*lov om privat byfornyelse*). This is aimed at single properties in three categories: private rented housing, private cooperatives and social housing. Indirect regulation is its basis. Owners are expected to take the initiative and, with tenants, decide what kind of renovation should be carried out. In the case of private rented housing, an important precondition is for the landlord and a majority of the tenants to reach agreement on the renovation scheme and on the resultant rent increase. Subsidies are available to reduce rent increases. The state pays 40% of the rent increase for the first eight years. After this, support is gradually withdrawn tapering to zero after 16 years.

Applications for subsidies are handled and approved by the Ministry of Housing. A private consultant has to guarantee that the renovation is within the list of items that can be subsidised. The local authorities are not normally involved, although they can help rehouse residents if necessary and provide information.

The programme allows annual subsidised investments of DKr2.4 billion, about a third going to each target group. From 1996 the programme has been reduced to include only private rental housing and to a limit on investment of DKr700 million per year. There are no formal cost limits for renovation projects, but to keep rents under market levels renovation costs normally have to be below DKr2-3,000 per square metre.

A second indirect programme, the grant for housing renovation (*tilskudsloven*), in operation from 1990 to 1994, had increases in employment in the building sector as its main objective. It ended in 1995 when activity in the building sector was thought to have reached a satisfactory level. This programme was aimed at smaller improvements in all kinds of housing. Applications took their turn with approvals given until the yearly cost limit was reached. Grant applications were processed by local authorities to be registered in a national database.

Subsidies were only on labour costs, and not for building materials. The subsidy level was between 40 and 50% minus DKr2,000. The maximum grant was DKr10,000 per dwelling, although properties preserved for their architectural value could attract a maximum grant of DKr50,000. These grants generated an annual investment of about DKr4-5 billion for a total grant of DKr1.5 billion.

In the 1980s, the renovation programme for social housing estates built in the 1960s and 1970s was mainly implemented through subsidies for new loans with lower annual payments along with grants from a common fund.

As part of the government's energy policy, a programme of subsidies for installation of central heating systems with water-based heat supplied from electric power stations has also been established.

## Changed strategy

Previously, Danish strategy for urban renewal and housing rehabilitation was based solely on the Urban Renewal Act, and earlier on the slum clearance law, both of which used direct regulation. This strategy has been changed with the introduction of indirect regulation programmes and there is increasing interest in further legislation relating to different tenures to promote private housing rehabilitation without official interference.

## The role of local authorities

Historically, local authorities have had an important role in direct regulation. They retain this role, with powers to implement their plans. The Urban Renewal Act makes it possible for local authorities to renew housing in specified districts, to renew open spaces in housing areas and to demolish properties. These decisions are taken without reference to central government. The local authorities often work through consultants, in practice mainly one of the two predominate urban renewal companies in Denmark.

Central government's role has been reduced to setting limits to each authority's expenditure within the national budget and to setting out procedures for the implementation of subsidies. The latter are mainly funded by central government, with local authorities also contributing a considerable amount.

Owners are generally left to organise renovation of their individual properties. However, local authorities often use their powers of expropriation for buildings needing extensive renovation.

In contrast, local authorities play only a minor role for programmes using indirect regulation. Central government determines the subsidies, sets guidelines and establishes the main priorities. The remaining decisions are taken by owners. Allocation is through a queuing system.

## Evaluation of the results of the urban renewal and housing rehabilitation policies

In a study of urban renewal strategies made for the Nordic Council of Ministers in 1992 (Hansen and Skifter Andersen, 1993), the effects of the housing rehabilitation policies of the Nordic countries in the 1980s were evaluated. The following utilises figures and conclusions from this study with additional information on recent developments incorporated.

Very little is known about the changes over time to housing quality in Denmark. There are no periodical surveys on the state of repair of the buildings, as in some other countries, only registration of the changes in dwellings lacking modern amenities. Figure 5.2 shows how the proportion of housing lacking modern facilities has changed in recent years.

**Figure 5.2: Changes in the number of dwellings in Denmark lacking amenities**

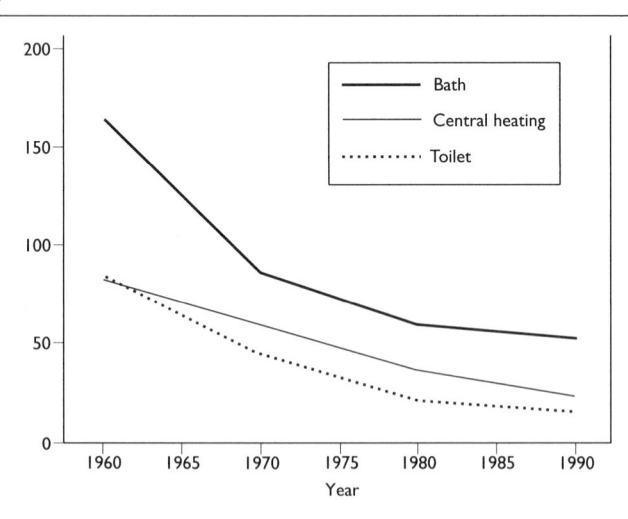

The large renovation programme of the 1960s targeted dwellings without bathrooms through improvement or demolition, concentrating on older blocks of flats. By the 1970s, with this type of housing modernised, improvement activity slowed down. As Figure 5.2 shows, very few new bathrooms were installed during the 1980s.

But even by the beginning of the 1990s, 12% of dwellings were still without indoor bathrooms, 4% lacked toilet facilities and 11% did not have central heating. Dwellings lacking amenities tended to be private rented housing, older cooperatives and local authority stock.

These figures indicate some failure on the part of the Danish government's strategy for housing rehabilitation in the 1970s and 1980s. As described above, during this period there was only one programme with one type of regulation, that of direct regulation under the Urban Renewal Act. Subsidies were increased considerably during the 1980s but, as Table 5.3 shows, the effect was quite limited.

Just over 5,000 dwellings per annum were improved under the Urban Renewal Act by the beginning of the 1990s. This is about 1,000 dwellings per one million inhabitants or 0.2% of the stock. However the cost of renovating each dwelling was quite high at an average of around $70,000, partly due to the poor condition of many dwellings requiring extensive renovation. But renovation work may have been more extensive than necessary as the legislation provided no incentives for local authorities or owners to minimise costs. The capitalised value of the direct subsidies from state and local authorities are calculated to constitute more than 60% of the costs. The strategy in the 1980s was inefficient. Regulation of the housing market, especially in the private rented sector, meant that private renewal activity almost came to a halt because owners could not

Table 5.3: The 1982 Danish Urban Renewal Act (1990)

|  | Number | Per million inhabitants | DKr | $ | % of costs |
|---|---|---|---|---|---|
| Number of dwellings improved | 5,200 | 1,000 |  |  |  |
| Investments (millions) |  |  | $59 | 2,150 | 357 |
| Cost per dwelling (000s) |  |  | 413 | 69 |  |
| Rent increase Year 1 |  |  |  |  | 35 |
| Direct subsidies |  |  |  |  | 64 |

recoup the costs through increases in rents. Indirect regulation to encourage private regeneration was not available to the government or local authorities. Furthermore the Danish Urban Renewal Act did not encourage cost-efficient renovation, which partly explains why only comparatively few dwellings were improved at a high cost.

However, urban renewal was popular with Danish residents. They were involved in decisions regarding the renewal of their neighbourhoods and their own dwellings and were given the right to veto certain improvements. Favourable subsidies have made it possible for nearly all residents, irrespective of income, to stay in their dwellings after renewal.

New subsidies for housing rehabilitation introduced in the early 1990s were originally part of employment policies, not a change in urban renewal strategy. Our research on the effects of these subsidies (see Skifter Andersen, 1994) shows that only a small proportion of this money was used for the housing stock most in need of rehabilitation, because there were few limitations on who could receive subsidies and on the use of subsidy.

Experience with the new Private Urban Renewal Act has been better to an extent. It has been difficult to interest private landlords in the programme, but research (Skifter Andersen, 1995b) shows that the law is working well in those properties where it has been utilised. More important structural problems in these buildings are being repaired and essential improvements made. The tenants have considerable involvement and seem satisfied with the rehabilitation.

## Most recent changes in policies

In 1997 the Danish Parliament passed a new legislation on urban renewal and housing rehabilitation. This new legislation will not, in the shorter term, result in dramatic alterations in the way public supported housing renewal is carried through, but it can, over time, mean fundamental changes.

The first major change compared to earlier legislation is an intention to separate the administration and support for urban renewal from that of housing renewal. From now on it is possible for local government to get state support for general regeneration and vitalisation of urban districts threatened by decay. This support can be used for both physical upgrading of infrastructure and for social, cultural and organisational improvements.

The other major change is that more importance is attached to the fact that the initiative for housing renewal comes from owners and tenants and less planning and control should come from local authorities. The control of local governments shall to a greater extent be a result of giving incentives and information to owners and the local authorities are – under certain conditions – allowed to decide what building works should be supported and how much. Moreover the legislation called 'Private Urban Renewal' has been made permanent as a part of the general legislation under the heading 'Agreed housing renewal'.

This legislation means a step towards less direct and more indirect regulation. How fast and extensive the changes will be depends, however, on what local governments are going to do. They can choose to follow the same track as before if they want to. Moreover it can in turn lead to measures used against the old housing stock in the central part of the cities being joined together with measures used to solve problems in newer deprived social housing estates in the suburbs.

SIX

# Urban renewal and housing rehabilitation in Switzerland
Roland Haari

## Historical overview

The unfolding of the postwar era in Switzerland is characterised by three particular features:

- Switzerland did not suffer any noticeable war damage either in its production facilities or in its housing stock;

- as a result of the above, the country's economy recovered somewhat earlier than that of most European countries;

- consequently Switzerland had experienced a large inflow of immigrants by the 1950s, partially explaining the population growth from 4.5 million in 1950 to the current 6.9 million (see Table 6.1).

Despite the different points of departure, the development in Switzerland is strikingly similar to that in other Western European countries. The immediate postwar period was preoccupied with satisfying the increasing demand for housing and also the requirements of a rapidly growing number of private cars. As time progressed, large-scale projects with multi-storeyed buildings appeared beside the two- to three-floor units in the newly constructed areas. Older and even medieval buildings in the cities were replaced by modern structures.

The first signs of disenchantment with the impact of a prosperous economy appeared when public concern was directed to traffic pollution, to the replacement of dwellings by offices, to the protection of historic sites and to the housing conditions in mountainous and economically disadvantaged regions.

Table 6.1: Population growth since 1950 (000s)

| Year | 1950 | 1960 | 1970 | 1980 | 1990 | 1992 | % |
|---|---|---|---|---|---|---|---|
| Swiss | 4,430 | 4,844 | 5,190 | 5,421 | 5,682 | 5,644 | 82 |
| Foreigners | 285 | 585 | 1,080 | 945 | 1,246 | 1,244 | 18 |
| Population total | 4,715 | 5,429 | 6,270 | 6,366 | 6,874 | 6,908 | 100 |
| Development in % (base year 1970=100) | 75 | 87 | 100 | 102 | 109 | 110 | |

Source: *Schweizerische Volkszählung* [Population statistics] (1990)

Continuous social processes cannot be attributed to a specific date. However, 1974, the year of the oil price shock, may be remembered as the turning point for a change in the attitude of the general population. There was a new appreciation of the buildings and the neighbourhoods of the late 19th and early 20th centuries. Simultaneously, citizens' movements showed a growing interest in urban renewal and the protection of the environment. Campaigns were raised to protect the residential areas against traffic pollution and the negative impact of large-scale projects. House owners frequently opted for renovation measures instead of wholesale modernisation of their buildings. On the whole, the maintenance of the existing housing stock found new impetus and the deindustrialisation of cities and towns focused attention on the use of obsolete factory buildings or derelict industrial areas for new purposes. Energy conservation and economical use of land became an increasing concern.

The recession, which characterises the last decade of the 20th century, may eventually signify another turning point in urban renewal and housing renovation. The desire to promote business and to strengthen economical potential leads to the streamlining of the building and the planning codes. The quest of the ecologists for effective environmental standards meets the support of otherwise unlikely allies. Economical land use is seen by the landowners as a signal for an intensified utilisation of their properties. The absorption of environmental costs in traffic prices has sharpened the appetite of the public authorities who see the issue in terms of additional revenues. The 1990s have proved to be a challenging time for urban renewal and housing renovation.

## General social conditions

Around half of Switzerland's land mass of 41,284 square kilometres is mountainous, meaning that most people live in a densely populated strip of land between the Alps and the Jura, which enjoys a mild continental climate. There are four different languages spoken in this relatively small area. The topographic and cultural structure of the country has not allowed for dominating urban and political centres and the five large cities (Zurich, Basel, Bern, Geneva and Lausanne) are therefore of modest size, despite the fact that two thirds of the inhabitants live in these urban settlements. The federal system of government reflects this structure. Many tasks and responsibilities rest with the 26 cantons and their respective communities. The federal government ensures, for example, the execution and the coordination of the cantonal planning. The individual cantons set a broad framework with their local communities at liberty to pursue their own goals. A peculiarity of the Swiss political system is that the zoning regulations and building codes of the cantons and their communities are subject either to a facultative or to an obligatory public vote.

## Housing market and general housing policy

In Switzerland eight salient features characterise the housing market:

1. Private ownership is predominant with close to 70% of dwellings in this category. Investment trusts of different denomination (such as insurance, real estate funds and foundations) control nearly a quarter. Housing cooperatives own about 5% of the apartments and the public authorities 3%.

2. The ratio of owner-occupied houses is small and approximately 70% of houses are for rent.

3. The proportion of substandard housing is insignificant – 95% of all houses have bathrooms and 90% have central heating of one form or another. Only one third of the occupied houses was built before 1947.

4. The available housing space per inhabitant has increased greatly over the last 20 years. While in 1970 the occupants outnumbered the total number of rooms (not counting the kitchen, bathroom and corridor)

in 20% of the apartments, in 1980 the figure was 10% and in 1990, 7%. The average surface area per person was, in 1995, 39 square metres.

5. In view of the high wage level of the workforce, rents are usually moderate at approximately one fifth of income. In 1990, for example, half of the apartments with three to four rooms were rented for prices ranging between CHF600 to CHF999 per month; one quarter was below CHF600 and another quarter above CHF1,000. However, dwellings of the same size, advertised in newspapers, can cost between CHF1,500 and CHF2,500 per month. An inexpensive rent has to be acquired through long duration of the tenancy.

6. The number of vacant dwellings is insignificant. One reason is that the population increase before 1970 easily absorbed the number of newly constructed habitations. Since the population growth appears to be tapering off, it is prosperity that now boosts demand. The impact of the current recession is evident in the percentage of vacant dwellings: 1990 0.44%, 1993 0.92%, 1994, 1.2%.

7. In earlier stages of the housing market, demand usually exceeded supply. Real estate is generally regarded as a safe investment, since the increase in property value remains above the level of inflation in the long run. The owners are therefore motivated to keep their property in good repair. Around 40% of dwellings built before 1961 have been renovated within the last 10 years. In many cases the owners have ready cash and are therefore able to finance the maintenance of their properties themselves. Unlike their counterparts in other countries, the Swiss banks dispose of readily available funds and are willing to give low-interest loans to finance house renovation. In the case of extensive reconstruction of buildings the banks exert considerable influence since they check each project for soundness and viability.

8. The legislation concerning house ownership subscribes to a liberal order and regulates two main aspects:

- The building has to be properly maintained and secured against any possible danger to the public.

- The contract between landlord and tenant, seen primarily as an agreement between two private persons, has to abide by strict rules against unfair practice. Important points include the usable conditions of the premises, rent and rent increases, sufferance of building works and the notice periods of the lease. However, these regulations are only enforced when either the tenant or the landlord takes legal action.

In certain respects some of these assertions need to be differentiated. Private ownership and the ratio of owner occupied dwellings, for example, diverge between rural and urban regions. In rural areas, 85% of the apartments are privately owned and approximately half are occupied by their owners. In the cities these figures are 61% and 23% respectively. Slight changes in the composition of ownership over the last 20 years show a proliferation of associations and funds from 4% to 8%; this tendency being more pronounced in the urban areas. Although substandard housing, measured by construction standards and amenities, is rare, the impairment of environmental qualities is widespread.

The improvement of housing accommodation does not affect all social groups equally. In one fifth of the apartments occupied by foreigners, the inhabitants outnumber the total of rooms, a figure which was common for Switzerland in the 1970s (see Table 6.3). Housing costs also differ.

**Table 6.2: Development of the housing stock since 1970**

| Year | 1970 | 1980 | 1990 |
|---|---|---|---|
| Number of dwellings | 2,207,093 | 2,722,432 | 3,173,322 |
| Development in % | 100 | 123 | 143 |
| Annual number of new constructed dwellings | 63,590 | 40,876 | 39,984 |
| Annual number of new dwellings in % from stock dwellings | 3 | 2 | 1 |

Source: *Eidgenössische Volkszählung* [statistical publication] (1990)

**Table 6.3: Occupied dwellings and inhabitants per room (%)**

| | 1970 | 1980 | 1990 | | |
|---|---|---|---|---|---|
| Inhabitant per room | | | Swiss | Foreigner | Total |
| -0.50 | 27 | 37 | 46 | 50 | 27 |
| 0.51-1.00 | 53 | 53 | 47 | 46 | 55 |
| 1.01+ | 20 | 10 | 7 | 4 | 18 |
| Total | 100 | 100 | 100 | 100 | 100 |

Source: *Eidgenössische Volkszählung* [statistical publication] (1990)

Rents in rural areas and in older buildings are lower than those in urban areas or in newer housing. However, the high rate of renovation and modernisation, coupled with the attractiveness of older constructions is gradually beginning to reverse the picture. In the long run, it can be expected that the existing differences in housing conditions between rural and urban areas or between Swiss and foreign nationals will diminish considerably.

The overall view of the situation in Switzerland reveals three main aspects of the housing policy: housing supply, quality of living in urban areas and environmental protection. Each of these three themes has peculiar ramifications linked to the conditions in the housing markets.

- The issue of **housing supply** arises partly because of the pressure of demand and of the scarcity of lodgings. Another cause is the fact that the majority of people live in rented apartments. Many measures try to address the problem: protection of tenants against the arbitrariness of landlords, preservation of the older (and inexpensive) apartments facing demolition or change of usage, quota of residential space in zoning regulations, subsidising the purchase of land and construction costs in order to reduce rent prices, abolition of building hindrances, promotion of ownership, and so on. The general thrust is not directed against housing deterioration, but towards the protection of tenants against scarcity of dwellings and excessive rent increases.

- The **quality of life in urban areas** is the result of the proliferation of private cars. Alleviating the impact of traffic remains the main goal for improvement in urban settlements. Prosperity not only brought the availability of private transport for everyone but it also promoted a new sensibility to a neighbourhood's surroundings. Consequently, the demand rose for traffic restrictions, as well as for open spaces and the elimination of various nuisances caused by the mixture of business and residential use in inner-city areas.

- **Environmental protection** in housing policy terms mainly means energy conservation. Actions include insulation of houses, for example, modernisation of heating systems and the use of alternative energy sources.

The delineation of a general housing policy has to take into consideration the different roles of the federal, cantonal and communal governments.

The federal authorities concern themselves with tenant protection, reduction in prices of newly built dwellings and the subsidising and modernisation of rural habitations in mountainous regions. Planning, despite a national planning code, is essentially a cantonal task. As mentioned before, the communes are at liberty to pursue their own policies within the framework of the cantonal planning. Since problems of urban renewal do not particularly occupy the cantonal government, public housing becomes a communal task, for example, in the city of Zurich. In the cantons of Geneva and Basel both dominated by a large city, communal and cantonal tasks are not easily distinguishable from one another.

Housing renovations are seen as the duty of the owners. A forceful policy, which encroaches on the prerogative of the proprietors is not found on the agenda of either of the three levels of public authorities. An explanation of the tasks of the different levels of government shows that Switzerland does not really possess a national housing policy. Each of the larger communes retains its own housing policy. Smaller communities often do without it altogether. There exists nevertheless an informal understanding on the part of the concerned parties that leads to some similarity of action in different parts of the country.

## Urban decay and housing deterioration

Urban nuisances originate from economic prosperity or the lack of it. Affluence causes crises of adaptation while economic sluggishness leads to the abandonment of buildings either through lack of demand or through lack of means.

Switzerland possesses a strong economy and a prosperous population. The decrease of the primary sector and the deindustrialisation of the economic system were in the past compensated for by the growth of the tertiary sector. These changes, together with the increasing consumption of housing space, created several problems with different manifestations. The reader has therefore to keep in mind that the following description of urban problems generally represents conflicts in a lengthy and unending process of adjustment. This fact is the main reason why urban renewal and not urban decay is the issue in Switzerland. It also explains the interest of the concerned parties in housing renovation rather than in the subject of housing deterioration.

*The urban fabric*

Change of land use, increased consumption of dwelling space and growth of traffic all influence one another, leading to a cluster of interrelated problems that characterise the different urban areas. One striking feature is the suburbanisation of Switzerland. The newly built-up areas not only have unsatisfactory facilities but they also lack sufficient public transportation. The centres and the inner-city neighbourhoods experience an influx of services, offices and traffic congestion. Houses of the last century and those of the first half of this are torn down and replaced by modern buildings. Increased density follows as a corollary. Conflicting land use (commerce, habitation) and the lack of open space impairs the quality of life. Traffic pollution in the inner-city areas is inevitable, but it also troubles many parts of the suburbs and even the countryside.

Economic transformation had also brought the obsolescence of trades, industries and rural buildings. The disuse of older factory buildings and industrial areas within the towns and cities is a comparatively new and frequent challenge for urban renewal in Switzerland. Public authorities and private developers see this change as a chance for upgrading the urban quality, either by inner-city housing projects or by commercial facilities. Rural buildings within the agglomerations became habitations for suburbanites and in the countryside they are renovated as weekend houses or holiday homes. The multiplying number of weekend houses and holiday homes, which are only temporarily occupied during the year, use up an increasing share of scarce natural resources. They have therefore become a much discussed topic of environmental protection.

## Housing stock

Dilemmas over housing stock in Switzerland have three causes: obsolescence because of change of values or demand, construction faults, and the attitude of the proprietors and political conflicts.

Obsolescence, because of the change of values or demand, is the most widespread housing issue. In the countryside many buildings still lack modern equipment. In the urban areas, the claim to larger accommodation renders older buildings (initially built for lower status groups) unsatisfactory. This is especially true of lodgings built before 1960; their sleeping, living and auxiliary rooms are too small. Environmental goals are another cause of the dilemma. They involve the insulation of houses as well as the installation of heating systems. Construction faults are a new phenomena. They apply mostly to buildings from the 1960s,

1970s and 1980s, which have made much use of new technologies. Flat roofs, prefabricated elements, synthetic fabrics and new materials head the list of complaints.

Dilapidation has its basis in the wear and tear of different parts of a building. Neglect, however, is a most important and decisive intermediate variable which determined whether deterioration actually occurs. As mentioned before, Swiss landlords are generally interested in the maintenance of their properties and the banks dispose of sufficient funds to give out loans for the renovation of houses. However, there nevertheless exists several specific circumstances that harm the upkeep of buildings. One of them is age of the building. In advanced years, landlords may leave necessary renovations to their heirs. Difficulties may also occur with public authorities who administer real estates; here the lengthy process of finding political consent leads to temporary neglect of buildings. Other complications arise from the objections of citizen groups that agitate and win public support, for example, against large scale projects in inner-city neighbourhoods.

## Social conditions

As mentioned before, the maintenance of the building stock is satisfactory. The question is rather whether the renovation of houses is too excessive. The scarcity of sub-standard or plain housing affects certain social groups negatively. Young families with children have a comparatively low income and often live in overcrowded conditions and under strained financial situations caused by high rents. Immigrant families also often dwell in crowded quarters, although the burden of high rent is somewhat alleviated because many of the members of a household are wage earners. Older people, on the other hand, frequently live in the older, inexpensive and commodious lodgings. These houses are often renovated and upgraded and the rent increases may put added pressure on that segment of the population who live on fixed incomes. Low status groups reside in traffic polluted areas with conflicting usage of land.

Moreover, there are social problems which affect certain neighbourhoods. For example, large-scale developments with multi-storeyed houses from the 1970s and 1980s in the fringe areas of the cities are problematic. These projects are not at all popular with the mainstream population because they have frequently attracted immigrant families and borderline groups. Although the houses are spacious and comfortable, the settlements suffer from overcrowding and shabbiness and insolvency and forced removal are frequent.

The meeting places of drug addicts in inner-city neighbourhoods give rise to another major problem. Initially the addicts are tolerated, then they are resisted, forcibly evicted and removed — only to reappear somewhere else. This cycle is an added burden to residential areas that are already heaving under traffic pollution and the inappropriate use of land.

*Future developments*

Present problems are so overbearing and so real, that symptoms and causes cannot be clearly identified. However, urban decay and housing deterioration do not appear overnight, since real estate and the urban infrastructure are of a remarkable longevity. A long process of wear and tear has already taken place before the marks of dilapidation become noticeable. In the face of these facts and in the current economic state of Switzerland, doubts arise over the future development of urban housing.

The present situation was characterised as a crisis of change. A relatively successful economy made widespread prosperity possible. Unemployment remained low and only small groups had to live on the fringe of society. Population growth and an increase in purchasing power ensured that demand usually outgrew supply in the housing market. Real estate was a safe investment and entrepreneurs and landowners could expect that the increase in value of their properties would in the most part exceed the rate of inflation. Interests rates were low and loans readily available. The legal framework was relatively liberal and did not fetter the activities of either proprietors or of the investors.

Deviation from this simplified picture has begun to appear. Unemployment is much higher nowadays and this trend may persist despite an upswing in the economy. The wages of the workforce trail behind the cost of living and the unemployed find work with new salaries well below 15% of their previous earnings. The number of vacant apartments is on the rise and now approaches 1.5%. Newspapers publicise the names of banks that are facing difficulties because of bad loans.

In the future, real estate may well lose its role as a safe and interesting investment and the demand will fall short of supply. One part of the existing housing stock will not appreciate in value while another will be preferred thus bringing in high rents. Proprietors will neglect the less favoured buildings, choosing to use them as cash cows. In one or two decades spots of urban decay and housing deterioration will proliferate among well-maintained middle class or fashionable neighbourhoods. Although dilapidation will bring an abundance of inexpensive dwellings, a significant proportion of the population will need public assistance to pay the rent.

## Policy objectives

The comments on the general housing policy have already given a first impression of the general aims. The main objectives are accommodation with inexpensive homes, promotion of the quality of life in urban areas and the protection of the environment. A more specific view shows three additional concerns: preservation of the older residential districts and the maintenance of historic buildings; smoothing economic cycles in the building industries; and simplified procedures for planning and building permissions. Each of these targets will be briefly summarised.

The goals concerning **supply of inexpensive dwellings** have a two-pronged approach:

- The construction of new lodgings is subsidised. Dwellings for different social groups, for example elderly or handicapped people, obtain additional benefits.

- Inexpensive, older apartments are safeguarded against demolition or change of usage and their modernisation and maintenance are promoted. Special arrangements are made concerning the building stock in the mountainous regions. In the face of the scarcity of apartments and the weak position of the tenants some provisions for the protection of the latter are included in the regulations.

The issue of **quality of life in urban areas** aims at alleviating the impact of traffic in residential areas, eliminating the nuisance caused by the mixing of residential areas, commerce, industry and services and the creation of sufficient green, open spaces especially within the confines of inner-city blocks.

**Environmental protection** is focused on energy conservation through the insulation of houses, improved heating systems, a changed modal split in transportation, the reduction of air pollution and traffic noise, economising on land use in built-up and development areas and the preservation of farmland.

**Preservation of older residential districts and maintenance of historic buildings** is mainly concerned with the aesthetic appearance of districts, streets and buildings within towns and cities.

**Smoothing economic cycles in the building industries** will avoid the repeated destruction of production capacity.

**Simplified procedures for planning and building approvals** are directed towards two objectives: the removal of impediments in order to promote the construction of new dwellings and the rehabilitation of older housing.

## Regulations and programmes

### Preliminary remarks

Switzerland has no national policy for the improvement of built-up areas and for the rehabilitation of building stock. The renovation and modernisation of housing are usually considered to be the responsibility of the owner. However numerous federal, cantonal and communal regulations and programmes impinge on urban renewal and housing renovation. While these activities are mainly uncoordinated, an informal unity of doctrine persists. Moreover the policy differs in accordance with the political persuasion of the legislative bodies. The larger cities or the cantons in the French-speaking part of Switzerland, for instance, are generally more likely to resort to codification or governmental programmes. Thus, while the canton of Zurich may pursue a mainly liberal approach, the city of Zurich can see a need for stricter rules within its jurisdiction.

The presentation of the different policies in Switzerland proves to be cumbersome and confusing although, with the proper expertise, this confusion could be somewhat eliminated. The following sections depict the situation on the federal level on the cantonal and communal levels. The exposition of cantonal and communal policies may regrettably do some injustice to the subject especially since urban renewal and the renovation of housing take place at the communal level.

### Federal regulations and programmes

At the federal level a variety of laws, programmes, applied research and efforts considering information and education encroach upon urban renewal and housing renovation. Although regulations set a framework, much effort is put into applied research, information and education. The reason for this is that such information may help those involved to prevent urban decay and housing dilapidation.

## Legislative framework

The federal law stipulates that the proprietor has to maintain a building to the standard where the structure does not in any way compromise the public safety. Cantons and communes can specify additional regulations against hazardous conditions, for example, fire protection, constructional safeguards and sanitation. The federal law also states that landlords are responsible for the maintenance of rented premises in habitable conditions.

The regulations on renting are part of the civil law. The rent can be freely negotiated between the landlord and the tenant and there is no federal control or supervision of the process. The principle of freedom of notice also applies. The legislator, however, provides protection against unfair practice. With regard to the renovation of houses, three aspects are worth noting: notice of the lease; sufferance of construction work; and increase in rent because of improvements or increase of mortgage interest rate.

The tenant has, within certain limits, the possibility of demanding a prolongation of a lease if he does not find satisfactory lodgings. The regulation may on the one hand accord a temporary delay on the renovation procedures but it may on the other hand permit the precautionary termination of a lease. The code concerning sufferance of construction works gives the tenant very limited opportunities of redress. He can however defend himself against undue hardship. The rules also stipulate that measures which add value to the building justify an increase in rent whereas maintenance work does not call for such an action. The maximum of 70% of the added value can be charged to the rent. This clause may protect the tenant from paying twice for the maintenance of the building but it does not provide a barrier against excessive and unnecessary renovations.

## Subsidies for the renovation of houses

Two ordinances deal with the question of renovation of houses. One is the law concerning the improvement of housing in the mountainous regions of 1970. The other legislature of 1974 focuses on the promotion of housing and house ownership. In addition two federal decrees of 1976 and 1993 aim to promote employment in the building trades.

### Law concerning the improvement of housing in mountainous regions of 1970

The regulations to amend housing in the mountainous regions allow grants between 10-30% of the construction costs. An additional requirement is that the cantons assume a share of the financial assistance. The combined financial assistance of the federal government and the canton range between 15-50% of the eligible improvements. The aid can go towards the renovation of dwellings, supply of water and electricity, drainage of waste water, plumbing and electrical installation and additional dwelling space in relation to family size. In certain circumstances new dwellings can be erected in unused buildings, new construction may be added or housing may be purchased. Those entitled to financial assistance have an annual income of CHF40,600 – and capital of CHF121,000 – or less. Special provisions are made for families with children, aged or handicapped persons. One stipulation is on the sale or change of purpose of the premises within 20 years. In the 25 years since the law has been in force, 40,000 dwellings have been subsidised.

### Law concerning the promotion of housing and house ownership of 1974

The second legal instrument of the federal housing policy is the law of 1974 concerning the promotion of housing and house ownership. Although the thrust of authorisation is directed towards new development and new buildings, the regulations do not exclude subsidies for renovations. In order to provide favourable conditions for housing construction, the regulations provide for measures of assistance in the acquisition of land reserves and in the development of land for building purposes. This is achieved through guarantees and interest subsidies. The support for non-profit housing cooperatives and their associations is achieved through loans and guarantees which are tied to specific projects, low and interest-free loans and shareholdings in organisations with supra-regional importance. The construction of affordable apartments and properties is achieved through guarantees on mortgage loans of up to 90% of the total investment, through repayable loans to reduce the initial level of rents and owners' costs (basic reduction) and through non-repayable grants to further reduce rents or costs for lower income groups (supplementary reductions).

The rationale for this system of government subsidies is to reduce the initial rent below the amount that would be required to cover effective costs. The rent gap between old and new lodgings is thus narrowed. The 'basic reduction' loans have to be paid back. Several increases of the rent ensure that the necessary level is achieved to cover the effective costs. In contrast to traditional promotion systems, the rents here do not remain blocked but are dynamically adjusted to the actual development of costs and to the economic performance of the occupier.

The law of 1974 specifies requirements that concern the financial status of the occupier as well as the building project. However guarantees and basic reduction are granted to everybody, while supplementary reductions are restricted to persons with an annual income of CHF50,000 – and capital of CHF144,000 – or less. Special provisions are made for families with children, aged or handicapped persons and students of different denominations. The obligations in regard to the dwellings include size and necessary rooms of the apartment as specified in an evaluation form, insulation, and particular stipulations for aged and handicapped persons. Additional guidelines specify the admissible costs for the housing project.

The renovation of housing generally follows the regulations described above. The buildings should be at least 20 years old and inexpensive compared with the cost of new construction. In accordance with the specific situation the regulations connected with building requirements can be relaxed.

The above described instrument is currently the main tool of the federal government. Compared with foreign measures its importance in the housing market remains relatively modest. This is because the supply and distribution of housing are for the greater part achieved by free market forces. In the long run the number of dwellings constructed with the aid of public funds is less than 10% of the total building output. As a result of changed economic circumstances, public support increased temporarily during the last couple of years and one third of new dwellings are currently involved in the federal scheme. Since 1974, 6,000 renovated apartments obtained financial assistance, this number most probably represents a minor part of all renovated lodgings.

### Federal decrees to promote employment in the building trades of 1976 and 1993

The federal decrees about financial aid for the renovation of existing lodgings from 1976 also deserve some attention. The rationale behind these was not the need for the renovation of houses nor was it for achieving social goals with regard to tenants. It was simply the struggle against economic recession in the building sector at the time. A fund of CHF50 million was made available to subsidise 12% of renovation costs over a period of six years and about 10,000 dwellings were rehabilitated as a result.

In 1993 the recession in the building sector brought about new federal decrees with the aim of promoting employment in the building trades. Beneficiaries of this action were non-profit housing cooperatives and owner-occupiers of single-family houses or apartments. The loans, at a low interest rate of 3%, were given for new constructions and housing rehabilitations. As a general rule the credits do not exceed 10% of the construction costs for new buildings and 30% for renovations. The mortgages are limited to CHF700,000 for apartment buildings and CHF80,000 for single-family houses or owner-occupied apartments. An additional stipulation is that the building project has to conform to the regulations of the law of 1974 concerning the promotion of housing and house ownership. In the years 1993 and 1994, federal loans of CHF50 million promoted the construction or rehabilitation of about 2,500 dwelling units and the credits triggered an investment of about CHF626 million. The average costs amounted to about CHF250,000 for each flat, indicating that the subsidies went mainly to new constructions.

## Applied research and information

The prevention of urban decay and housing dilapidation is the foremost goal of the federal policy in urban renewal and housing rehabilitation. The liberal legislation sees the upkeep of housing as the responsibility of the owners. Applied research, information and education are therefore required to stimulate the concerned parties to the desired course of action.

Several offices with different purposes are involved in applied research, information and education. The above mentioned law concerning the promotion of housing construction and house ownership includes research and information in the building sector as the responsibility of the Federal

Office of Housing. During the last 20 years many studies and activities regarding the renovation of housing have been undertaken. In the fulfilment of their assignments, the Federal Office of Planning, the Federal Office of Energy and the Federal Offices of Economic Conditions concern themselves equally with issues that relate to urban renewal and/ or renovation of houses. In addition, the Swiss National Science Foundation runs some national research programmes that touch on the improvement of urban areas and housing conditions.

The results of research are published in different papers. The most important of these reports are *Schriftenreihe Wohnungswesen* and *Arbeitsberichte Wohnungswesen* by Forschungskommission Wohnungswesen and by the Bundesamt für Wohnungswesen; reports of the *Impulsprogramm Bau* by Bundesamt für Konjunkturfragen; studies of the national research programs *NFP 22: Nutzung des Bodens in der Schweiz* and *NFP 25: Stadt und Verkehr* by the National Science Foundation.

The above mentioned agencies work together in a multitude of groups, commissions and personal contacts. The network also includes cantonal and communal authorities or non-governmental associations like the Swiss Association of National Planning or the Swiss Association of Housing. The manifold contacts lead to a coordination of the activities in research and information. However, the different institutions may sometimes compete with each other, hence the need to give an overview of the issues that have emerged during the last 10 to 15 years. For the sake of convenience the issues will be organised under the five headings: urban renewal, housing renovation, participants and social groups, legal instruments and background reports.

**Urban renewal**
In the domain of urban renewal there are two conspicuous subjects that attracted much attention: land use and traffic. Both have environmental protection as a common denominator. With regard to land use, the preoccupation was on economising the consumption of land used for settlements. Much ingenuity was put into the question of how additional demand could be directed in the already built-up areas, especially within the suburbs and in the less densely populated neighbourhoods of towns and cities. Considering the examples of different types of localities, investigations show the potential of intensifying land use without distressing the inhabitants.

The bulk of the studies about traffic aims at internalising travel costs.

One of the solutions was a road pricing project for Bern. The purpose was to reduce traffic by means of more expensive transportation prices. Additional topics taken up were the promotion of cyclists and pedestrians within the traffic system and the reduction of land consumption for streets and highways.

Other concerns in applied research were planning methods in urban renewal and the improvement of the urban fabric. The studies about planning methods concerned themselves with the course of the planning process and data gathering. It was realised that urgent difficulties demand immediate responses but that their complexities do not allow for cursory solutions. The research relating to the urban fabric are concerned with evaluation of the environment on the one hand and with models for the improvement of neighbourhoods on the other. In this later category fall the upgrading of backyards, arrangement of streets and reduction of traffic.

**Housing renovation**

The research relating to the renovation of housing has three main objectives. The first includes manuals and instruments for the planning of house renovation, such as a fast method for estimating the cost of renovation or the making of a planning manual. The second focuses on the renovation of specific types of building, including factories, apartments, multi-storeyed houses or rural habitations. A multitude of examples proves that factory buildings could be converted into dwelling houses and that multi-storeyed houses could be amended. The third field is the protection of the environment. In an extension of similar studies on urban renewal, the researchers scrutinised the potentials of increasing the utilisation factor of buildings and of land plots. Other themes are the insulation of houses, building techniques and the recycling of building materials.

**Participants and social groups**

Urban renewal and the renovation of housing are usually treated as projects devoid of human beings. In the best case the experts give cursory attention to measures to alleviate drawbacks for disadvantaged social groups. In this context it is noteworthy that there are empirical studies about participants and social groups within the process of urban renewal and the renovation of the housing stock. The research into urban renewal concerns itself with topics such as the attitudes of the population towards economic utilisation of land, the mobility of different social groups, the possibilities of changing public behaviour regarding transport, the situation of children in cities and the participation of the populace in the planning process. Even studies in housing renovation deal with the effect of such work on tenants. Proposals look at the participation of tenants in housing improvements which in reality, is a rare occurrence.

A related question is the behaviour of the proprietors. Since this is far from being a homogenous group, the investigation addresses the divergent behaviour of the different types of owners, for example, private, public, funds and building cooperatives.

**Legal instruments**

Legal instruments, technical specification, planning and building codes have been seen as favouring new construction and therefore hindering urban renewal and housing renovations. One problem was that the renovation of buildings brought about additional costs, because new technical standards such as fire protection, electricity and plumbing had to be compulsorily implemented. Another hindrance relates to the adaptation of existing houses to novel needs. Similar questions addressed investigations concerning the better use of built-up areas. The studies proposed more flexibility by relaxing the standards for urban renewal and housing renovation procedures. The easing of standards aimed firstly at the promotion of renovation of houses, secondly at protection of the environment through economical land use and thirdly at reducing rents after renovations. The third problem was also the main concern of an 'expert commission on the renovation of houses'. The Commission suggested a better adaptation of the federal legislation that up to now served mainly to lower the cost of rents in newly built lodgings.

Proposals to use a firm's pension funds to promote house ownership of the employees were implemented in 1995. The possibility of taking loans on one's own credit or to use the accumulated capital helps greatly in the construction of one-family houses. The new regulation may to a lesser extent help in the renovation of existing buildings.

**Background reports**

A number of miscellaneous studies fall under this heading and include some framework information for the public policy. The questions involve social justice and the protection of the environment, investors and ground market, quality of life in the cities or the future of small towns. Some other reports address more specifically the issue of urban renewal and housing renovation. The researchers concerned themselves with displacement of trades and artisans in inner-city neighbourhoods or with the saturation of the housing market and the lack of investment therein. The last theme has already been dealt with in a study in 1991 and it may prove to be a point of interest in the future.

## Cantonal and communal regulations and programmes

The activities of cantonal and communal authorities touch in different ways on the domain of urban renewal and the renovation of houses. The avenues of influence include building and planning codes, the execution of public planning, public property and social and tax legislation. The federal structure of the political system naturally causes many variations. The following outline gives a general picture, which does not necessarily apply to any specific place. As a rule it may be said that in large cities and urbanised regions the multitude of regulations is on the increase.

### Building, planning and environmental codes

The national law sets a framework which requires the cantons to establish plans and to abide by general objectives and procedural standards (such as the publication of plans and public consultation) as well as to differentiate between a general master-plan and specific zoning and building regulations. There exists no federal, cantonal and communal law governing urban renewal and housing rehabilitation. However, there are problems that must be dealt with by the authorities. In contrast to many other countries, the obstacles to be overcome do not pertain to the neglect of buildings but arise rather from the demolition or the excessive renovation of inexpensive dwellings. The cantonal and communal authorities usually try to solve the dilemma by means of the planning, building and zoning laws or by the ordinances on preservation of historic sites and buildings.

One of the initial approaches was to impede the demolition of (inexpensive) family lodgings or their use as business premises. The different modifications of the zoning regulations serve a similar purpose. The neighbourhoods built around the turn of the century experienced a growing appreciation during the last two decades. Many cantons and communes utilised the building and planning codes to regulate the preservation of older buildings and the urban fabric of built-up areas.

The restrictions may range from the adaptation of new buildings to suit the appearance of a neighbourhood to the complete protection of a particular house. Although aesthetic considerations are paramount, a less publicised purpose of the preservation laws is to put a brake on the destruction of inexpensive dwellings. This agenda also plays a role when zoning regulations reduce the density of built-up sections. The proprietors are induced to maintain the existing structure, because new construction is likely to reduce the utilisation of the land.

Regulations that prescribe the percentage of lodgings within defined areas control displacement by commercial premises. The logic behind this is that residential use yields less than commercial use and the residential areas therefore have to be protected. One of the goals of these regulations is to provide a sufficient supply of housing in the inner-city areas. Another objective is to make the demolition of older buildings and the subsequent erection of new buildings less attractive. The overview shows that the legislation primarily sets a framework to control the activities of the private owners. The public authorities cannot play an active role in so far as private property is concerned.

During the past 20 years legislation to protect the environment and conserve energy proliferated. Laws requiring improved protection of oil tanks against leakage are compulsory. New constructions have to have an improved insulation. Heating costs have to consider the individual consumption by each tenant. Subsidies are available for sound-proofing windows. This legislation fell on fertile ground and proprietors insulated a large proportion of the existing housing stock or installed energy efficient heating systems.

**The execution of public planning**

In the realm of public streets, plazas, parks and buildings the cantonal and the communal authorities not only have a planning authority but can also execute their plans. The main objective of these plans is to lessen the negative impact of traffic, a major concern of the general public. The measures taken – as well as the political controversies surrounding them – are quite similar to those in other countries. They include new thoroughfares to relieve residential areas from through traffic, traffic regulation such as one-way or speed limits to reduce noise and air pollution. Other actions are the creation of residential streets with recreational areas and vehicle barriers or pedestrian areas within the commercial centres of the cities.

The authorities are embarking on a mission to improve the appearance of their villages, towns and cities, irrespective of whether this is combined with traffic planning. Examples of such aesthetic improvements are street design, the creation of parks, plazas and pedestrian walks. Similarly they are promoting the greening of front and backyards or the maintenance of the building exteriors, though without much power to implement their ideas. The inability of local governments to impose their concepts has obliged them to rely on communication, education, persuasion and incentives to achieve their objectives.

Recent developments in built-up areas have influenced urban improvement. Large neglected areas such as desolate public facilities, industrial or railroad tracts have to be developed for new utilisation. All of a sudden it is possible that a large number of apartments can be constructed within the city. Another opportunity exists in promoting economic growth through commercial or trade centres. The need to change zoning regulations provides the administrative boards with some leeway to influence developments in the desired direction. Private persons and public authorities may even actively seek ways to cooperate. In some large-scale projects private developers meet with opposition from the local population and the executive bodies get a chance to play the role of mediators.

**Public property**

Communities, towns and cities own a sizeable proportion of the real estate within their boundaries. Included in this are public facilities, historic buildings and quite often communal housing as well. Sometimes the rehabilitation of buildings provides the opportunity to improve the surroundings or to experiment with energy measures.

Some cantons and municipalities possess specific funds for buying and reselling property for the purpose of urban improvement. By reselling property they bind the new owners into fulfilling certain obligations.

**Social and tax legislation**

Switzerland is using subsidies of land and construction costs in order to alleviate high rent costs. As an extension of the federal law on the promotion of housing and home ownership, many cantons have created their own legislation. The public have likewise often supported housing cooperatives. Another approach was to build communal housing in the city of Zurich. In some cantons and municipalities, however, certain disadvantaged groups, for example, elderly people or large families, have the possibility of obtaining assistance with the cost of rent.

Tax legislation does not play a prominent role in the renovation of dwelling places. The owner can deduct the costs of maintenance but not those of improvements from their tax assessment. The system varies in different parts of the country with some cantons allowing a flat deduction. Other cantons demand an exact inventory of the costs. Occasionally the owner can choose between the two types of tax assessment.

## Evaluation of the effect of policies

The three main goals of urban renewal and house renovation during the last two decades were supply of inexpensive dwellings, quality of life in urban areas and protection of the environment. This list conforms somewhat to the chronological order with which the goals appeared on the political agenda, and this will be used to enumerate the following evaluation. At the end of the chapter some thoughts concerning the maintenance of the building stock and the efficacy of research will be examined.

An evaluation of the effects of policies demands information as to the number of goals achieved as well as what part can be attributed to the effects of policies. Unfortunately there are no similar studies that could further enlighten this matter. The following comments therefore have to be understood as a broad overview.

### Supply of inexpensive dwellings

During the last decade the inhabitants have experienced a tremendous improvement in the housing supply: increase in dwelling space, bathrooms, warm water and central heating. Homelessness is largely unknown in Switzerland. Rents at 20% of income is seemingly bearable. However, the newspapers, however, a less favourable picture, with stories about the difficulties of finding apartments and the exorbitant costs of rent. The advertisements show that rents are high and that inexpensive dwellings are difficult to find.

It appears that subsidies for new constructions have a minor effect on the housing market. Even renovated older apartments are costly. The question arises whether all the painstaking efforts of protecting existing apartments against demolition and change of usage are conducive to reasonable rents for the majority of people. The answer is doubtful. There are two other more convincing reasons.

- Inflation, even at a moderate rate, has rendered once expensive dwellings economical. The yield of assets remains satisfactory.
- Most proprietors in a stable situation show some hesitation about large rent increases. Therefore the gap between old and new apartments widens.

*Quality of life in urban areas*

Quality of life in the urban areas mainly refers to the immediate surroundings of the dwellings. Here the efficacy of policies is ambiguous. Measures to enlarge pedestrian zones in the city centres and were initiatives to reduce traffic in the residential areas. The undertakings had some measure of success and the beautification of inner-city neighbourhoods with green open spaces and new road surfaces has advanced progress. The opportunities offered by desolate industrial areas were also taken up.

On balance consideration must be given to the fact that parts of the urbanised area, especially along the main streets, are afflicted by heavy traffic pollution. The topography of the land does not often offer solutions other than the stringent restriction of traffic, a measure that is not usually taken. The improvement of backyard surroundings remains, despite many attempts at information and education, a sluggish affair. Material interests, coupled with the varied approaches of private owners puts restrictions on the development of projects.

*Environmental protection*

The protection of the environment concerns urban renewal as well as housing rehabilitation. In the first domain, reducing traffic, changing the economical use of land are front runners in the quest for lessening the negative impact on the quality of the environment. In the second domain, energy conservation through the proper insulation of houses or improved heating systems, has an important role to play.

**Urban renewal**

The traffic indicators show that the movement of transport went on increasing, that rides became longer than before and that the number of cars continued to grow. Whether conditions, without the efforts to restrict traffic, would be worse remains doubtful. A certain latitude with regard to changing the behaviour of road-users seems possible. However, to a large extent the choice of transport is forced upon the population by the existing urban structure or the available means of transport. Such factors change rather slowly.

The evaluation of the attempts to economise the utilisation of land will have to wait, simply because the effects of such a new policy are not yet noticeable. Generally it can be said, however, that the instruments which measure the efficacy of urban renewal and house renovation, are presently still missing.

**Housing renovation**

The proposed goal of energy conservation got a favourable response from house owners. There is every reason to believe that the number of older buildings that benefited from energy improvements is large and still growing. This may be due more to the interests of the proprietors to preserve and augment the value of their real estate than to the policy of the authorities. This is especially so, since the owners have ready cash available and are able to use the added values of their houses as an excuse to increase rents. The energy measures were just another convenient outlet that served the interests of the land owners.

## Maintenance of the housing stock

The housing stock in the urban areas is generally well maintained and modernised (Table 6.4). Violation of the law regarding adequate maintenance of property hardly occurs. Conflicts are more likely to arise in the drive for excessive rehabilitation and modernisation or the replacement of old facilities by new buildings. This statement also holds true for lower class neighbourhoods with ethnic minorities and environmental problems. The causes are to be found in the motivation and interests of the proprietors as well as in the high rents and the adequate purchasing power of the tenants. Another reason is that the instruments of public policy respect the effects of market forces. For example, the law of 1974 concerning the promotion of housing and house ownership attempts only to reduce the initial rent below the amount that would be required to cover effective costs. In the following

Table 6.4: Occupied dwellings with year of construction and renovation (%)

|  | Year of construction | | | | | |
|---|---|---|---|---|---|---|
| Year of renovation | pre-1900 | 1900-20 | 1921-46 | 1947-60 | 1961-70 | 1971-90 |
| 1961-70 | 12 | 9 | 7 | 3 | | |
| 1971-80 | 21 | 19 | 19 | 10 | | |
| 1981-90 | 41 | 41 | 39 | 39 | 35 | 10 |
| No renovation | 26 | 31 | 35 | 48 | 65 | 90 |
| Total | 100 | 100 | 100 | 100 | 100 | 100 |
| No of dwellings (000s) | 396.8 | 211.3 | 320.8 | 445.0 | 543.8 | 882.9 |

Source: *Eidgenössische Volkszählung* [statistical publication] (1990)

years several rent increases ensured that the necessary level of return was achieved to cover the effective costs. Finally, the building trades themselves make vigorous efforts in their own self-interest to induce the owners to renovate their properties.

However, the current economic situation could change the conditions favourable to the maintenance and modernisation of the housing stock. One of the tasks ahead will therefore be to monitor the factors that affect housing renovation.

## Efficacy of research

The federal government carries out its policies on urban renewal and housing renovation largely with the help of applied research, information and education. There is little knowledge as to whether these efforts are having any effect. Uncertainty exists even with regard to the impact of results on different groups such as owners, tenants, architects, civil engineers, city planners and the building trades. Future studies must therefore deal with the efficacy of these approaches.

SEVEN

# Distributing the responsibilities – urban renewal in Vienna
*Wolfgang Förster*

## Introduction

Urban renewal and urban development cannot be considered without due regard being paid to the social environment and, in particular, the nature of the city concerned. This is especially true in the case of Vienna, which has a number of characteristics that distinguish it from other European cities of comparable size and character. As Austria is a federal republic and Vienna is one of nine autonomous provinces, the city can to a large extent develop its own housing policies to meet local needs. This includes the provision of housing subsidies, policies on housing renewal and levels of housing allowances. The federal constitution thus generates nine different housing policies in Austria, with nine very different approaches to urban renewal. Only the Tenancy Act, which guarantees tenants' rights to a much greater extent than in most other European countries, remains a state responsibility.

In Austria as a whole, the federal government continues to be the most important provider of funds for housing, raised from various taxes, but this does not interfere with the autonomy of the provinces in policy terms. The majority of resources for housing provision are provided by the state, with the funds provided for direct subsidies generated by means of earmarked taxes and contributions from income tax and distributed to the nine federal provinces. However, in Vienna, the city contributes more to new housing and housing renewal than comes from state sources. In 1994 about ASh18 billion came from the city budget, compared to ASh6 billion from the state.

This chapter concentrates on Vienna's urban renewal policies rather than describing those of Austria as a whole. However, as Vienna is by far the largest Austrian city with renewal problems on a much greater scale than most other areas of the country, most innovative policy developments in this field have been developed there. Unlike most other European capitals, Vienna is still characterised by the products of massive housing construction during what is called the age of promoterism. Almost 40% of the current housing stock dates back to the period before 1918 (see Table 7.1), with most of these houses being owned by private landlords and rented out to tenants. One third of the city's housing stock, 280,000 out of a total of 850,000 units, falls into this category. Many flats still lack modern amenities such as central heating (these are referred to as category B units according to the State Rental Act), or are even without a bathroom (category C) or a toilet (category D) (Table 7.2 shows further details). Since 1919, nearly all new housing has been provided either by the city itself or by non-profit housing associations, so privately rented housing can, with very few exceptions, be found only in the oldest building sector. This is a significant difference from the rest of Austria, especially the rural areas. Nevertheless, non-profit housing associations and cooperatives play an important role in the Austrian housing market, providing approximately 10% of the total housing stock, or approximately 20% of dwellings in multi-storied buildings and about 50% of the social rental sector.

The city itself participates actively in the construction of council houses to an extent virtually unrivalled by any other city in its class. This commitment has its roots in Vienna's pioneering municipal housing construction schemes of the inter-war period. At the same time significant sums of money from public sources are made available to maintain and improve the mostly private stock of old houses. The city authorities have never undertaken any large-scale clearance and renewal schemes of the kind which have given rise to so many problems in other European cities. This was due in part to Vienna's long period of marginalisation at the eastern edge of free Europe and the resulting reluctance of private investors to commit large sums of money to renewal. As a result, one city was able to benefit from the insights gained from policies observed elsewhere. In addition, tenants' rights are more strongly protected by legislation and precedents than in most other countries, so that there has been a tendency to develop renewal strategies which give greater recognition to these rights.

It was not by accident that, at the very beginning of urban renewal programmes in Vienna, an instrument was provided which deliberately

Table 7.1: Vienna housing stock: periods of construction

|  | Number of dwellings |
|---|---|
| Before 1919 | 321,750 |
| 1919-44 | 101,411 |
| 1945-60 | 114,770 |
| 1961-80 | 236,224 |
| after 1980 | 79,936 |

Table 7.2: Vienna housing stock: technical standards

|  | Number of dwellings |
|---|---|
| Central heating, bathroom, WC | 479,158 |
| Bathroom, WC | 75,194 |
| Water supply, WC | 47,998 |
| WC or water supply outside the dwelling | 136,612 |

took a small-scale and tenant-oriented approach: the 1969 Law on Housing Amelioration. Especially since its amendment in 1971, it has been one of the most impressive models in Europe of modernisation with tenant interests at heart. Drawing on the regulations of the law governing tenancies, which granted extensive rights of choice to tenants, about 160,000 dwellings have been improved to date. The Law on Housing Amelioration reflected the basic philosophy that it should be the tenant who decides about the future standard of his or her flat, and hence the extent of any increase in rent. Observing this principle goes a long way to ensuring that social displacement or 'crowding-out' and social segregation can be avoided.

It is also symptomatic that the Austrian 1974 Urban Renewal Law, the only redevelopment instrument which paid less regard to tenants' rights, has de facto never been applied in Vienna. In many respects the 1974 Law was a copy of the German law on town-planning promotion which has been used to undertake area-wide redevelopment (pulling buildings down and erecting new ones, resorting to coercive means if necessary).

Dissatisfaction with that approach led to a policy of 'gentle' urban renewal, a process which has led to the development of the Vienna model for urban renewal.

## The Vienna model

Not all the possible technical solutions are, at the same time, socially desirable. This principle has determined Vienna's urban renewal policies from the very beginning. *Sockelsanierung* (basic renewal) is the form of revitalisation which gives most emphasis to tenant views and this accounts for the majority of investment. The principle of 'soft urban renewal' means first of all to adapt to the wishes and possibilities of the people living in densely built-up urban areas. Similarly 'socially comprehensive urban renewal' means directing public and private investments into those areas where existing economic sources are too weak to stop the social and technical processes of degradation.

This policy can be characterised as an anti-segregation strategy and emphasises a strong role for the city in the field of housing, a high degree of public investment, and a strong priority for social aspects and inhabitants' participation. This interference in the private housing market is widely accepted in the city and may be explained by a long tradition of public housing policies dating back to Red Vienna in the 1920s. The benefits are that 'luxury modernisation' combined with gentrification and the eviction of sitting tenants can more easily be avoided.

The pillars of housing policies are the tenancy laws and the concept of social housing. The Tenancy Act that has been in effect since 1919 protects tenants against tenancy termination, limits rent increases and contains provisions requiring landlords to maintain dwellings. This has helped to prevent the deterioration of the stock and avoided large-scale demolition and the displacement of residents. It has also made a substantial contribution to avoiding gentrification and social segregation. A further stabilisation of the housing market was achieved by public housing schemes. Vienna reacted to the drastic housing shortages and massive unemployment following the First World War with a large municipal housing programme. Since the 1920s the city of Vienna has built 220,000 rented flats, becoming the most important landlord in Austria and one of the largest in the world.

In its rehabilitation efforts Vienna has been able to benefit from experience abroad. The city decided not to rely on demolition, new construction and the eviction of residents, but it had become obvious that the extremely low rents – based on the 1917 Rental Act – made it impossible to maintain old houses. As a consequence, most buildings in both the private and public sectors continued to deteriorate with nothing being done to improve the housing standards. Low rents had been defended with social as well as economic arguments. They had made it possible to pay lower wages, for assistance, helping Austria's then rather weak economy to compete – a situation which has, of course, changed. Tenants' rights, however, had become an important political issue, and for a long time the political parties hesitated to raise rents, making it necessary to provide subsidies for urban renewal projects.

In 1984, the Housing Rehabilitation Act laid the foundations for a new urban housing policy. The act summed up the subsidy options provided for old buildings, making them more uniform, while guaranteeing comparable public grants for the fields of housing rehabilitation and new housing. The objective is to preserve and improve houses and apartments, both in the public and private rental sectors, while protecting sitting tenants.

In 1994, 2,691 assistance applications were recommended for acceptance. Basic renewal accounted for 1,177 while only 139 were cases of total or comprehensive renewal involving much larger-scale building work. Single improvements such as the installations of lifts and maintenance works are included in the programme. About 104,000 dwellings have benefited so far. The volume of redevelopment investment, totalling about ASh28.9 billion, has not only made a major contribution to the preservation of older and relatively low-priced housing, but has also stimulated the building trade, creating jobs.

## The subsidised housing renewal schemes in Vienna

The goals of soft urban renewal may be specified according to the objectives of housing rehabilitation:

1. Soft urban renewal

- priority of social criteria
- avoiding social segregation or gentrification
- avoiding forced change of ownership
- affordable rehabilitated housing.

2. *Sockelsanierung* (renewal of inhabited buildings)

- distribution of responsibilities between owner and tenants
- tenants' participation
- tenant-oriented modernisation schemes
- substitute housing offers.

3. Subsidies

- subsidy level depends on existing standard of apartments (up to 98% of total building costs)
- allowances to low-income households
- controlled and limited rent increases
- Vienna Land Procurement and Urban Renewal Fund (WBSF)- point system: priority by social, technical and urban criteria
- equal subsidies to privately and publicly owned rental buildings.

4. Single building approach/area-oriented renewal

- no designated renewal areas with special subsidies
- *Gebietsbetreuung* (area renewal offices to stimulate rehabilitation measures and to coordinate improvement of public spaces)
- *Blocksanierung* (block improvement schemes including housing renewal, improvement of public spaces and ecological measures).

The most significant renewal strategy is *sockelsanierung* (basic renewal), that is, preserving, improving and modernising older housing without moving tenants. Projects involve the renovation and improvement of the building and modernisation of flats in accordance with tenants' wishes. At the same time, installation of electricity and/or gas mains and disposal pipes prepare for the implementation of future improvements including merging small flats into larger ones, again taking into account the individual wishes of tenants. Consequently, this has become the most popular rehabilitation scheme, with 60% of all subsidised renewal activities falling into this category. Others include *totalsanierungen* (overall renewals, or the rehabilitation of empty buildings), *einzelverbesserungen* (single improvements, like the installation of lifts, heat insulation or district heating) and *erhaltungsarbeiten* (maintenance works). With few exceptions – like lifts for handicapped tenants or environmental measures such as district heating systems – subsidies are only given to dwellings lacking amenities (categories C and D mentioned earlier). High quality buildings are subject to private, non-subsidised renewal activities financed by higher rent incomes, but rents for sitting tenants are only raised with approval from a municipal department.

In the 1990s the policy of urban renewal offers the property owner sufficient financial incentives while remaining socially oriented through the high level of public subsidy. Up to 90% of rehabilitation cost is borne by the public sector through bank loan subsidies. The amount depends on the type of improvement selected and on the standard of the building, the principle being that the worst condition houses receive the greatest subsidy. The subsidy on loans is highest, for instance, for the elimination of substandard dwellings (flats without bathrooms or a WC). To repay the loans, rents may be increased temporarily to a level set and controlled by the city authorities, accompanied by individual allowances to tenants if necessary. No further rent increase may be made during the 15-year period of the subsidy. One out of five dwellings in Vienna is located in a building that either has been refurbished, is in the process of being refurbished or will be in the near future. There is still a lot to catch up with, and funds are limited. Urban renewal has also turned out to have major economic potential for the building industry.

In 1984 the WBSF was initiated by the city government. The Fund handles and examines applications for subsidies and coordinates all rehabilitation activities (see Figure 7.1). Its second major task is to purchase land for social housing projects. Building companies applying for grants for new social housing, more than 90% of all new housing projects in Vienna, must purchase land via the Fund thereby helping to stabilise real estate prices and rents. The WBSF currently has a staff of 74 (see Figure 7.2). It is a corporation under the Fund Act and a financially independent non-profit-making institution.

## Distributing the responsibilities

Careful distribution of responsibilities and active participation are required in the current renewal process (see Figure 7.3). This leads to a new and broader form of public–private partnership distributing responsibilities between all parties involved – city administration, local authorities, landlords, tenants, and so on. For example, landlords, private and public,

**Figure 7.1: Process of *Sockelsanierung* (overall rehabilitation of inhabited buildings)**

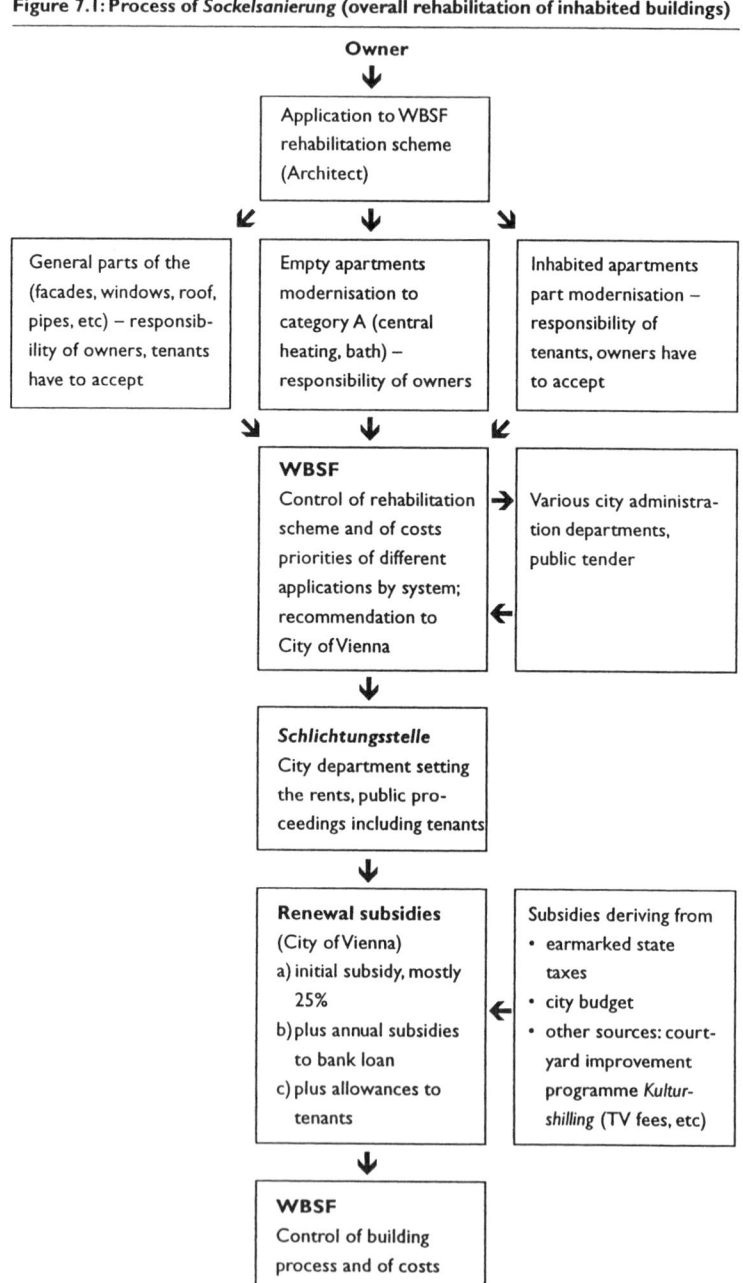

```
                               Owner
                                 ↓
                    ┌──────────────────────────┐
                    │ Application to WBSF      │
                    │ rehabilitation scheme    │
                    │ (Architect)              │
                    └──────────────────────────┘
              ↙                  ↓                  ↘
┌───────────────────────┐ ┌───────────────────────┐ ┌───────────────────────┐
│ General parts of the  │ │ Empty apartments      │ │ Inhabited apartments  │
│ (facades, windows,    │ │ modernisation to      │ │ part modernisation –  │
│ roof, pipes, etc) –   │ │ category A (central   │ │ responsibility of     │
│ responsibility of     │ │ heating, bath) –      │ │ tenants, owners have  │
│ owners, tenants       │ │ responsibility of     │ │ to accept             │
│ have to accept        │ │ owners                │ │                       │
└───────────────────────┘ └───────────────────────┘ └───────────────────────┘
              ↘                  ↓                  ↙
                    ┌──────────────────────────┐
                    │ WBSF                     │     ┌──────────────────────┐
                    │ Control of rehabilita-   │ →   │ Various city         │
                    │ tion scheme and of costs │     │ administration       │
                    │ priorities of different  │     │ departments,         │
                    │ applications by system;  │     │ public tender        │
                    │ recommendation to        │ ←   │                      │
                    │ City of Vienna           │     └──────────────────────┘
                    └──────────────────────────┘
                                 ↓
                    ┌──────────────────────────┐
                    │ *Schlichtungsstelle*     │
                    │ City department setting  │
                    │ the rents, public pro-   │
                    │ ceedings including tenants│
                    └──────────────────────────┘
                                 ↓
                    ┌──────────────────────────┐   ┌──────────────────────────┐
                    │ **Renewal subsidies**    │   │ Subsidies deriving from  │
                    │ (City of Vienna)         │   │  • earmarked state       │
                    │ a) initial subsidy,      │   │    taxes                 │
                    │    mostly 25%            │ ← │  • city budget           │
                    │ b) plus annual subsidies │   │  • other sources: court- │
                    │    to bank loan          │   │    yard improvement      │
                    │ c) plus allowances to    │   │    programme *Kultur-    │
                    │    tenants               │   │    shilling* (TV fees, etc)│
                    └──────────────────────────┘   └──────────────────────────┘
                                 ↓
                    ┌──────────────────────────┐
                    │ WBSF                     │
                    │ Control of building      │
                    │ process and of costs     │
                    └──────────────────────────┘
```

Figure 7.2: Vienna Land Procurement and Urban Renewal Fund (WBSF)

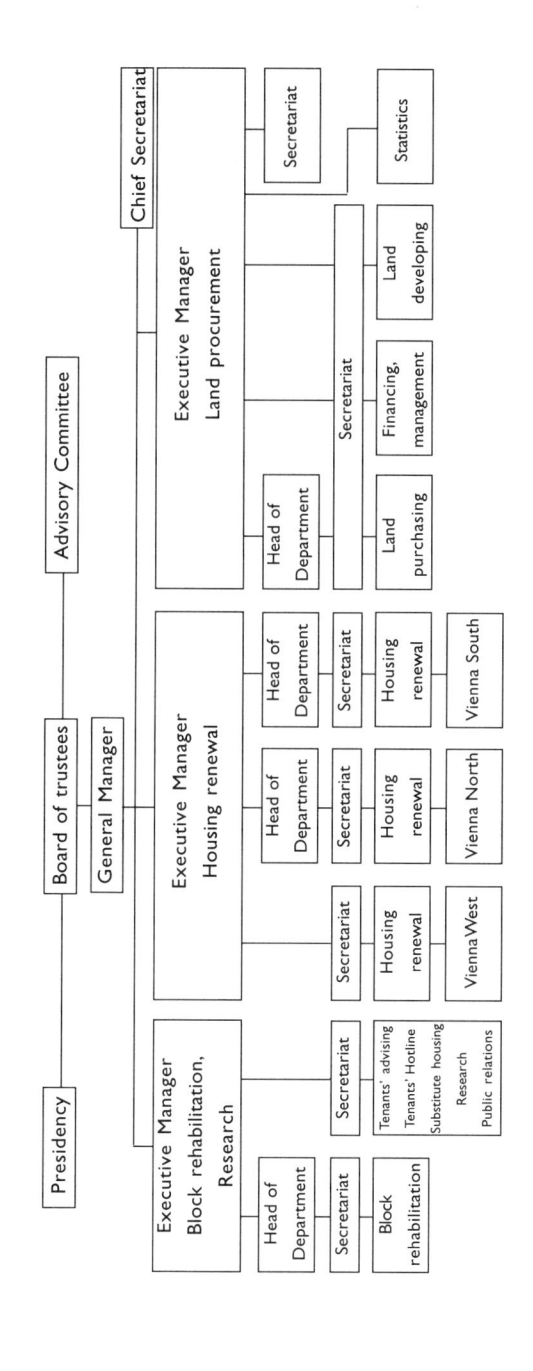

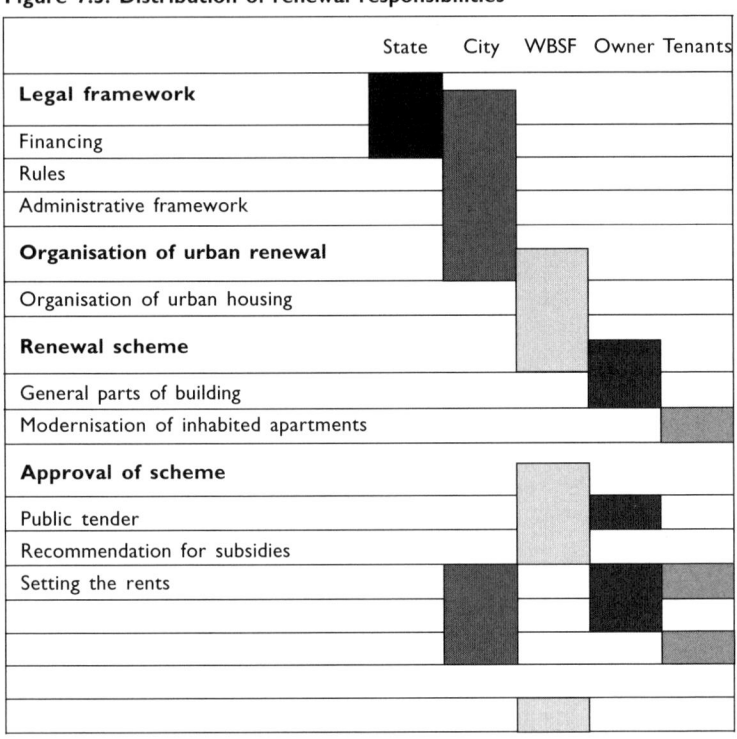

**Figure 7.3: Distribution of renewal responsibilities**

| | State | City | WBSF | Owner | Tenants |
|---|---|---|---|---|---|
| **Legal framework** | | | | | |
| Financing | | | | | |
| Rules | | | | | |
| Administrative framework | | | | | |
| **Organisation of urban renewal** | | | | | |
| Organisation of urban housing | | | | | |
| **Renewal scheme** | | | | | |
| General parts of building | | | | | |
| Modernisation of inhabited apartments | | | | | |
| **Approval of scheme** | | | | | |
| Public tender | | | | | |
| Recommendation for subsidies | | | | | |
| Setting the rents | | | | | |

are responsible for building maintenance; tenants decide upon the improvement to their apartments. Special intermediary organisations such as the WBSF, local area renewal offices, block rehabilitation officers and local business advisory teams all create platforms for decision making and compromise.

## From housing rehabilitation to urban renewal

A first step towards an area-based approach to urban renewal, targeting those buildings in urgent need of repair often with poorer inhabitants, was taken as early as 1974 with the establishment of the first *Gebietsbetreuung* (area renewal office). These offices counsel tenants and owners in matters of housing improvement, encourage public and private investment and are involved in district development and urban planning. There are currently 14 *Gebietsbetreuungen* in densely built-up areas of Vienna. They are regarded as neutral partners in the decision-making process and do not carry out any building activities themselves in their designated areas.

Block improvement schemes, that is, the improvement of whole blocks of buildings with different owners along with additional works such as laying out green spaces and traffic reduction schemes, started in 1989. Landlords, shop owners and residents are all involved in developing the block improvement project from the outset. Information, expert advice and specific project management is provided, ensuring that there is every opportunity to participate. The project management is by area renewal offices or by special block improvement officers appointed by the WBSF. Both aim at establishing new platforms for decision making and for conflict management. It is seen as important to have conflicts, whether arising from contradictory interests or simply from a lack of communication. They are not avoided but discussed openly, allowing an equal opportunity for everybody to take part, including older people and minority groups.

## The role of research

The role of research in urban renewal continued to grow in importance. Supported by WBSF, Vienna Housing Construction Research was set up in 1991 when house-building promotion came under Austria's individual provinces. It supplies useful data on technical, financial and social aspects of urban renewal. Attention is focused on the affordability of dwellings and to the evaluation of revitalisation in residential buildings. One of the most ambitious projects is the development of a Viennese housing-market model, made by WBSF.

Environmental aspects of urban renewal are also becoming more significant, with town planning as a starting point. By making the administrative districts slightly denser, targeted rebuilding, and through enlarging attics, high-quality dwellings can be created in districts already well-supplied with infrastructure. Counteracting segregation in these areas would be a welcome side-effect. At WBSF's suggestion, there has been more public promotion of adding extra storeys to buildings and the extension of attics since 1991. The latter are being developed through block revitalisation in the large city-owned residential buildings constructed between the wars.

Environmental improvements can be implemented during block redevelopment (eg, landscaping), and other environmental measures are undertaken in the case of smaller basic renewal projects.

*Urban renewal in the future*

Not least because of the prospect of Austria becoming part of the European Union, Vienna reached a turning-point. Increased population mobility and social segregation, compounded by an amendment to the rent control legislation which for the first time takes into account a flat's location, point to future problems of cumulative decay. Along with increasing dwelling costs, this could result in the development of slums. Many studies indicate that urban renewal will have to perform a primarily social task to avert unfavourable developments. Publicly assisted new housing tends to be aimed at the middle classes, which may reduce tensions at the lower end of the housing market. However, public urban renewal should directly benefit the underprivileged. The conflict in the current Tenancy Act between protecting the stock with old tenancy agreements and allowing market rents in new lettings impacts on redevelopment. Sitting tenants tend to be regarded as socially needy. Revisions to housing policy along the following lines will have to remedy this situation:

- Housing policies have to increasingly fight speculation, especially in the sector of the private rental market which serves mainly low-income immigrants (many of whom are illegal immigrants and therefore cannot defend their rights). Anti-speculation measures can include stricter controls of tenancy contracts and of rents as well as compulsory purchasing procedures.

- Those districts of Vienna with the worst residential quarters should get public resources, in accordance with the idea of compensatory urban renewal, so that they can carry out improvements to their public spaces and enhance their image.

- Faced with an increasingly pluralistic society to which a generally valid housing model will soon no longer apply (planning and building is focused on the standard family which in fact is about to become a minority in cities), a broad range of urban renewal experiments should be tried in order to prepare for future changes.

Demands for deregulation and a radical reduction of state intervention are often made but can only be partly approved from the point of view of social-minded urban renewal. What remains undisputed, though, is the policy of increasing public investments primarily where there is no private initiative at all or where it does not suffice. Housing policy should be interpreted as an interlocking system which takes in town planning, the local government's social policy and strategies of economic policy and which manifests clear-cut orientation towards the needs of the weak and underprivileged in society.

In a situation where the problems faced in renewal areas are getting more and more complex, urban renewal increasingly becomes crisis management. Neutral units of mediation are thus more imperative than ever. Planning processes, together with teams of area services, must work closely with the people concerned and efforts in the field of block redevelopment will have to be improved and redoubled.

EIGHT

# Strategies and policies for urban renewal and housing rehabilitation in France

*Anne-Marie Fribourg*

## Historical development

Among the many urgent problems at the end of the war, France was faced with a housing crisis. This was not only because of bombing (about 500,000 dwellings were destroyed and close to a million damaged to varying degrees), but also due to an inadequate building programme during the inter-war years which had not taken the massive rural exodus into account. This situation was compounded by an almost continuous policy of rent freezes which had discouraged private investment.

The first measures taken in 1945 led to one million partially-damaged dwellings being repaired, with compulsory purchase of vacant premises. However, awareness of the adverse effects of rent freezes on building maintenance and the need for public support led the government to levy a charge on rented property which went towards a National Fund for the Improvement and Maintenance of Rural and Urban Housing. This became the FNAH (National Fund for Housing Improvement) under Crédit Foncier de France's management and in 1971 became the ANAH (National Agency for Housing Improvement).

A law passed in 1948 introduced means-tested rent increases, with the aim of allowing owners to improve housing stock. This period was dominated by growth in new construction: first in rebuilding then, from 1950, in the resurgence of public building programmes through the *Habitations à loyers modérés* (HLMs) or social flats. New construction surged from 70,000 dwellings completed in 1948 to 320,000 in 1959. There were no specific central government measures directed at housing improvements, except for rural housing. The rural housing improvement grant was introduced in 1955 and is bolstered by Crédit Agricole loans.

In France, housing policy was developed through a series of national plans. Originally an objective of the 3rd Plan (1958-61) was to clear about 15,000 dwellings per annum. This figure was increased towards the end of the plan to take into account the 450,000 slums recorded in 1954. Repair of dwellings was touched on only in relation to rural housing. The plan also provided for semi-annual rent increases at a rate which would 'balance' the markets in new and old housing by 1965.

The 4th Plan (1962-65) included a section on building maintenance, improvement and restoration and underlined the need to conserve buildings of special interest. Owners were encouraged to double the level of maintenance and improvements by allocating a portion of rental income to improvements. At the same time, changes occurring in cities and urban problems led to plans for the reconquest of the city centre. Over the course of the preceding plan, urban renovation measures had been initiated, and in 1962 the Malraux law created conservation areas and encouraged the restoration of quality buildings in these areas. Urban renovation is the construction of new blocks, usually residential, after the demolition of existing buildings. Fifteen thousand new dwellings were planned in projects launched before 1961. The 4th Plan forecast the construction of 50,000 dwellings in projects to be launched in 1965, and 100,000 dwellings per annum between 1970 and 1975.

The 5th Plan (1966-70) set the objective of improving 200,000 dwellings per year, with the establishment of minimum standards for habitation. Raising a property to the required standards would be the necessary condition for rent rises. With the 6th Plan (1971-75) a slowdown in urban growth was endorsed and the need to restructure city centres was emphasised. The plan said that controlling changes to the existing urban fabric would call for intervention in the most run-down areas, and in city centres local authorities would need to define and carry out complex and coherent local policies of renovation and rehabilitation.

The improvement of housing quality became a priority only in the 7th Plan (1976-80) and it was over the course of this plan that policies currently in force were developed. Economic conditions in 1975 also favoured setting up a new policy. The Ministry of Economic Affairs, Finance, Development, and Housing commissioned the Nora Report which concluded that the traditional approaches of urban development and local partnership should be combined to prevent housing issues being sidelined. The new policy rested on incentives. Prevailing rents did not permit the normal maintenance of rented housing, whether private or public. The distinction between private and public housing was, moreover, partly academic. The 1948 law, by regulating rent levels, had created public housing de facto. Units of housing with controlled rents were often poorly maintained for financial reasons despite ANAH subsidies.

Procedures previously available were improved and reinforced:

- The projects grouped under building restoration, which constituted the first attempts at block improvements, were replaced by OPAHs (Planned Projects in Housing Improvement). As an incentive, state aid was made available to municipalities to implement these projects. Aid was set up for owner-occupiers (PAH), and landlords could benefit from increased ANAH subsidies in return for a nine-year rent-control agreement.

- Ancillary projects (sidewalks, frontage restoration, facilities) were encouraged by financing set up under the FAU (Urban Facilities Fund).

- At the same time, mechanisms to improve the large HLM estates were strengthened. As a government report clearly emphasised, this particular type of property needed diverse intervention strategies of varying complexity, for example, upgrading, humanising and maintaining.

State subsidies for upgrading and improvement, including rent-control agreements and aid to individuals, were extended. The programme of Social Life and Housing was brought in for HLMs. Blocks were situated in dehumanised urban settings but the problems went far beyond those of bricks and mortar to the social malaise resulting from a policy of housing allocation which did not take account of social factors. The new policy relied to a large extent on the willingness of elected officials to act. With respect to private housing, the creation of OPAHs and their fine-tuning has produced substantial qualitative and quantitative results (between 1976 and 1990, 1,600 OPAHs were created of which 600 are still active). It could also be said that the procedure has in some ways become an automatic one, partly independent of the state, which is a sign of success.

The 8th Plan (1981-85) prioritised the improvement of living conditions in existing housing, specifically in large blocks suffering deterioration, a policy which relied on the Social Life and Housing procedure initiated at department level. The 9th Plan (1984-88) set out an implementation priorities programme for better urban living with the rehabilitation of existing housing, particularly social housing, and the social development of areas, and its main focus (700,000 social dwellings to be rehabilitated over the course of the plan, 148 areas to be subject to neighbourhood upgrading agreements). The 10th Plan (1989-92) emphasised the need for agreement and cooperation in urban social development and municipal contracts.

In conclusion, in this way over the last decade, the State has thus put effort into social housing and problem areas. Decentralisation, introduced in 1982, put initiatives for improving private housing stock at the local level. Rehabilitation projects have been set much more ambitious goals than just building renovation in being expected to repair the social fabric as well.

## General conditions for housing rehabilitation

France is a country with relatively high population growth by European standards. In 1993 there were 57.5 million inhabitants and about 27 million dwellings. Household size, around average for Europe, showed a small decline in the past decade. The number of dwellings has increased in line with the population, but not with household formation. France's gross national product (GNP) (1991) is the second highest in the EU, but the fourth on a per capita basis ($14,000 per capita in 1991). After a period of high inflation and negative real interest rates in the 1970s and 1980s (which favoured private housing investment), the economy is now characterised by low inflation and high real interest rates which could be a problem for housing investment. The unemployment rate is high.

## Housing policy and the housing market

Housing responsibilities in France are not decentralised. Public financing of housing is the responsibility of the State, although in practice this is shared between the State and the territorial authorities. Local authorities exercise control over urban development and local housing policies, the two factors essential to an effective housing programme, especially in providing building land for construction purposes. France is also characterised by the existence of the HLMs as already mentioned, which are the main source of social housing. There are 1,000 such organisations, of which 250 are public agencies under the control of local authorities and 360 are limited liability joint stock companies. They are equivalent to housing associations in Britain.

There is a relative balance between homeowners and tenants in France. Of the total population, 54% live in owner-occupied dwellings while tenants are apportioned more or less evenly between the social and the private sectors. Table 8.1 outlines some background figures on the housing situation in France.

The general principles of housing policy are focused in two directions:

1. **To enable everyone to live in dignity:** the notion of the right to accommodation is written into the legislation of 1989 as fundamental. This includes the possibility to own or to maintain oneself in proper accommodation and is the result of a compromise between three contradictory objectives:

    - a low residual rent for the tenant (condition of access to accommodation);
    - the quality of the accommodation (which has a cost factor);
    - the level of public assistance which society is capable of accepting.

2. **To offer a true freedom of choice for all** in matters of accommodation, as far as occupation as well as the type of accommodation and location are concerned.

These two directions – the right to accommodation and freedom of choice – imply a **sufficient supply of accommodation** – both in quantity

Table 8.1: Housing market indicators, France (1992)

| | |
|---|---|
| New dwellings per year per 1,000 inhabitants | 4.9 |
| New dwellings per year per 1,000 inhabitants (1985-90) | 5.6 |
| Number of dwellings in stock per 1,000 inhabitants | 471 |
| Average dwelling size (square metres) | 86.4 |
| Dwelling without bath (% of stock) | 6 |
| Dwellings built before 1949 (%) | 37 |
| Average rent per year per square metre (FF) | 320 |
| Rent/disposable household income (%) | 14.3 |

(otherwise poor people are not accommodated) and in quality in a broad sense. They also imply a diversity of occupancy status (with a balance between owner-occupancy, social tenancy and private tenancy) and diversity of occupancy (with the avoidance of concentrations of social dwellings and spacial and social segregation).

## Problems of urban decay and housing deterioration

Two main types of locality are particularly affected by the deterioration process:

- older areas either built well before 1900 or at the start of the century;
- urban developments from the 1960s.

The nature of the deterioration process varies considerably according to the date of construction. In older housing, the basic structure needs reinforcing and dwellings lack basic amenities. In the more recent developments, problems relate to poor construction, dampness, leakages and poor insulation. The regulation of private rental housing was limited to buildings constructed before 1948, in effect introducing a two-tier housing market and limiting property upkeep.

## Dwelling tenure and rehabilitation needs

Table 8.2 shows a breakdown of housing condition by tenure in France in 1992. As it indicates, dwellings lacking amenities are almost equally found in tenanted and owner-occupied housing. About 46% of tenants in dwellings built before 1948 lack amenities, but this has decreased from 53% in 1988. There are no statistics on the state of buildings apart from the presence or lack of amenities such as running water, a bathroom or central heating.

## The effects of housing policy on tenure

Since 1977, one focus of French housing policy has been the development of home ownership. The effects of this are evident in an analysis of changes in occupier status between 1978 and 1988. In 10 years, the percentage of owner-occupiers has climbed from 46.6% to 54.3% while the percentage of private sector tenants has declined, mainly due to apartment sales to tenants (see Table 8.3).

Table 8.2: Dwellings by tenure and amenity level, France (1992)

|  | No water or with water only | | No toilet or no bathroom | | Comfortable, no central heating | | Comfortable with central heating | | Total | |
|---|---|---|---|---|---|---|---|---|---|---|
|  | 000s | % | 000s | % | 000s | % | 000s | % | 000s | % |
| Owner-occupier (outright) | 226 | 4.0 | 306 | 4.6 | 1,017 | 15.2 | 5,115 | 76.3 | 6,705 | 100 |
| Owner-occupier (mortgagee) | * | 0.4 | 36 | 0.7 | 572 | 11.0 | 4,582 | 88.0 | 5,208 | 100 |
| Social tenant | * | 0.3 | 47 | 1.2 | 221 | 5.9 | 3,498 | 92.7 | 3,775 | 100 |
| Private sector tenant | 178 | 3.9 | 180 | 3.9 | 948 | 31.7 | 3,254 | 71.3 | 4,561 | 100 |
| of which of building constructed pre-1948 | 171 | 7.5 | 162 | 7.1 | 714 | 31.2 | 1,245 | 54.3 | 2,292 | 100 |
| Other tenures | 182 | 9.7 | 145 | 7.7 | 334 | 22.7 | 1,221 | 64.9 | 1,882 | 100 |
| All housing | 655 | 3.0 | 714 | 3.2 | 3,092 | 14.0 | 17,670 | 79.8 | 22,131 | 100 |

* Not significant.

Source: INSEE Housing Survey (1992)

Table 8.3: Changes in housing tenure, all households (1984-92) (000s)

|  | October 1984 | | October 1998 | | November 1992 | |
|---|---|---|---|---|---|---|
|  | Actual | % | Actual | % | Actual | % |
| Owners non-mortgage | 5,360 | 26.3 | 5,829 | 27.4 | 6,612 | 29.9 |
| Owners mortgage | 4,963 | 24.4 | 5,410 | 26.1 | 5,301 | 24.0 |
| **Total owner-occupier** | **10,323** | **50.7** | **11,387** | **53.6** | **11,913** | **53.8** |
| Social sector | 3,362 | 16.2 | 3,622 | 17.0 | 3,775 | 17.1 |
| HLM | 2,978 | 14.6 | 3,189 | 15.0 | 3,376 | 15.3 |
| Other social housing | 384 | 1.9 | 433 | 2.0 | 399 | 1.8 |
| Private sector | 4,570 | 22.5 | 4,291 | 20.2 | 4,550 | 20.6 |
| **Total tenants** | **7,933** | **39.0** | **7,913** | **36.8** | **8,336** | **37.7** |
| Other | 2,109 | 10.4 | 1,957 | 9.1 | 1,882 | 8.4 |
| **Total** | **20,384** | **100.0** | **21,256** | **100.0** | **22,131** | **100.0** |

Source: INSEE Housing Survey (1992)

## Tools of analysis

Housing surveys and, to a lesser degree, population censuses, are the two principal sources for investigating the housing stock. The assessment of housing quality rests almost exclusively on one sole indicator: comfort. This is limited to sanitary amenities such as cold and hot water supply, separate inside toilet, bathroom with bath or shower and heating. With economic growth and an increase in purchasing power, these amenities have become widespread, although in 1990 about two million dwellings still did not have all modern sanitary facilities. Nevertheless, a dwelling can be completely 'comfortable' yet still be unsuitable for habitation because of dampness, rain penetration and disrepair.

Housing surveys include questions relating to the situation and environment of the dwelling (aspect, neighbourhood, noise levels, soundproofing), but these indicators have never been put to use. Householders are also asked to rate their living conditions as very good, good, fair, poor, or very poor. Only the 1988 survey asked about problems with the dwelling (size, quality, surroundings, isolation, price). Inadequate quality was the most frequently cited: 28.2% of all households found that their dwelling was of poorer quality than they expected. This assessment was based on comfort, age and also usable area. In conclusion, French statistics do not tackle the question of the quality of the dwelling except through measuring comfort. However, attempts are being made, particularly at the CNRS (National Centre for Scientific Research), to improve the quality of information on housing quality. Under discussion are:

**Table 8.4: Amenities in principal residences (1990)**

|  | Number of dwellings | Number of people |
|---|---|---|
| Characteristics of dwelling |  |  |
| No bath, no shower, no internal toilet | 814,755 | 1,428,824 |
| No bath, no shower, with internal toilet | 596,246 | 997,232 |
| Bath or shower, no internal toilet | 575,486 | 1,321,197 |
| Bath or shower, internal toilet, no central heating | 3,270,386 | 8,458,503 |
| Bath or shower, internal toilet, central heating | 16,278,804 | 43,164,607 |

Source: Population Census

- the distinction between the physical quality of the dwelling (intrinsic quality) and its adequacy as a dwelling for the household (size and financial accessibility);
- the intrinsic quality of the dwelling cannot be assessed in only static terms. The problem is also to assess changes in the quality of existing dwellings. Improvements which do not manifest themselves as visible changes must be taken into account for a proper follow-up of quality.

## Rehabilitation needs in private housing

It is difficult to evaluate the real rehabilitation needs of the private housing stock, as the censuses and housing surveys show only the lack of certain elements of comfort: toilets, bathrooms, central heating. However, other rehabilitation needs do exist and the nature of the work required is known, even though precise evaluation is not possible.

These include needs resulting from the state of regulations in force at the time the dwellings were constructed. Building standards have taken into account certain requirements of comfort or safety only gradually since 1960. Energy conservation has been included since 1975, while accessibility for physically disabled people, and soundproofing followed later. Many buildings need works to bring them up to current standards even where financial or tax incentives have allowed improvements to part of the property (especially in energy conservation). There is a need for major repairs not only to pre-war properties but also to more recent ones. Local surveys have found that the upkeep of a property has not always been taken into account in buildings often considered new by their owners. According to local surveys, the need to replace or bring up to standard obsolete facilities is particularly marked in rented properties and those with owner-occupiers of modest means. These needs have been behind changes to housing improvement policy, such as aid to owner-occupiers for major repairs, energy conservation, works to improve accessibility and the extension of ANAH aid for dwellings more than 15 years old.

### Links between regional economic changes and housing rehabilitation

There is little regional information available about the links between rehabilitation and the economic vitality of the regions. However, in older industrial regions where the housing market is slack, the rehabilitation of old housing is more selective. By contrast, these regions are well provided with social housing which benefits from the same rehabilitation policies as other regions.

## The distribution of responsibility for rehabilitation

Rehabilitation policy for social housing is the responsibility of the state, which lays down rules for subsidies allocated through decentralised agencies. These can be augmented by the regions, mainly as part of state regional planning agreements. Aid to owner-occupiers (PAH) is also the responsibility of the state, with implementation also devolved to decentralised agencies. Aid to landlords is the responsibility of the ANAH. Policy is set by its administrative board, on which the state has a seat, with implementation devolved to decentralised state agencies. The regions, the départements and communes can, within limits, develop policies to aid housing rehabilitation. Landlords are responsible for the condition of their properties and can be required to effect works to maintain their rented property in good condition.

## Regulation mechanisms

### Controls on private renting

New lettings are for three years for individuals. This can be reduced to one year if the property is required by the landlord for family or professional reasons. The rent is determined by negotiation according to whether the dwelling is new or is being rented for the first time and meets the standards of comfort or if it is comfortable and has been brought up to standard, or if at least a year's rent has been spent on it in the last six months. In other cases, if the rent demanded is higher than the rent charged to the previous tenant, it must be determined by reference to rents normally charged in the neighbourhood for comparable dwellings. The tenant has two months to contest the rent figure before a departmental arbitration commission. Special arrangements for reducing rents can be made by order of the Council of State in geographical areas where abnormal conditions apply, such as Paris. This legal framework does not apply to dwellings covered by the rent controls of 1948, but there are relatively few of these (less than 400,000, situated mainly in the large urban centres), and they are for the most part 'uncomfortable'. Their occupants benefit from regulated rents and security of tenure.

*Policies set up to promote regular maintenance*

This policy has two facets:

- Construction codes lay down the general building regulations for residential buildings along with maintenance required to ensure safety standards. Provisions relate to:

  - elevators (lifts);
  - heating systems, gas appliances;
  - collective gas-controlled mechanical ventilation systems;
  - garage doors;
  - detection systems, smoke extraction, fire protection.

  To ensure that these obligations are met, owners must sign up to maintenance contracts, some of which are laid down in bylaws. Special maintenance obligations ensure safety in high-rise buildings and those open to the public. Companies also offer landlords and co-owners maintenance contracts for facilities that include elements susceptible to ageing such as taps, water softeners, movable blinds and shutters, roofs and terraces.

- Legislation introduced in 1989, dealing with the rental sector, lays down the responsibilities of landlords and tenants. The landlord is required to provide the tenant with a usable dwelling in good repair, to maintain the premises in a fit state and to effect all necessary repairs for the upkeep of the premises rented. The tenant is required to accept the costs of ongoing maintenance for the dwelling and the fittings mentioned in the contract and of the repairs (both individual and communal) apart from those resulting from decay, poor workmanship or construction defects. The tenant pays recoverable costs for professional maintenance work done at the request of the owner. This provision is aimed mainly at charges arising from maintenance contracts.

## Programmes with financial support

### OPAH

Planned Projects in Housing Improvement (OPAH) were created in 1977 as the instrument of housing improvement policy in older areas. Agreement is produced between the state, the ANAH and a commune or intercommunal cooperation body, and relies on goodwill and support from local residents and owners. The latter are encouraged to make improvements through grants, from the state for owner-occupiers of modest means, and from the ANAH for landlords.

*Tax reductions for outlay in respect of large repairs, thermal insulation and certain improvements*

Tax allowances are available for up to 25% of costs up to FF10,000 for single persons and FF20,000 for a married couple, with further allowances for children.

Private landlords benefit from subsidies granted by ANAH for improving the comfort of dwellings over 15 years old. The subsidy varies between 25% and 70% depending on the nature of the works involved and the owner's commitment to rent levels. The annual budget of ANAH is financed by a tax on landlords. The ceiling can, in exceptional cases, be increased to FF130,000 per dwelling if it increases the habitable area by at least 10% for dwellings finished 31 December 1960.

## PALULOS

Social housing is eligible for improvement grants through the PALULOS scheme which provides state subsidies at a rate of 20% for construction works, with a ceiling of FF85,000 per dwelling. There is also a grant for dwelling improvements for low-income owner-occupiers at 20% of the cost of the works to a ceiling of FF14,000. The subsidy can be increased to 25%, with a ceiling of FF175,000, in cases of coordinated projects under the OPAH scheme; up to 35%, with a ceiling of FF24,500 for low-income owners; and up to 50%, with a ceiling of FF20,000 for work for disabled people.

Social tenants are eligible, based on their income, for personal assistance as a function of the household's housing costs. The ceiling for subsidisable works is FF85,000 per dwelling.

## ANAH

Since its creation in 1971, the ANAH has played an executive role in housing improvement policy in the private rental sector within the framework of global housing policy. It gives subsidies for improvements to rental housing in return for a commitment to rent levels from the landlord for 10 years. The dwellings have to be over 15 years old and subject to the supplementary leasehold tax at 2.5%. The ceiling for subsidisable works is FF2,580 per square metre and FF22,500 per dwelling; in PST projects (schemes to help house the homeless) the subsidisable expenses have a ceiling of FF750 to FF1,500 per square metre of private areas and FF1,000 per square metre for common areas.

ANAH subsidies can represent 40% to 70% of subsidised works, up to a ceiling of FF1,700 to FF2,500 per square metre. Between 1990 and 1993, the total value of subsidies awarded rose from FF1,860 million to FF2,437 million, and generated works rising from FF6,800 million to FF8,746 million, respectively. The number of dwellings subsidised increased from 105,000 to 141,300 of which 8,600 to 9,680, respectively, were linked to low interest loans. In 1993, OPAH and PST subsidies represented over 40% of the ANAH budget covering 32,700 dwellings. Post-1948 housing stock only uses a small part of the budget: 8.6%. Financing for housing rehabilitation comes from the State, the regions, the departments and communes, and from the owners themselves. Funding for ANAH is raised through TADB (supplementary leasehold tax). The tax is applied to buildings over 15 years old. Landlords pay 2.5% of the rent charged allowing then access to ANAH subsidies.

Subsidies are available only for dwellings intended for residential use, including commercial and professional premises converted to dwellings with special fittings. Work must be for improvements to safety, health or fittings, energy conservation, soundproofing, access or alterations for physically disabled people.

This improvement work is only subsidised in dwellings or building which lack amenities or need to be brought up to general standards. Works to make good, to repair or replace fittings are not subsidised. However, in the case of extreme obsolescence, the replacement of one or more fittings can be allowed as part of a global improvement project. Subsidy is calculated as a percentage of the work covered up to a ceiling which varies by region. The rate of subsidy is normally 25%, but can be increased in projects contracted with municipalities or for highly social-oriented projects for disadvantaged tenants.

## PAH

Owner-occupiers of dwellings more than 20 years old are eligible for home improvement grants (PAH) which are means tested. The PAH finances works to improve safety, health, home fittings, energy conservation and accessibility for disabled people. Its rate is 20% of the cost of works subject to a ceiling of FF14,000. This rate can be increased to 25% of a FF17,500 ceiling in the case of coordinated projects (OPAH), to 35% of a FF24,500 ceiling for owners with very limited resources, or to 50% of FF20,000 ceiling for works involving disabled people.

As indicated above, there is aid available to owner-occupiers with meagre resources (PAH). However, certain blocks built in the 1960s pose maintenance problems and are given special consideration. There are tax reductions equal to 25% of the expenses, to a ceiling which during the period 1990-95 was FF10,000 for a single person and FF20,000 for a married couple, plus allowances for children. These allowances are for major repairs to dwellings completed more than 15 years ago, thermal insulation and regulation of heating, improvement expenses, installing a security door or intercom, works to improve accessibility for the disabled and the installation of elevators.

Overall, state efforts have been sustained despite the ups and downs of the economy and even reinforced over the most recent period in social housing (see Table 8.5).

### Other kinds of help to landlords and tenants

No means tests are applied, but landlords and tenants with meagre resources can obtain increased subsidies. By contrast, the owners of large properties must sign special agreements and may receive reduced subsidies. The allocation of subsidies is decided by departmental commissions which bring together the parties concerned: owners, tenants and state

Table 8.5: The flow of public subsidies (FFmillions)

|  | 1984 | 1985 | 1986 | 1987 | 1988 | 1989 | 1990 | 1991 | 1992 |
|---|---|---|---|---|---|---|---|---|---|
| PALULOS | 1,684 | 1,738 | 1,811 | 1,638 | 1,527 | 1,727 | 1,476 | 1,672 | 1,798 |
| ANAH | 955 | 952 | 1,198 | 1,294 | 1,434 | 1,447 | 1,329 | 1,241 | 1,241 |
| PAH | 427 | 297 | 272 | 253 | 336 | 321 | 349 | 375 | 375 |
| Total | 3,066 | 2,987 | 3,281 | 3,185 | 3,297 | 3,495 | 3,154 | 3,288 | 3,414 |

Source: Housing records

representatives. The commissions have the power to increase assessments in the light of local conditions.

ANAH also allocates subsidies for diagnostic surveys (eg, on thermal and acoustic requirements) to indicate to the owner intending to make improvements what work would be desirable, its cost and expected lifetime. Priority in the granting of aid, including the reservation of credits, is given to contractual policies carried out with the local authorities: the Planned Projects for Housing Improvement (OPAHs) and the Special Social Programmes (PSTs).

The principal aim of the OPAHs is to improve the housing stock and maintain social housing in existing areas. A three-year agreement between the state, the ANAH and a municipality is produced. To encourage the private provision of low-rent housing, the ANAH increases the subsidies when the owner commits himself to limiting the rent of an improved dwelling. The tenant attracts housing aid in the form of Personal Housing Aid (APL).

PSTs are social projects in the private rented sector following a law of 31 May 1990 to promote the right to housing. As with OPAHs, a three-year agreement between the State, the ANAH and a local authority is produced. Their aim is to improve the 'uncomfortable' housing stock occupied by the disadvantaged (young, single-parent households, old people) and bring vacant dwellings back into use.

Social targeting of these projects is through two measures:

- the owner is obliged to sign an agreement with the State which stipulates a rent ceiling and allows the tenant to receive the APL;

- a system for follow-up and mediation is set up: a specific schedule of allocation for the dwelling, mediation between the owner and tenant, social support agency help for the tenant, guarantees for the owner.

## Treating the problem as a whole

Policy for social development has been set up for certain areas, mostly with social housing, where it is felt that more than renovation is necessary. The lack of facilities needs to be addressed while dealing with problems arising from poverty. The Minister for Cities leads and coordinates policy in these areas, with various administrations implementing the decisions. At national level, the CIV (Interministerial Committee for Cities and Urban Social Development), chaired by the Prime Minister, develops policy and allocates resources. At the local level, coordination is through a project chief paid by the municipality and with financial support from central government. Direct intervention credits (aside from rents) into these areas have been consolidated in order to facilitate their implementation, 90% of which are delegated to department/prefect level. It is the project chief, with the help of a coordinating structure, notably contacts with the prefecture, who ensures links between the initiatives taken in the various fields. Initiatives can be developed locally and there are national policies designed for specific situations.

As for personal safety in urban areas, commissions for the prevention of delinquency bringing together all the officials concerned have been set up at departmental level, and community policing (specially-trained police officers who know an area and patrol it regularly) has been developed by the police authorities under the aegis of the Ministry of the Interior. As for economic development, central government agencies such as the ANPE (National Employment Agency) have been mobilised to encourage integration through local employment in these areas (setting up local centres to foster youth employment) and to bring them back into the economic life of the city by seeding them with new activities.

A systematic partnership with the private sector does not exist, but here and there, initiatives have been taken. At national level, leaving aside central government administration, two partnership programmes have been set up, one with the FAS (Social Action Funds, which manages aid to immigrants and people in difficulty). The CDC (a state bank which manages national and local community funds) has a 'development through solidarity' programme which provides low interest loans (7%) through the local authority to finance investment and land acquisitions. There are many other local initiatives to help rebuild the social fabric including the setting up of community associations involving people in the on-going maintenance of their housing stock, teenage students helping younger children with learning difficulties and activities for women.

*Rent support policy*

The are two main types of personal housing allowance (see Table 8.6 for details regarding recipients):

- housing allowance (AL) which itself is split into family housing assistance (ALF) and social assistance (ALS);

Table 8.6: Number of recipients of personal housing allowance at 31 December 1991 (in millions of households)

|  | Renting | Owning | Total |
|---|---|---|---|
| APL | 1,658 | 855 | 2,513 |
| ALS | 1,054 | 26 | 1,080 |
| ALF | 857 | 205 | 1,062 |
| Total | 3,569 | 1,086 | 4,655 |

- housing allowance targeted at particular dwellings (APL).

Their allocation is means-tested but calculated in different ways. APL is generally more generous than AL. APL applies, whatever the characteristics of the family or the age of the occupants, to a particular set of dwellings. ALF is allocated essentially to households with dependants (children, old people) in dwellings for which APL is unavailable; ALS is allocated to households that have no right to either APL or ALF. The two types of assistance, in contrast to aid for bricks and mortar, vary greatly according to income (increase an average FF20 per FF100 income drop) and according to family size (increase an average 33% per extra child).

## Results of policies

Table 8.7 traces the distribution of investment between 1984 and 1992, showing that investment has come essentially from the private sector.

In relation to OPAH projects, there has been a gradual transfer of responsibility to the communes (with a role in urban development since the decentralisation) with the state (responsible for housing finance) becoming a partner to guarantee that objectives are met, especially for the most disadvantaged. There has also been an emphasis on social objectives, seeking to keep locals in their communities, increasing accessibility and preventing the creation of intractable problems. The policy has also widened to include consideration not only of the actual dwelling but of its environment and context, that is, the relationship of the block to its area and to the rest of the city. The notion 'older areas' has been extended to the postwar housing stock which is displaying deterioration and problems with quality of life affecting social integration policies, especially in blocks built in the 1960s.

Table 8.7: Distribution of investment in housing (1984-92) (FFmillions)

|  | 1984 | 1985 | 1986 | 1987 | 1988 | 1989 | 1990 | 1991 | 1992 |
|---|---|---|---|---|---|---|---|---|---|
| **New dwellings** | | | | | | | | | |
| HLM | 20.4 | 22.6 | 24.2 | 21.6 | 20.2 | 16.9 | 15.6 | 17.5 | 20.6 |
| Other social landlords | 5.0 | 5.1 | 5.5 | 5.5 | 6.2 | 7.4 | 6.9 | 6.6 | 6.6 |
| Other legal persons* | 8.0 | 6.7 | 9.4 | 18.1 | 23.5 | 25.5 | 28.5 | 29.6 | 29.0 |
| Natural persons | 139.4 | 135.0 | 140.5 | 150.7 | 159.6 | 172.8 | 171.2 | 146.7 | 128.2 |
| **Second-hand dwellings** | | | | | | | | | |
| HLM | 0.7 | 0.7 | 0.6 | 0.7 | 0.6 | 0.5 | 0.5 | 1.0 | 1.2 |
| Other social landlords | 0.8 | 0.9 | 1.2 | 1.5 | 1.7 | 2.0 | 2.2 | 2.1 | 2.0 |
| Other legal persons* | 1.4 | 1.6 | 2.0 | 2.6 | 2.9 | 3.2 | 3.7 | 3.5 | 3.3 |
| Natural persons | 128.3 | 140.6 | 174.7 | 215.7 | 241.0 | 279.0 | 303.4 | 274.9 | 259.7 |
| **Works** | | | | | | | | | |
| HLM | 9.7 | 10.9 | 12.1 | 13.1 | 14.5 | 15.4 | 15.9 | 17.7 | 20.0 |
| Other social landlords | 0.8 | 0.9 | 0.9 | 1.0 | 1.2 | 1.7 | 1.5 | 1.6 | 1.7 |
| Other legal persons* | 1.3 | 1.3 | 1.6 | 1.6 | 1.7 | 2.0 | 2.3 | 2.1 | 2.0 |
| Natural persons | 91.6 | 96.7 | 101.4 | 106.2 | 115.2 | 121.6 | 124.1 | 125.8 | 121.7 |
| Total | 407.4 | 423.0 | 474.1 | 538.3 | 588.3 | 648.0 | 675.8 | 629.1 | 596.0 |

Note: *Legal persons are generally private, this category including insurance companies and banks and also other welfare landlords.

Source: Housing records

Further changes were introduced in 1991. These lay down principles for policy to encourage social cohesion, preventing or helping to eradicate segregation. The law gives the OPAH a legislative content and a principal aim 'to maintain housing, especially social housing, in old areas'. This procedure aims not only to improve the availability of housing but also to take into account all living conditions in the broad sense: public spaces, local services, transport and shops. Prior to the launch of an OPAH, the mayor leads a consultation exercise with local residents, the relevant contracting authorities and representatives of tenants' associations, to find common ground. The results are presented to the municipal council and then to the prefect. The OPAH draft agreement has to be delivered within a month to allow the general public to express its views.

Since 1977, close to 2,200 OPAHs have been set in motion. Since 1988, slightly under 200 OPAHs have been launched each year. Over 60% are in communes of less than 10,000 inhabitants, where they constitute the interface between housing policy and local development, and contribute to the development of intercommunality.

More than half of the urban OPAHs involved average-sized areas (fewer than 100,000 inhabitants), and a third involved large urban centres (more than 100,000 inhabitants). Greater Paris accounted for less than 10%. Over the last years (1992-95), the value of ANAH commitments in OPAH came to a little less than FF700 million per year, representing FF2,500 million of works and about 25,000 dwellings improved (of which 4,000 were linked to low-interest loans). PAH credits represented FF200 million per year involving more than 18,000 dwellings. The OPAHs place flexible incentives at the disposal of local authorities, including financial commitments by the state. To produce a balance sheet or evaluation is somewhat difficult as these projects involve many aspects and some may have succeeded from one point of view while not from another. In quantitative terms, many of the projects have allowed the effective improvement of a large number of dwellings. In qualitative terms, these procedures have allowed the economic revitalisation of many areas. However, the social effects of the projects are not always positive. Housing rehabilitation projects can result in rent rises which despite precautions and new subsidies, have led to the eviction of the poorest residents. Insofar as rather contradictory objectives were being followed – that is, to bring market forces back into play while keeping the residents where they were – this result is not surprising.

*The rehabilitation of social housing*

The rehabilitation of social housing over the last 15 years has had mixed results. On the whole the procedure has worked satisfactorily. Enterprises have gained skills, knowledge and learned to negotiate with tenants. The almost exclusively technical approach of the early years has now expanded to take social considerations into account. Nevertheless, the general view is that results are fragile. The effect of investment in buildings is often short term – in some areas, having to be redone five years later. Local elected officials are not sufficiently involved to make meaningful contributions to solving problems of peripheral estates. The success of urban social development policies varies with districts, each having weak and strong points. It is difficult to measure the outcomes of these policies. Local inhabitants tend to be ambivalent, although some enthusiasm is evident.

NINE

# Urban renewal and housing rehabilitation in The Netherlands
*René Teule*

## Introduction

Most cities in The Netherlands currently find themselves in a favourable situation. There are no large-scale deteriorated residential areas and no extensive abandoned industrial zones. This is largely the result of outstanding efforts in urban renewal and housing in recent decades. Both the national government and the private sector have invested a great deal to tackle urban decline in Dutch cities.

To deal with these problems, a balanced policy programme seems to be of crucial importance. Successful cooperation and strong coherence between urban renewal and housing, between national and local government and between government and the private sector have contributed considerably to these quite 'healthy' residential areas and living conditions in the cities. Obviously, it would be best not to change this kind of successful policy programme in the near future. However, national government is thinking about withdrawing from urban renewal policy. From the description of the urban renewal and housing rehabilitation policy in The Netherlands in this chapter, this would appear not to be a wise step.

After a short introduction to The Netherlands, the third section of this chapter deals briefly with Dutch housing policy and the housing market. The next section clarifies the relationship between urban renewal and housing rehabilitation as well as the exact definition of urban renewal. Subsequently, the fifth section goes into further detail about the urban renewal achievements in the recent past. Urban renewal in the future is then examined. The chapter ends with a discussion and evaluation of policy.

## Background

In 1995, The Netherlands had 15.4 million inhabitants living on 41,500 square kilometres of land. Between 1985 and 1990 the number of inhabitants grew from about 14.5 million to 15.0 million. Population density grew from 428 inhabitants per square kilometre in 1985 to 456 inhabitants per square kilometre in the 1990s (see also CBS, 1995).

During the period from 1985 to 1990 the gross national product (GNP) in The Netherlands grew from DGl425.35 billion to DGl573.84 billion. Converted into GNP per inhabitant, this means an average of DGl29,355 in 1985, DGl34,480 in 1990 and DGl37,530 in 1993. Although in absolute terms the GNP grew, relatively speaking this was not the case. During the period 1989-93 the annual growth decreased gradually from more than 4% in 1989 to 0.7% in 1993. However, in 1994 the growth of GNP increased again to about 2% (CBS, 1994a; 1995).

Interest rates have been falling since the beginning of the 1990s. In 1990 and 1991 mortgage interest rates were higher than in the years before (about 9% versus 7%). Since then this mortgage interest level has declined to about 7% or 7.5% in 1994 (Ministerie van VROM, 1994).

At the end of the 1980s inflation in The Netherlands was very low (between 0% and 1%). In the 1990s it was somewhat higher, between about 2.5% (1990 and 1993) and about 3% (1991 and 1992).

Finally, it is important to mention that in 1993 the growth of disposable household income was lagging behind inflation. In 1993 the average disposable household income was DGl43,500, while a year before it was DGl42,900 (Trimp, 1994). In 1993 income inequality grew somewhat (see Table 9.1). The income contribution of the lowest decile groups decreased at the same time as the contribution of higher decile groups increased.

## Housing and the housing market in The Netherlands

The Netherlands has a long-standing tradition of creating housing opportunities for lower-income groups. The Housing Act of 1901 created the basis for the development of the non-profit housing sector and housing market regulation in general. In the first decades of this century social rented housing was occupied by registered members of housing associations. Members were often those in skilled or semi-skilled occupations rather than the very poor. Until the 1950s the lower-income groups remained largely in the private sector of the housing market,

Table 9.1: Income distribution of households in decile groups (1991-93)

|  | Decile groups (10%) | | | | | | | | | |
|---|---|---|---|---|---|---|---|---|---|---|
|  | 1st lowest | 2nd | 3rd | 4th | 5th | 6th | 7th | 8th | 9th | 10th highest | Total |
| 1991 | 2.2 | 4.5 | 5.8 | 7.0 | 8.4 | 9.7 | 11.2 | 13.0 | 15.5 | 22.7 | 100.0 |
| 1992 | 2.1 | 4.5 | 5.8 | 7.0 | 8.4 | 9.8 | 11.3 | 13.0 | 15.5 | 22.6 | 100.0 |
| 1993 | 2.0 | 4.4 | 5.7 | 7.0 | 8.4 | 9.8 | 11.3 | 13.1 | 15.6 | 22.6 | 100.0 |

Source: CBS (1994b)

Table 9.2: The development of dwelling stock according to tenure (1947-94) (%)

|  | Owner-occupiers | Housing corporations associations | Central/local government | Individual landlords | Private investment companies | Total | Number (000s) |
|---|---|---|---|---|---|---|---|
| 1947 | 28 | 9 | 3 | 54 | 6 | 100 | 2,117 |
| 1971 | 35 | 24 | 13 | 20 | 8 | 100 | 3,729 |
| 1981 | 41 | 34 | 9 | 9 | 5 | 100 | 4,816 |
| 1989 | 43 | 38 | 6 | 6 | 6 | 100 | 5,612 |
| 1991 | 46 | 36 | 5 | 6 | 6 | 100 | 5,892 |
| 1994 | 48 | 36 |  | 16* |  | 100 | 6,118 |

Note: * Total % for central/local government, individual landlords and private investment companies.

Source: van der Heijden (1993); Ministerie van VROM (1994)

because they could not pay the rents for new good-quality housing in the non-profit sector.

Only with the growth of the non-profit rented housing sector after the Second World War (see Table 9.2) did the social sector begin to meet the housing needs at the bottom end of the housing market (Dieleman, 1993). Until recently the growth of the non-profit rented sector went together with a more gradual growth of the owner-occupier sector and a shrinkage of the private rented sector. Since the beginning of the 1990s this movement has shifted towards a stabilisation of the non-profit sector and an ongoing growth of the owner-occupier sector.

Dutch housing is in a period of transition, partly as a result of the implementation of the *Housing in the 1990s* memorandum, published in 1989. The main topics in this memorandum were (Ministerie van VROM, 1989):

- a reallocation of responsibilities and associated financial risks between the (market) parties involved in housing (towards a more self-sufficient non-profit sector and a more market-oriented housing policy);
- more targeted financial support from central government (a decrease in the level and number of subsidies for social housing);
- rents that cover more of the costs (market rents);
- a shift in the central focus of housing policy towards the regional and local level (decentralisation).

House building in the social sector will be replaced more and more by commercial house building. In the social sector attention will focus on target groups, that is, the households below modal incomes. In 1990 this applied to about 40% of all households, including many elderly people, single-parent households and single people.

Another important topic covered in the *Memorandum* is the 'mismatch' in the Dutch housing market. This is one of the main problems that the central government wants to combat. Many households with a relatively high income are living in non-profit housing. About 38% of the cheap rental dwellings (< DGl490 per month in 1990) are occupied by households with an income above the modal level (about DGl30,000 in 1990). At the same time 40% of the more expensive dwellings (> DGl650 rent per month in 1990) are occupied by income groups beneath the modal level (Ministerie van VROM, 1994). This existing mixture of households of different income groups in the non-profit housing sector in The Netherlands is also reflected in a low level of spatial segregation by income. Attempts to alter this pattern may increase social and spatial segregation in housing. At the regional and local level this maldistribution is not felt so explicitly.

Within the non-profit rented sector there are two groups active in the construction of and provision of housing: housing corporations (associations) and local authorities. Over four fifths of the social dwellings are in the hands of housing associations ('approved institutions'), about 15% are the property of local authorities and the remaining are owned by other non-profit institutions which do not have the status of approved institution.

Within the social rented sector, the housing associations' share is steadily increasing, whereas that of local authorities is declining (Priemus, 1990). The government encouraged the privatisation of local authority housing by hiving it off to existing housing associations or by local authority housing organisations becoming housing associations. After 1997 no financial support was to be given to municipal companies, with the expectation that all these companies would be transformed into housing associations by that time.

In 1985 there were 317 local authority housing organisations and 854 housing associations. By 1992 the former had reduced to 195, whereas the number of housing associations stayed the same. In 1992 most local authority organisations were very small in size: 64% had less than 600 dwellings. Only 6% of these organisations owned more than 4,000 dwellings. Housing associations were typically larger. In 1992 about a quarter of the associations were small (less than 600 dwellings) and 18% possessed more than 4,000 dwellings (Ministerie van VROM, 1994).

The property of housing associations and local authorities mainly consists of 'Housing Act Dwellings'. These are subsidised and are primarily intended for people on low incomes. Until recently the loans necessary to finance the construction of Housing Act Dwellings were provided by the national government (Boelhouwer and van der Heijden, 1992). Nowadays, Housing Act Dwellings no longer exist. Since 1995 the national government has stimulated social housing only via small fixed subsidies for new building activities or housing rehabilitation.

*Housing subsidies*

Housing subsidies in The Netherlands can be divided into two categories: consumer or subject subsidies (housing allowances) and producer subsidies (object or property subsidies) for the maintenance of existing dwellings and the construction of new ones (van Kempen et al, 1992). Formerly, the focus in housing policy was on producer subsidies which were supposed to keep housing affordable (for instance, by building new Housing Act Dwellings). One of the major drawbacks of the programme was that households with higher incomes could also benefit from low-cost housing. This was one of the reasons for cutting back producer subsidies at the beginning of the 1990s.

This has left the housing allowances as one of the key policy instruments. Its objective is to target subsidies specifically at lower-income groups. From the beginning the programme was a huge success when measured in terms of number of recipients. These numbers expanded rapidly, partly because of increasing housing costs, partly because of the stagnation in the growth of personal incomes. The number of recipients grew from 348,000 in 1975/1976 to 920,000 in 1992/1993. The average allowance subsidy also grew; from DGl974 per year in 1975/1976 to DGl2,021 per year in 1992/1993 (Teule, 1994; Ministerie van VROM, 1994). In 1989, just over half of all households with a minimum income were enrolled in the housing allowance programme, receiving an average payment of DGl75 per month.

However, housing allowances have not rectified the major financial inequity of the housing system, with lower-income groups still paying a disproportionate share of their income for housing. Minimum-income households pay almost twice as much for housing (in relative terms) as households earning two or three times the modal income (van Weesep and van Kempen, 1993). There is also a big difference in housing costs between the rental sector and the owner-occupier sector (see also Tables A9.1, 9.2 in the Appendix of this chapter). As already indicated, tenants in the social sector belong to a broad spectrum of income groups, and in terms of other characteristics represent a wide cross-section of society. On average their incomes are higher than those of tenants living in private rented dwellings built before the war (Boelhouwer and van der Heijden, 1992).

In recent years the housing allowance programme has also been subject to cutbacks. Accessibility is being reduced and subsidy conditions tightened. The programme management at the national level has also been improved. A major result is the stabilisation or even a slight reduction in the number of eligible recipients to about 920,000 households. The average level of the allowance is, however, still growing.

## Urban renewal and housing rehabilitation: history and definition

Urban renewal and housing rehabilitation are strongly connected in The Netherlands. Especially since 1985, when a comprehensive urban renewal policy programme was established, the rehabilitation of the dwelling stock in the inner-city areas and the early 20th century neighbourhoods has been a major factor.

The historical development and definition of both these activities are combined in this section. After a short historical description of urban renewal policy, recent developments in housing improvement will be presented. Finally, an important problem of definition within the framework of urban renewal will be pinpointed.

The beginning of Dutch urban renewal dates from the 1960s. A number of small and especially medium-sized cities started developing reconstruction schemes and slum clearance schemes for their inner areas. Selective clearance of slums was started to allow for large road schemes that would increase access to the inner city.

During the 1970s these demolition operations were financially supported through regulations developed by the national government. The most important of these was the *Interim Saldo Regeling* (ISR or Interim Balance Regulation) which came into effect in 1977. The ISR implied that for a few municipalities the total deficit of slum clearance activities and reconstruction activities was paid for by the national government. Under the regulation at first six, later eight and finally 14 municipalities received this preferential treatment (Priemus and Metselaar, 1992).

Only since 1981 has there been a coordinated national policy concerning urban renewal. This was set out in the *Memorandum on Urban and Village Renewal* (MUVR) (Ministerie van VROM, 1981) which estimated the national need for urban renewal. Moreover, this estimate was dynamic with the continuing ageing of the built environment and the outcome of policies taken into consideration. This eventually led to the production of two models for the urban renewal task. It was estimated that by doubling efforts urban renewal would be completed in the year 2000, that is, within 20 years, whereas with an unchanged policy it would take more than 50 years, finishing long after 2030. Urban renewal was seen as a comprehensive finite project, dealing with the improvement of dwellings, residential environments, monuments, traffic and welfare problems, sewage systems and so on. At that time it was especially focused on inner-city areas.

It was not this memorandum but the Urban and Village Renewal Act (UVRA), which came into effect on 1 January 1985, which formed the national basis for urban renewal. Its introduction meant more political freedom for local governments to develop their own urban renewal policy, in complete contrast with the centralised character of the earlier ISR. Moreover, while the ISR referred to only a small number of municipalities, in principle the UVRA covered all municipalities.

Through the introduction of the UVRA, 19 subsidy schemes, mainly from the Ministry for Housing, Physical Planning and the Environment, supplemented with some regulations from the Ministry of Economic Affairs and the Ministry of Welfare, Health and Cultural Affairs, were abolished and incorporated into a national fund for urban renewal (De Vries-Heijnis, 1990). This fund amounted to about 1 billion guilders a year.

Until 1995 this sum was calculated annually using a formula called the 'urban renewal key' among municipalities and provinces in The Netherlands. The 1990 formula for the urban renewal key was as follows:

$$\frac{s(a+i) + b + h}{C^2} = \frac{s(a + B10\ fw) + b + (\tfrac{1}{2}p + 2m)}{C^2}$$

where:

$s$ = urbanisation factor, ranging from 1 to 2

$a$ = number of dwellings, built before 1945, present at 1 January 1988

$i$ = 'business factor'

$B10$ = number of businesses in industry with more than 10 employers

$f$ = factor 2 for the four largest cities: factor 1 for other municipalities

$w$ = relationship between the number of dwellings built before 1945 and the total number of dwellings in a municipality

$b$ = number of multi-family dwellings, built before 1931, present at 1 January 1988

$h = \tfrac{1}{2}p + 2m$ = historical factor

$p$ = number of dwellings in an indicated or still to be indicated protected city area or village area

$m$ = number of monuments in the entire municipality, if the municipality is a 'protected scape' or will be indicated as such

$C$ = relationship between the average income in a municipality and in the whole of The Netherlands in 1984.

Municipalities that owned a share of more than 0.1% in the fund for urban renewal according to this formula received the contribution directly from the fund (the 'direct municipalities'). The other municipalities received their financial contribution via the relevant province, the latter acting as a shareholder for these non-direct municipalities.

The different components of this urban renewal key were considered to be essential in fulfilling the urban renewal task. Within the pre-war housing stock the attention was focused on multi-family dwellings built before 1931. Private rented dwellings of poor quality especially had to be improved. Attention was also focused on low-income groups. The bulk of the urban renewal activities was still concentrated in the inner cities, especially those of more than 50,000 inhabitants. However, neighbourhoods built at the beginning of this century were also being tackled by the 'urban renewal machine'.

### Recent developments in housing rehabilitation

After the Second World War, emphasis on dwelling improvement in The Netherlands lay on restoration of war damage, the division of dwellings into apartments (to cope with the housing shortage) and the installation of sanitary facilities. However, the subsidies available and investment elicited were not large. New construction had priority over improvement (van der Schaar, 1991).

Criticism of the large-scale inner-city demolition activities of the 1970s led to better subsidies for improvement of the existing housing stock. It is important to make a distinction between the improvement of private rented dwellings and that of social rented dwellings. For years separate subsidy systems existed for private and social rented dwellings which, in general, were less favourable for private landlords.

The following types of subsidies were in use, almost all of which directly promoted maintenance and renewal (Papa, 1992):

- contributions to the operating deficit after improvement (especially for pre-war social rented dwellings);

- lump-sum contributions (notably for postwar social rented dwellings);

- premiums expiring after 10 or 20 years (for commercial rented dwellings and owner-occupier dwellings).

The subsidies were not attractive enough for private landlords, however. In Amsterdam, Rotterdam, The Hague and Utrecht, where there were many poor-quality multi-family private rented dwellings, project-based approaches to dwelling improvement proved to be impossible (van der

Schaar, 1991). In those cities, poor-quality dwellings were purchased and then refurbished (first without, later with government subsidies). This strategy is still used in the four largest cities.

In the late 1980s, subsidies were more streamlined, partly due to the introduction of the urban renewal fund. In 1985 the subsidies for improvement of owner-occupier dwellings were placed in this fund, and transferred to municipalities. In addition, the separate schemes for private and social rented dwellings were integrated into one direct subsidy scheme for dwelling improvement. This meant the end of differences in regulation. One of the important characteristics of this new scheme was that only lump-sum contributions were provided. Moreover, the maximum investment costs for dwelling improvement were raised from 80% to 100% of comparable new construction costs.

At the beginning of the 1990s a new system of subsidies for construction and dwelling improvement came into effect (the Dwelling-linked Subsidies Order). Responsibility was decentralised to the municipal level, though, for smaller municipalities (less than 30,000 inhabitants) the province acted as budget-holder. The distinction between major and minor dwelling improvement also became important, with a limit on investment of DGl50,000 (van der Schaar, 1991). The minor improvement of private rented dwellings (in many cases postwar) was abolished. In addition, subsidies for major improvement of pre-war private rented dwellings were also transferred to the urban renewal fund, destined for the four large cities (see below). Decentralised annual budgets for major improvement of (pre-war) social rented dwellings remained until 1995 but have now also been replaced by incentive contributions (to the amount of DGl5,000). These contributions can be used to encourage major improvement of social rented dwellings or for new constructions of social rented and owner-occupier dwellings.

Table 9.3 shows how many subsidised and unsubsidised improvements took place in the different housing sectors from 1980 to 1990. It also indicates the investments involved. It is clear that nearly half the improved dwellings (49%) and nearly half the total investments (47%) were subsidised. Subsidies in the social rented sector were very important with almost 85% of the dwellings improved with some kind of subsidy. Shown in DGl, the 'subsidy addiction' is even more striking with more than 86% of investment subsidised. Within the owner-occupied sector it is the other way around. Here only 11% of the dwellings were improved with the help of subsidies (ie, 3% of total investment).

**Table 9.3: Housing rehabilitation in the 1980s**

| Housing sector | Number of improvements | Investments (DGl billions) |
|---|---|---|
| **Social rented sector** | | |
| Subsidised | 531,400 | 14.4 |
| Unsubsidised | 100,000 | 2.3 |
| Total | 631,400 | 16.7 |
| **Private rented sector** | | |
| Subsidised | 49,200 | 1.2 |
| Unsubsidised | 109,400 | 3.3 |
| Purchased by local government | 83,200 | 3.2 |
| Total | 242,800 | 7.7 |
| **Owner-occupiers** | | |
| Subsidised | 69,600 | 0.6 |
| Unsubsidised | 550,100 | 16.7 |
| Total | 619,700 | 17.3 |
| **Total** | | |
| Subsidised | 737,500 | 19.4 |
| Unsubsidised | 759,500 | 22.3 |
| Total | 1,497,000 | 41.7 |

Source: Kuiper Compagnons (1990)

Thus, direct public intervention for housing rehabilitation, via housing associations and local authorities, was concentrated on the social rented sector. Parts of the private rented sector were also improved through direct or indirect intervention.

## The definition of urban renewal

Urban renewal can be defined in different ways. According to the 1981 memorandum, urban renewal was defined as "an intensified adaptation of the living, working, production and social environments to benefit those who work and live in rundown areas (built up before 1971) by meeting their present needs and customs; maintenance and management issues are not included" (Ministerie van VROM, 1989). Urban renewal was seen as a comprehensive programme focusing on a broad range of issues, targeted on a specific part of the built-up environment constructed before 1971. It is important to note that by this definition, urban renewal would be finished only when the present needs and customs were met. However, these needs and customs continually develop and change.

In the 1985 UVRA, urban renewal was defined more broadly as the "systematic effort both in town planning areas and in social, economic, cultural and environmental protection areas, aimed at preservation, restoration and improvement, redivision or slum clearance of built-up parts of the municipal territory" (UVRA, Article 1, Paragraph 1). Defined in this way, urban renewal is an on-going process with no clear beginning or end. Moreover urban renewal seems to be less targeted on a specific part of the built environment. Because decentralisation was an important topic of the 1985 Act, different municipalities worked out their own more specific definitions of urban renewal, according to their problems, means and possibilities. They also chose their own urban renewal areas, generally neighbourhoods in the inner cities.

In 1997, the government evaluated its urban renewal policy and assessed the remaining need for urban renewal. The results were set out in the document *Future Urban Renewal Policy* (Ministerie van VROM, 1992). This explicitly stated that urban renewal is a finite process, with national government concern in this respect is planned to come to an end around 2005. This referred back to the above-mentioned definition of urban renewal in the 1981 Memorandum on Urban and Village Renewal accentuated by adding the words 'at present still existing' when speaking about the arrears to be combated. Clearly the national government wanted to map everything needed for finishing the urban renewal task. Unexpected tasks that might present themselves in the near future, as happened during the 1980s with soil pollution, were excluded. Here the national government applied double standards: what is finished was counted (1980s), while the things that still have to be done only count to a limited extent (1990s). Thus the broader definition of urban renewal as mentioned in the official 1985 UVRA was ignored. The national government wanted to abolish this broad legal definition because it bound it for too long a period and would cost too much money. Urban renewal at the national level would thus be defined in a very static way in the future, and would only relate to arrears or disrepair which were formulated in 1981. Possible new problems related to urban renewal were ignored. If they occurred in the future, they would have to obtain a new place on the political agenda.

## Urban renewal achievements during the 1980s

Against this background we can now look at the urban renewal achievements in the recent past. In 1990 the national government evaluated urban renewal policy during the 1980s. The evaluation analysis concluded that "urban renewal is well on schedule" and about halfway through (Ministerie van VROM, 1990).

During this decade DGl105 billion (at a 1980 price level) was invested in urban renewal (see Figure 9.1). The greater part of this amount was spent on dwelling improvement (DGI 41.7 billion or 39%, Table 9.3), house building for substitution (17%) and new supplementary housing development (28%). The DGl29 billion that were invested in new supplementary housing development (211,000 dwellings) was more than expected. This was especially due to physical planning policy focused on the cities (the 'compact city policy').

Figure 9.2 shows who produced all these investments in the past decade. Although the government has made a substantial contribution (DGl38 billion, or 36%), private investors in particular are the ones who have nourished urban renewal policy financially. No less than 61% of all investments in urban renewal were accounted for by the private sector.

**Figure 9.1: Investments in urban renewal according to activities in the 1980s**

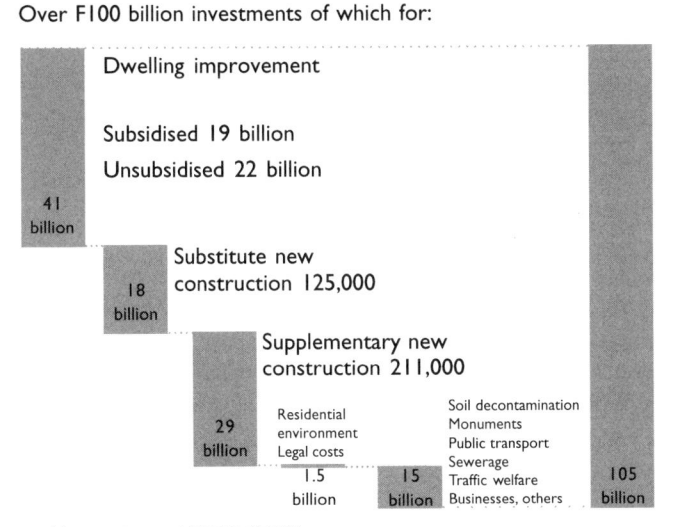

Over F100 billion investments of which for:

| | | |
|---|---|---|
| 41 billion | Dwelling improvement<br>Subsidised 19 billion<br>Unsubsidised 22 billion | |
| 18 billion | Substitute new construction 125,000 | |
| 29 billion | Supplementary new construction 211,000 | |
| 1.5 billion | Residential<br>environment<br>Legal costs | |
| 15 billion | Soil decontamination<br>Monuments<br>Public transport<br>Sewerage<br>Traffic welfare<br>Businesses, others | |
| 105 billion | | |

Source: Ministerie van VROM (1990)

**Figure 9.2: Investments in urban renewal according to cost centres in the 1980s**

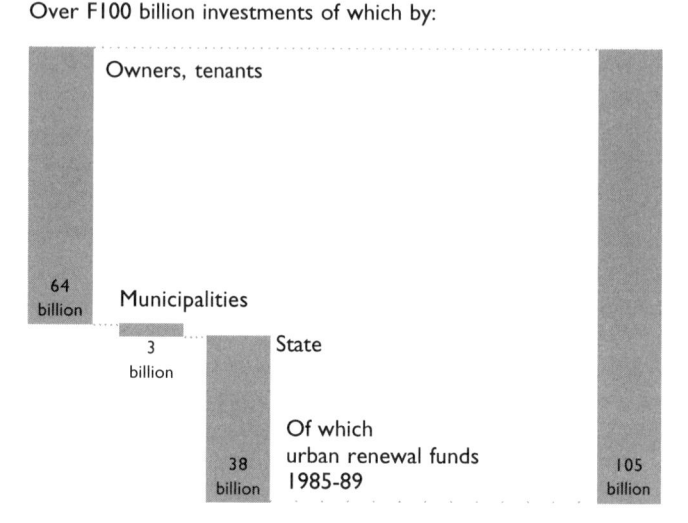

Over F100 billion investments of which by:

- Owners, tenants: 105 billion
- 64 billion
- Municipalities: 3 billion
- State: 38 billion
- Of which urban renewal funds 1985-89

Source: Ministerie van VROM (1990)

These include the investments of owner-occupiers and tenants themselves. Government investments in urban renewal appear to have exerted a generating effect, but the private sector invested DGl1.68 for every guilder invested by the government.

What is clear is that only a minor part of government investment took place through the urban renewal fund (Figure 9.2). A large part of investment in housing improvement and the construction of new dwellings was via producer subsidies (mentioned earlier). The various investments and subsidies mentioned in Figures 9.1 and 9.2 are set out in Table 9.4 (see also RIGO, 1990).

Though this conclusion may apply to urban renewal as a whole, there is more differentiation for various urban renewal activities. Five groups of urban renewal activities are distinguished: 'above expectation', 'on schedule', 'disappointments', 'windfalls' and 'future'. Figure 9.3 gives a summary (Ministerie van VROM, 1990).

Differences occur not only between urban renewal activities but also between the characteristics of municipalities. The evaluation of urban renewal policy during the 1980s led to the following characterisation (Priemus and Metselaar, 1992).

Table 9.4: Investments and subsidies in Dutch urban renewal in the 1980s (DGlmillions at 1980 price level)

|  | Investments | | Subsidies | | |
| --- | --- | --- | --- | --- | --- |
|  | 1980-89 | 1981-89 | 1980-89 | 1981-89 | % |
| **Housing** | | | | | |
| Repair and improvement subsidised | 19,400 | | 105,000* | | 54* |
| Repair and improvement unsubsidised | 22,300 | | | | |
| Substitute new construction | 17,954 | | 6,810† | | 38† |
| Improvement of residential environment | 783 | | 783 | | 100 |
| Process costs | 870 | | 870 | | 100 |
| Subtotal | 61,307 | | 18,963 | | 31 |
| Supplementary new construction | 28,643 | | 9,767† | | 34† |
| **Other policy sectors** | | | | | |
| KSBS-type aid‡ | | | 187 | | |
| Modernisation of shopping centres | | | 34 | | |
| Rehabilitation of environmentally hazardous business | | | 131 | | |
| Sewerage | | 659 | | | |
| Public transport infrastructure | | | 3,280 | | |
| Motor traffic facilities | | | 97 | | |
| Cycle traffic facilities | | | 18 | | |
| Built parking facilities | | 146 | | | |
| Restoration of monuments | | | 914 | | |
| Welfare facilities and other activities | | | 110 | | |
| Regional and economic policy | | | 30 | | |
| Soil decontamination | | | 1,159 | | |
| Noise pollution control | | | 187 | | |
| Road safety | | | 28 | | |
| Total | | 805 | 6,175 | | |

Notes: * The financial expenditures on housing allowances are excluded.
† Including the expenditures on housing allowances.
‡ KSBS is a general scheme for aid to businesses in urban renewal areas.

Source: RIGO (1990)

Figure 9.3: Summary of evaluation of urban renewal activities

| Above expectation | Disappointments | On schedule | Windfalls | Later/future |
|---|---|---|---|---|
| Improvement of pre-war social rented dwellings | Aspects of traffic | Improvement of pre-war social rented dwellings | Businesses in non-urban renewal municipalities | Improving the residential environment |
| New supplementary housing development in urban areas | Cycle infrastructure | Improvement of private rented dwellings | Process costs | Urban renewal in built-up urban areas in the more expensive sector |
| Accommodation for primary education | Already built parking facilities | Improvement of owner occupier dwellings | | Support to business |
| Connection to sewage system | Rehabilitation of environmental nuisance businesses | Demolition and compensatory new housing development | | Soil decontamination |
| Restoration of dwellings that are monuments | Replacement of sewage system | | | Aspects of welfare/education priority policy concentrations |
| | | | | Improvement of spatial-economic structure |
| | | | | Modernisation of shopping centres |
| | | | | Management |
| | | | | Public transport |
| | | | | Urban parks and gardens |
| | | | | Noise pollution |

- The *catchers-up* (such as Amsterdam, Rotterdam, The Hague, Utrecht, Zaanstad), which still have many neighbourhoods where demolition and substitute new construction or improvement will take place.

- The *urban developers* (such as Groningen and Tilburg): municipalities that are far advanced with improvement of the original urban renewal neighbourhoods. Urban renewal here is being succeeded by a municipal policy directed towards consolidation and prevention of decay.

- The *all-rounders* (such as Delft and Leiden): municipalities where much has been done in old districts, but where urban renewal can be extended to other districts.

- The *centre renewers* (such as Alkmaar and Terneuzen): municipalities that put the emphasis on renewal of the centre. This renewal includes house- building and dwelling improvement in this area.

- The *performers* (often smaller 'direct' municipalities, such as Hoogeveen and Dongeradeel): municipalities that have developed and implemented a number of smaller plans.

According to another study, urban and village renewal in the smaller municipalities often means the implementation of infrastructural works (Slootweg, 1989).

It also appears from research that the evaluation study of urban renewal during the 1980s made use of the wrong baseline, the Memorandum on Urban and Village Renewal (Priemus et al, 1991). The official 1985 UVRA contains a much broader definition. Secondly, because of the fact that many urban renewal needs have grown during the 1980s (obsolescence of building stock, environmental problems, infrastructural interventions, social problems in parts of some cities, etc), the achievements of the past decade have been overestimated and the present problems underestimated.

From an OTB investigation (Priemus et al, 1991) it appears that this is certainly true in the four largest cities (Amsterdam, Rotterdam, The Hague and Utrecht). In these cities the speed of dwelling improvement in the pre-war dwelling stock has been overestimated, and the problems of low-income households in urban renewal areas have been underestimated. Thus the question is whether the 'schedule' used for evaluating urban renewal during the 1980s has been the right one. Be that as it may, a great deal still has to be done in the larger cities, despite the fact that urban renewal has already made a substantial contribution to urban revitalisation and development in the past decade.

## Renewal and rehabilitation in the future

After evaluating urban renewal in the past decade, the remaining activities were specified by national government, making clear the finite nature of its financial concern. According to this point of view, urban renewal policies would be finished by the year 2005 (Ministerie van VROM, 1992).

### Urban renewal tasks 1990-2005

Until 2005, national government distinguished central tasks at national level. These were defined in a static way and were only concerned with smoothing away backlog situations which existed in 1990 in the pre-1971 areas. Estimates for the financial budgets for these tasks were made through calculations and assumptions. To a large extent these were based on the results of the evaluation of urban renewal during the 1980s (Ministerie van VROM, 1992).

**Land costs and revenues of house building**

As far as housebuilding was concerned, a distinction was made between the replacement of poor-quality dwellings by new ones and the addition of new dwellings in the inner city. Those areas built before 1970 in Dutch cities contained more than 170,000 poor-quality dwellings. It was assumed that 76,600 of these dwellings would be replaced with government grants. Furthermore it was expected that 85% of these dwellings (64,000) would be rebuilt on the site of demolition. The remaining 12,600 will be built elsewhere. It was also assumed that new housing for substitution would be built mainly in the social sector (65%). The remainder (35%) would only be lightly subsidised or not subsidised at all.

For new construction in the inner cities, a distinction was made between two types of locations. First of all there were locations where the function had changed or would change. Secondly, there were locations where density would increase. Changing the function means that vacant factories and former industrial areas (partly environment-polluting businesses) would be replaced by new dwellings. Typical of these kinds of locations is that a disadvantaged area is changed into a new residential neighbourhood. It was estimated that up to 2005 about 147,600 dwellings would be built on these locations.

The position over the second type of location was different. Generally these were undeveloped and used extensively as parks, parking lots, traffic areas or just fallow land. The utilisation of these potential building lots fitted into the already existing urban facilities and infrastructure. It was not a matter of arrears. The national government took the view that building on these potential lots would not form part of the urban renewal task.

For the realisation of the dwellings mentioned (76,600 substitution and 147,600 addition), calculations of the average costs and revenues per dwelling had been made. Compared to the 1980s the costs were expected to be higher because of higher acquisition costs, soil pollution and lower building densities.

The costs were estimated at DGl54,000 per dwelling as compared with DGl45,000 during the 1980s. However, the revenues were also expected to be higher (DGl26,000 per dwelling versus DGl18,000 per dwelling in the 1980s). The national government assumed that the private sector can shoulder a larger share of the costs.

### Land costs and revenues of non-house building

If new dwellings were built in the inner cities other facilities also had to be provided (schools, community centres, shops and businesses). Based on the national ratio between expenditure on residential and other facilities (92:8) and the number of dwellings presented above, a total number of square metres for non-housebuilding was calculated (1,950,000 square metres). It was assumed that the costs and revenues for each 100 square metres of non-house building were the same as for each dwelling (see above).

### Subsidised improvement of owner-occupier dwellings

This form of housing rehabilitation referred to owner-occupier dwellings in the inner cities built before 1945 and of very poor technical quality, which might not have been included in the new housing development for substitution. In total 16,500 poor-quality owner-occupier dwellings had to be improved, requiring an average investment of DGl75,000. A third of this investment would be subsidised.

## Subsidised improvement of private rented dwellings

The major improvement of very poor-quality rental dwellings was a housing matter with its own subsidy scheme. However, the non-radical improvement of dwellings in the private rented sector was part of urban renewal.

Most dwellings requiring improvement in the private rented sector were located in the inner cities, built before 1945 and of a moderate quality. It was expected that these would not be improved by the owners without subsidies, particularly in the case of dwellings owed by small private landlords. In total 51,000 dwellings had to be improved, requiring an average investment of DGl40,000. Half of this investment would be subsidised.

## Purchase of dwellings by local government for improvement

In the four largest cities in The Netherlands (Amsterdam, Rotterdam, The Hague and Utrecht) poor-quality private rented dwellings are purchased by the municipality. The owners of these dwellings do not invest systematically in their property and purchase by the municipality is often the only guarantee for continuation of the urban renewal process. The actual improvement of these dwellings is part of another programme. However, the purchase of these dwellings generally leads to operating deficits which are (partly) subsidised with an average budget of DGl15,000 per dwelling. In total there were about 32,000 such dwellings (mainly in the four cities mentioned).

## Renovation of buildings

There were buildings in the inner cities that had lost their function (eg, offices or churches), some of which have great character and were still of good quality. Within the framework of urban renewal, preference was given to rebuilding these structures instead of demolishing them, with partial subsidy of the costs.

## Improvement of the residential environment

The importance of a good-quality urban public environment was increasingly recognised, with attractive streets and squares forming an important feature. Within the framework of urban renewal the most urgent problems in the residential (public) environment would be tackled by the year 2005. Special attention would be paid to care for parks in the pre-war urban districts.

## Infrastructure

Urban renewal plans would also pay attention to concentrating traffic in certain areas and to excluding it in mainly residential areas. It was hoped that this would lead to less noise nuisance, traffic inconvenience and local air pollution.

## Support to businesses in urban renewal areas

During the urban renewal process, support was given to manufacturers, entrepreneurs and shopkeepers to compensate them for lost income. Financial help was also offered to construct special buildings in which businesses are gathered together, generally on the edge of urban renewal areas. This kind of business support was mainly given in the ISR municipalities.

## Rehabilitation of environmentally hazardous businesses

Environmentally polluting businesses have a negative influence on the residential environment because of noise, bad smells and other inconvenience. In Dutch cities more than 3,400 of these businesses had to be relocated. The majority (70%) were located in the smaller municipalities which are particularly badly affected by congestion and pollution. A limited number of these environmentally hazardous businesses would spontaneously seek another location so no subsidy would be needed.

After relocation some of the abandoned locations would be rebuilt with dwellings. The buy-out costs and land purchase costs are encompassed in the land costs for the new housing development. In these cases no extra urban renewal subsidy would be necessary. If the abandoned locations were not to be rebuilt with new dwellings, an average subsidy per relocated company would be calculated.

The possible soil pollution and soil decontamination costs did not fall under the urban renewal cost estimates. Attempts would first be made to have the perpetrator (partly) pay these costs or, failing that, there would be other possible course of redress.

## Welfare

Traditionally, welfare facilities form part of the urban renewal task, with special reference to the construction of social and cultural facilities in urban renewal areas.

**Process costs**

Process costs consist of urban renewal plan preparation costs, costs of participation and counselling in the urban renewal process and the costs of 'substitution dwellings'. The latter were intended as dwellings for inhabitants who temporarily have to leave their own dwelling. Since 1990 the costs of moving and furnishing were also counted as process costs.

The study of urban renewal achievements in the 1980s indicated that the process cost subsidies were most important for the success of the urban renewal process. Involving the inhabitants as much as possible in the planning and execution of the process was very important. It also meant that there was less resistance to the plans and less danger of passing problems on to other neighbourhoods.

*Investment in the future*

In total, it was estimated that another DGl136 billion had to be invested in urban renewal in the years to come (at 1990 prices), about 71% from the private sector. National government would contribute another DGl34 billion in total (25%). Of this, DGl11 billion would be distributed via the urban renewal fund among the municipalities in The Netherlands. The rest of the national contribution would find its way via various other subsidy schemes (see Table 9.5). All this implied that national government expected an even larger generating effect of the guilders invested by itself for the remaining urban renewal task than during the 1980s. It was expected that the private sector would invest DGl2.84 for every guilder invested by the national government in the 1990s.

This estimate of the need for urban renewal drawn up by the national government was not considered correct by everyone. Firstly, there was criticism that the national government's financial commitment was seen as a finite task. Also, there were serious doubts about the calculations and assumptions underlying the estimate of the national urban renewal task. Halfway through the period 1990-2005 (in 1997) the underlying assumptions and calculations were to be evaluated. If the assumptions and calculations were no longer valid the estimate of the remaining need for urban renewal would be adjusted.

It was also argued that some tasks were missing from the estimate. Specifically, conservation of monuments, rehabilitation of the sewage system, soil pollution and dealing with problems in the (early) postwar dwelling stock were not included. By including these missing tasks,

Table 9.5: Total investments in the remaining urban renewal (1990-2005) and the relevant cost centres (1990 price level)

|  | DGl billions | % |
|---|---|---|
| **Investments** | | |
| Dwelling improvement | 43 | 32 |
| New housing development for replacement (substitution) | 16 | 12 |
| New supplementary housing development | 48 | 35 |
| Residential environment/process costs | 3 | 2 |
| Other investments | 26 | 19 |
| **Total** | **136** | **100** |
| **Cost centres** | | |
| Owners, tenants | 97 | 71 |
| Municipalities | 5 | 4 |
| State: urban renewal fund | 11 | 8 |
| State: other subsidy schemes | 23 | 17 |
| **Total** | **136** | **100** |

Source: Ministerie van VROM (1992)

different parties involved in urban renewal have almost unanimously come to a similar conclusion. Instead of the DGl11 billion in the urban renewal fund calculated by the national government, the amount needed was twice as high (SOAB, 1992;Vier grote steden, 1992;VNG, 1992). Despite these arguments national government has stood by its own conclusions.

## Distribution of financial means

The national estimates of the remaining urban renewal needs were also apportioned at local level. Using national assumptions and calculations, the need was divided as follows:

- each of the four largest cities (Amsterdam, Rotterdam, The Hague and Utrecht);
- other municipalities with over 100,000 inhabitants;
- municipalities with 30,000-100,000 inhabitants;
- municipalities with fewer than 30,000 inhabitants.

The remaining budget of the urban renewal fund (DGl11 billion) was divided among these (groups of) municipalities (Ministerie van VROM, 1993). This meant that each of the four largest municipalities in The Netherlands had an estimate of the remaining need for urban renewal with a related budget. The distribution of the remainder was divided between each of the three remaining groups of municipalities, using a key which is an updated version of the 1990 urban renewal key. The threshold for being a 'direct municipality' is now where it has more than 0.15% in the urban renewal fund. Again, the provinces function as shareholders for those municipalities with a share lower than 0.15%.

However, the different components of this urban renewal key have almost nothing to do with the estimate of the remaining need for urban renewal in the period 1990-2005. For instance, an important component is the number of monuments. In the estimate monuments do not count at all. Similarly, the updated urban renewal key contains no component for the residential environment, despite the fact that the improvement of the residential environment is an important part of the estimate.

## Conclusion

In The Netherlands there is a long-standing connection between housing and urban renewal. In the 1960s and 1970s parts of the inner cities were confronted with poor living conditions. Dwellings were not water-tight and were too small, streets were dirty and unsafe, factories smelled or stood derelict. This was due partly to the ageing of the poor-quality housing stock built at the end of the last century. Maintenance lagged behind. Factories from the inner city moved out, leaving deteriorating areas. Those businesses which stayed behind were often a nuisance for the residential environment. Furthermore, the historical value of the city centres was ignored and there was an immense growth of motor traffic. Finally, the city centre with its shops and offices demanded new quality standards and other requirements of accessibility.

In the 1970s, medium sized cities started developing reconstruction and slum clearance schemes for the inner cities. This was the beginning of Dutch urban renewal. Halfway through the 1970s these operations were supported by regulations developed at the national level. The so-called ISR-programme involved direct regulation for slum clearance in a few municipalities which the national government financed.

In the second half of the 1970s, criticism of demolition led to better subsidies for improvement of the existing housing stock and rehabilitation in the rental stock was stimulated by direct government subsidies. For years different subsidy systems existed for private and social rented dwellings. Generally these were more favourable for social than for private landlords. In the four largest cities (Amsterdam, Rotterdam, The Hague and Utrecht) this distinction led to a special strategy for improving poor-quality multi-family dwellings owned by private landlords. The local governments purchased these dwellings and refurbished them (first without, later with subsidies) with the improved dwellings subsequently handed over to housing associations.

In the early 1980s a comprehensive urban renewal policy was formulated to cope with the inner-city problems in all municipalities (Memorandum on Urban and Village Renewal). In 1985 an official UVRA came into effect. Urban renewal was defined as a broad spectrum of activities (dwelling rehabilitation, improvement of residential environment and monuments, fighting traffic and welfare problems and so on). It was also seen as a continuous process with no clear end. Decentralisation to the local level was an important aspect. An urban renewal fund and an accompanying distribution key were introduced for all municipalities in The Netherlands.

At the same time, existing subsidies for dwelling improvements were streamlined. In the years following 1985, various subsidy schemes were placed in the urban renewal fund. Up to 1995 subsidies for radical improvement of pre-war social rented dwellings had a separate, exceptional position outside the fund. This subsidy scheme has been replaced by a system of incentive contributions to encourage radical improvement or new construction.

The comprehensive urban renewal policy introduced an amalgamation of different subsidy schemes for a diversity of activities (such as housing rehabilitation) into one fund.

At the beginning of the 1990s, national government evaluated renewal activities during the 1980s, providing a wealth of information about the achievements of urban renewal in the recent past. Although there was and still is discussion about the exact definition, the evaluation concluded that in general urban renewal was on schedule and about half complete. About DGl105 billion (1980 price level) were invested in urban renewal, with the private sector taking the largest share. It became clear that the centrally coordinated renewal programme introduced in 1985, with a decentralised policy performance and financial responsibility, had accomplished a lot. Government investments were found to have a significant in stimulating further activities.

In the early 1990s, national government announced that its financial involvement in urban renewal would come to an end in 2005, this finishing point legitimised by using an adjusted version of an old definition of urban renewal. Urban renewal seemed to disappear from the national political agenda. The remaining need for urban renewal was estimated, with a corresponding financial budget to be distributed among the municipalities. It was estimated that Dgl136 billion had to be invested in urban renewal up to the year 2005 (1990 price level). Compared to the 1980s, the private sector was expected to produce a larger share of the investments. The outcome was considered doubtful. Why should the national government expect private investments to increase when the termination of national public effort with urban renewal had been announced? The opposite seemed the more likely outcome.

Besides, why abandon a successful system of mixed responsibilities and investments that proved to be successful? It is clear that in The Netherlands housing and urban renewal are interdependent. The same applies to government and private investments in the process. Therefore, ignoring future problems in urban renewal has a negative influence both on housing and private investment. It may also mean that they will grow too large to be tackled with normal measures. Then again 'new' arrears might occur in some 'urban' areas as might the need for 'new' urban renewal. Continuously keeping such problems under control is of great importance not only within the scope of urban renewal, but also for other, adjoining sectors like housing and physical planning.

A balanced policy programme is required to combat urban problems. Coordination is needed at national level to set the framework and responsibility for financial budgets at local or regional level. Additionally, the correct mix of financial investments by the national government, local government and private sector is essential. Minimal government investment does not encourage sufficient private investment. Too much government investment can lead to subsidy addiction.

Since the arrival of a new government in 1994 urban problems have taken on a different social aspect. A separate minister was appointed to coordinate urban policy in large cities. The renewal process in large cities achieved a new place for itself on the political agenda. The near future will tell us whether this will have consequences for the investment readiness of the national government and, through that, of the private sector.

# Appendix to Chapter Nine: Housing costs and the rental and owner-occupier sector

Table A9.1: Monthly housing costs and household incomes of tenants (DGl) with and without housing allowances (IHS) (1 January 1986, 1990 and 1993)

|  | Gross rent | Subsidisable service charges | Basic rent | IHS | Net rent(DGl000s) | Net yearly household income | Net rent ratio |
|---|---|---|---|---|---|---|---|
| **With IHS** | | | | | | | |
| 1986 | 466 | 13 | 479 | 147 | 332 | 21.1 | 21.1 |
| 1990 | 497 | 9 | 506 | 157 | 349 | 20.9 | 21.8 |
| 1993 | 540 | 16 | 557 | 173 | 384 | 20.9 | 24.3 |
| **Without IHS** | | | | | | | |
| 1986 | 374 | 10 | 384 |  | 384 | 30.7 | 17.2 |
| 1990 | 438 | 8 | 445 |  | 445 | 33.1 | 19.0 |
| 1993 | 511 | 14 | 525 |  | 525 | 35.8 | 20.2 |
| **Average** | | | | | | | |
| 1986 | 393 | 11 | 404 | 31 | 373 | 28.7 | 18.0 |
| 1990 | 453 | 8 | 461 | 40 | 421 | 30.0 | 19.7 |
| 1993 | 518 | 15 | 533 | 45 | 488 | 31.9 | 21.2 |

Source: Ministerie van VROM (1994)

Table A9.2: Monthly housing costs and household incomes of owner-occupiers, with and without mortgage (1 January 1986, 1990 and 1993)

| | Gross mortgage costs | Additional housing costs* | State contrib- ution | Fiscal effects | Gross housing costs† | Net housing costs | Net yearly household income (DGI000s) | Net housing costs ratio |
|---|---|---|---|---|---|---|---|---|
| **With mortgage** | | | | | | | | |
| 1986 | 750 | 42 | 50 | -208 | 733 | 525 | 43.2 | 16.5 |
| 1990 | 750 | 42 | 48 | -175 | 742 | 575 | 48.5 | 15.8 |
| 1993 | 874 | 42 | 33 | -209 | 883 | 674 | 54 | 16.6 |
| **Without mortgage** | | | | | | | | |
| 1986 | - | 33 | - | 33 | 33 | 66 | 31.5 | 3.4 |
| 1990 | - | 42 | - | 33 | 42 | 75 | 33.4 | 3.3 |
| 1993 | - | 42 | 4 | 96 | 38 | 134 | 41.5 | 4.7 |
| **Average** | | | | | | | | |
| 1986 | 567 | 42 | 42 | -142 | 567 | 408 | 40.2 | 13.1 |
| 1990 | 575 | 42 | 33 | -125 | 583 | 450 | 45.0 | 12.9 |
| 1993 | 686 | 42 | 27 | -143 | 701 | 558 | 51.3 | 14.0 |

Notes: * Additional housing costs = building insurance, (permanent) ground lease and property tax.
† Through rounding off the gross housing costs are not always the same as the sum of the gross mortgage costs and the additional housing costs minus the state contribution.

Source: Ministerie van VROM (1994)

TEN

# National strategies for urban renewal and housing rehabilitation in Norway

*Solveig Aaen*

## Introduction

Planned urban renewal has a relatively short history in Norway. The first programmes were launched towards the end of the 1970s, and implementation gathered momentum in the mid-1980s. Postwar Norwegian housing policies had been aimed at providing sufficient housing, as the housing stock had decreased during the war and the urban population was growing.

Norway has three cities with urban renewal problems: Oslo, Bergen and Trondheim. This chapter will concentrate on the urban renewal situation in Oslo, where the need for urban renewal has been greatest and where the largest amount of activity has taken place.

Oslo has a population of 470,000. Following new urban renewal legislation introduced in 1976, Oslo's municipal planning authority identified priority areas, where there was an urgent need to improve housing and the surrounding environment. These inner-city areas contained about 70,000 dwellings, mainly built in the latter part of the last century. A few of these are small wooden houses of one or two storeys, some of which were transported from the countryside and reassembled just outside the original city boundaries. But mostly they are three- to five-storey brick-built tenements housing large families in small flats. They usually had shared toilet facilities, often in the yard. Some had further three- to five-storey dwellings in the backyard on sites originally for housing horses, pigs and chickens.

Previous urban renewal projects had concentrated on old and

dilapidated low-density buildings which were demolished and replaced with high tower blocks. In the postwar period, the local authorities' emphasis was on managing urban growth and planning authorities generally paid little regard to existing housing areas near city centres. Some areas were hit by 'planning blight', where plans for large-scale new developments, urban motorways, and so on, were still in the official plan but unlikely to be implemented. Because of this, property owners had no motivation to keep up repairs and maintenance, which led to further damage to properties and a general running down of the neighbourhood. There was also pressure for commercial development on the fringes of city centres, particularly in the 1960s and 1970s, which meant replacing housing with office blocks.

## Background

Norway covers about 324,000 square kilometres, almost half of the Scandinavian peninsula. It is sparsely populated with only 4.5 million inhabitants. Over the past 100 years, the proportion of the population living in urban areas has gradually increased, with approximately a quarter now living in the four main urban areas of the country, each of which has more than 90,000 inhabitants, 10% of the country's population lives in Oslo.

Industrialisation started later in Norway than elsewhere and it was still among the poorer European countries during the inter-war period. Since the Second World War it has experienced steady economic growth with an investment rate among the highest in Europe. The inflation rate was relatively high during the 1970s, for several years exceeding 10% with unemployment exceptionally low at around 1-1½%. In the first half of the 1980s, inflation was reduced, but unemployment rose. With a surplus of payments from the export of oil and gas, the economy was expanded and unemployment was reduced to between 1% and 2%. In the mid-1980s, the Norwegian economy boomed leading to increased activity in the building industry. Growing demand for housing coupled with financial deregulation resulted in large house price increases. In the latter half of the decade, growth in non-oil activities decreased while the oil price fluctuated. This lead to a historically high level of unemployment and a sharp drop in house prices, leading to problems of negative equity, ie, households had mortgage debts that exceeded the value of their homes.

In the early 1990s, the Norwegian economy stagnated, but the 1990s have seen a gradual improvement in the economy, a slow reduction of unemployment and improving confidence.

## Housing policy and the housing market in Norway

A large proportion of the housing stock in Norway is owner-occupied. In 1970, 65% of the dwellings were owned individually or in cooperatives. Urban areas had larger numbers of rented dwellings, with Oslo having the highest proportion (approximately 50% in 1970). The number of owner-occupiers increased steadily after the war, particularly in cities. By 1990, owner-occupation was 78% nationally and 75% in Oslo.

Norway does not have a subsidised housing sector as such. Instead there is a policy of attempting to integrate different socioeconomic groups so that it is not apparent externally who is on social benefits and who is self-sufficient. On the whole this is quite successful. However, it must be said that it has not completely prevented the formation of housing areas with lower status in some of the bigger cities.

Local authorities are relatively independent, receiving part of their funding from the state, but also being able to levy their own taxes and charges. They have a high degree of freedom and a high level of responsibility, with the central government adopting a 'carrot and stick' approach to housing policy. This consists of legislation making it mandatory for local authorities to provide housing for certain groups of the population, and loans and grants from the State Housing Bank for housing and other related provisions. In addition to local authorities, any owner of a building plot or a dwelling can apply for subsidised construction or improvement loans from the State Housing Bank, providing that the resulting dwelling meets minimum standards with a maximum housing cost and maximum size requirement.. One of the goals of the renewal policy is to facilitate former tenants to become joint or cooperative owners of the property after renewal. The price limits vary with building types, size and location of dwellings. A small dwelling in the city centre can have a higher cost per square metre than a larger, detached dwelling in the countryside.

## Problems of urban decay and housing deterioration

Housing standards in Norway are generally high. However, in the mid-1970s there was growing awareness of the poor housing and unsatisfactory living conditions in some of the larger cities. Equality between different groups of the population is an important goal in Norway, so the central government felt there was a need for a joint effort to solve the problems of decay in central, urban housing areas.

In our political and cultural context, these urban areas were not typically Norwegian. We have one of the smallest rental sectors in Europe, and owning your own house or flat, directly or through a housing cooperative, had been encouraged through low interest rates and tax benefits. However, in the urban renewal areas, rental markets had been established around the end of the previous century, becoming subject to strict regulation in the 1930s. A large part of this sector's rental housing was privately owned. The owners might be living in the property, or it could be owned by private investors, large companies providing housing for their employees, or just people who had inherited or somehow taken over a tenancy without any housing management experience.

Before the Second World War, private tenancies were subject to strict rent control. Property speculation, often with demolition and non-residential redevelopment, led to low standards of maintenance. When improvements were carried out, borrowing costs could be added on to the existing rent. Such rent increases could be very large when there was a need for substantial, and therefore costly improvements. In many circumstances, it was economically more advantageous for the tenants to take over the property and become owners before improvements were carried out.

Self-employed people got favourable tax treatment for deficits in their accounts, some achieving this through buying rent-controlled tenancies. But although tax and rent control regulations were meant to stimulate maintenance, they were insufficient in ensuring good management of the properties. At the same time, there was little incentive to invest in improvements as the area became more run down. This was part of the downward spiral.

The housing situation in central areas of Oslo in 1975 showed the following characteristics:

- more than 40,000 households were living in dwellings built before 1920;
- about two thirds of these were rented, mostly from private landlords;
- about 20,000 of these dwellings lacked basic amenities like indoor toilets and hot water;

- there were fire traps, partly due to disrepair and disorder, but also because it was not possible for modern fire-engines to get into backyards;
- more than half of the dwellings were small, containing only one or two rooms;
- the insulation was insufficient;
- many of the dwellings had not been properly maintained for decades;
- the environment was generally deteriorating with few places for children to play safely or older people to sit out and enjoy the sun;
- the increasing traffic made the streets dangerous and polluted;
- there were few public amenities like nurseries for children.

The population in the urban renewal areas had a higher than average proportion of the old and disabled, one-person households, people living on pensions or social security and the unemployed. At the same time, there was a lower than average proportion of families with children, people with higher education and car owners. Furthermore, the uncertain future of these areas led to a downward spiral where the negative effects further accumulated. In some areas those with adequate means started to move out and were replaced by population groups that further added to the problems.

## The goals of the urban renewal process

The basic aim of the urban renewal programme was to reverse the negative spirals into positive spirals, making urban renewal areas attractive living environments and creating improved and less dependant local communities. There was a gap, however, between what was considered a reasonable standard of living and the ability of the affected groups to pay for the necessary improvements.

These goals were:

- Urban renewal should first of all benefit those already living in the area, by improving their housing and environmental standard, thereby giving them a better quality of life.
- The costs of housing improvement should in principle be covered by the inhabitants, and therefore not exceed about 20% of average industrial wages.

- Low income households should be given a housing allowance to enable them to benefit from a better housing standard.

- Urban renewal should also turn tenants into owners. This would ensure that former tenants were able to benefit from the investments in the areas, instead of paying increased rents that would primarily benefit the landlord. It was also believed that ownership would give inhabitants the incentive to ensure better building maintenance and better environmental management.

- Urban renewal should in the longer run contribute towards a more 'normal' population structure, partly by improving the environment, outdoor facilities, social services, etc, and partly by providing more of the larger dwellings suited to families with children. It was felt that a more normalised population structure would ensure a larger degree of involvement in the local communities from families with small children, etc.

## Policy implementation: regulations and programmes

### Private rehabilitation and tenure regulation

As mentioned previously, a large proportion of rented housing was privately owned. For several decades there had been attempts at ensuring maintenance, repair and upgrading of the properties by allowing rent increases and offering tax incentives. In some properties this had reasonable results, in others the deterioration accelerated over the years. Up to the mid-1980s, demand for housing in cities far exceeded the supply, making it more profitable for owners to fill up vacant flats with short-term tenants who were exempt from rent control, rather than to start costly improvements.

When planned urban renewal started in 1977, changes in legislation promoted the idea of turning tenants into owners to ensure improvement of the property.

When an area was designated for urban renewal, improvement of the property was made possible in several ways:

- Owners had the opportunity to improve the property, if a majority of tenants supported the scheme. After the improvements had taken place, the property would normally continue as tenancy, or the owner could decide to sub-divide the property and give the tenants the opportunity to purchase their dwellings. Those who did not wish to purchase, could remain as tenants, but the flat may then be owned by a third party.

- The tenants could purchase the property before improvement if the owner agreed, carry out the improvements with financing from the State Housing Bank, and then own the property as a cooperative or sub-divide it.
- A majority of the tenants in a property could demand that the local authority or its urban renewal agency purchase the property, carry out the improvements and sell the property to the previous tenants as a cooperative at cost price.

New legislation in 1977 also gave local authorities first refusal or option to purchase tenancies offered for sale outside the designated urban renewal areas. This was intended to prevent speculation by private landlords and to enable tenants to become owners. The local authority could intervene in a contract and purchase at the contract price, either on behalf of the tenants or on behalf of an implementation agency

Further new legislation came into force in 1982 allowing the division of tenancies into individual dwellings, after a wave of speculative transactions by landlords which left buyers of so called 'rental rights' with little protection. The new legislation introduced minimum standards for amenities before division could take place, and gave the local authority the right to refuse division if thought necessary as part of the urban renewal programme.

A large part of housing developed since the 1930s consists of housing cooperatives, with each dwelling tied to a share of the property and the shareholders themselves living in the dwelling. Decisions to improve these dwellings with, for example, extra facade insulation, new windows, improved outdoor facilities, etc, were made jointly by the cooperative owners. Large, expensive improvements demanded a large majority vote to be implemented.

Property prices increased both in central urban areas and in the suburbs, particularly in the mid- to late 1980s. This made it more advantageous for individual and cooperative owners to improve properties, as new development became too costly. Large-scale improvements of postwar properties have taken place all over the city. The housing market collapse, with prices falling by 20-30% in the early 1990s, increased the pressure to improve postwar properties in order to keep up relative value.

Around 1990, unemployment increased, and a larger than usual proportion of the population started having debt problems. Some were evicted, and many had to sell their homes at a loss. In the inner cities this led to a demand for cheap rented accommodation, and for several years there was little incentive to improve tenancies. This trend now seems to have turned, as the economic situation is improving and unemployment is reducing.

## Norwegian State Housing Bank, loans and grants

Norway's State Housing Bank was established just after the Second World War. The principle was to provide reasonable loans for housing development in order to encourage building in general, and also to provide financing for households who would normally not be able to borrow from an ordinary bank. These loans had good security, being a first priority mortgage. Housing associations, housing cooperatives, private developers and single individuals are all eligible for a loan, providing that the development fulfils certain minimum technical standards and is of reasonable size and cost. In addition, low-income households can get extra loans and grants to enable them to buy a house or flat. The housing bank also channels the government housing support to low-income households.

The rest of the funding usually comes from private banks or credit institutions, along with personal savings. In large parts of the country, custom-built houses are common, with the owners undertaking parts of the actual building work themselves in order to provide the necessary private capital.

Government subsidies are reduced step by step over a period of eight years with down payments starting after eight years and then gradually increasing. This proved to be good for young families when they first settle down and expect their household income to increase as they get into middle age. Also when inflation was quite high, the amount paid in interest and down payments would, after a few years, be quite low in real terms.

The lowering of interest rates 1994-95 meant that the economic problems which arose from booming house prices have been reduced. In the case of housing cooperatives, whether free standing or joined to a housing association, the loan covers up to 80% of the total cost of purchasing and repairing the property. The shareholder then has to find the remaining 20% in a private credit institution or from their savings.

## Financing urban renewal

The model of housing finance used in the State Housing Bank was adapted for urban renewal. Work to a flat in an improved dwelling should have a calculated cost of no more than 75% to 80% of a similar new dwelling. In addition the Housing Bank may give special grants in order to cover extraordinary costs of repair, backyard clearance, or to preserve antique facades. This grant may also be given to environmental improvement projects, where it should cover 80% of the costs. In Oslo, the local authority has given special grants to encourage quick installation of indoor toilets.

The Oslo local authority also established a generous extra urban renewal housing allowance to enable the original tenants to remain in their flats after renewal. This was necessary because the state grant did not take into consideration the generally higher level of housing expenditure in the cities.

Since 1982, the government grant for urban renewal has nearly trebled, in order to encourage local authorities to complete the necessary tasks. The local authority has also been given greater freedom to decide in which areas and properties the grants will have the largest strategic impact on the urban renewal process, and to allocate larger grants if that is deemed necessary. It can also use part of the grant to rehouse affected tenants.

## Institutional and organisational framework

Local authorities are responsible for implementation of urban renewal and can establish agencies to carry it out. All of the three major cities in Norway did this in the period from 1978 to 1985. The agencies were shareholder companies where the local authority owned 51%, the banks, housing associations, etc, holding the rest. Over a period of 12 years the agency, Oslo Urban Renewal, participated in, or was directly responsible for, just over a third of the Oslo's urban renewal activities. It was a non-profit organisation and, apart from its funding capital, which was quite low, it was meant to cover the running expenses directly from charges on the projects and not require support from the local authority. The local authority originally had the right to take over the finished renewal projects and nominate residents to them. These were primarily people who had originally lived in the properties or those displaced when dwellings were demolished in other renewal projects.

Housing associations were also directly involved in renewal and redevelopment and are responsible for just under a third of the urban renewal during this period. They were also working under the same premises, development was non-profit making, and the original tenants should be able to stay on or move back after improvement.

The remaining third of renewal was carried out under the different models described previously: directly by private landlords, by tenants' housing cooperatives or by the owners of the few remaining individual, small detached or semi-detached houses.

Tenants' associations were given grants by the local authority to interview the tenants as to their wishes, inform them of their rights and take part in discussions with private landlords and the local authority. Associations of homeowners and landlords were funded to provide information to owners and assist in their discussions with tenants and authorities.

*Legal instruments*

The 1976 law of urban renewal made urban local authorities responsible for defining priority urban renewal areas where improvement of housing and/or the environment was urgent. The local authority is responsible for land use planning, traffic management plans, environmental improvement programmes, etc, sufficient to enable implementation of urban renewal. They are also responsible for development of childcare facilities, improvement of educational facilities and health and welfare services, as well as development and maintenance of technical infrastructure, which have also been part of urban renewal programmes. The local authority was also made responsible for the implementation of urban renewal, with the possibility of special implementation agencies being set up for practical purposes. All the three major local authorities chose to use this strategy.

This legislation for the first time made possible planned urban renewal that included both clearance/redevelopment and improvement. The implementation programme had to set out which buildings which were for improvement or demolition. The latter was necessary in some places to ensure sufficient light and space for outdoor recreation and children's playgrounds. In other areas it was necessary because existing structures were in such poor condition that the cost of repair and improvement was too high. And in some areas demolition was planned because the site was poorly developed and the local authority felt a higher density was desirable. The usual strategy was for the site to be purchased by the local authority, its implementation agency or a local housing association, who would then carry through the development.

Enforced improvement of existing housing is now possible for local authorities through improvement programmes. These can be enforced whether the building is owned by a private landlord or a cooperative formed by tenants purchasing a tenancy, or whether it is an individual small house badly in need of repair. If the owners do not comply with the order, the local authority can institute compulsory purchase measures on behalf of the tenants or on behalf of the implementation agency.

The urban renewal legislation of 1976 did not make explicit tenants' rights in taking part in the urban renewal process. This right was reserved for the owners of the properties. In Oslo, the local authority nevertheless developed a comprehensive participation process which involved tenants. In revision to the legislation in 1986, urban renewal was integrated into the general planning legislation and tenants' rights to participation was included.

The Oslo local authority included a further stage in the improvement process whereby a private landlord who wanted to improve the dwelling above ordinary maintenance levels had to get the approval of at least half the tenants. If they had no confidence in the landlord, there was the possibility of the tenants taking over the property and forming a housing cooperative. Alternatively, the local authority could intervene on behalf of the Oslo Urban Renewal agency, who would then carry out the improvements and transfer the property to the tenants. The original owner is, of course, compensated at the market price for his property.

## *The building code and its exceptions*

Working in cooperation, the local authorities and the State Housing Bank established a 30-year standard, and have made an exception to the stricter specifications of the building code. This is intended to ensure the necessary repairs, better fire safety, certain minimum amenities and improvement standards.

### Legislation on housing associations and cooperatives

Existing legislation on housing associations and housing cooperatives has been actively used. This means that a housing cooperative can either be set up by a group of tenants, or the housing association can set up a cooperative and sell the shares to interested housebuyers. One person can only hold one share, and there are strict limitations on sub-letting. Usually the housing cooperative will remain linked to the mother housing association, who will assist with bookkeeping, maintenance etc. Up to the mid-1980s, this also meant regulations on who could buy shares and at what price. Independent housing cooperatives can also be formed.

## Policy evaluation

When planned urban renewal started at the end of the 1970s, it was felt that there was a comprehensive package of legislative, financial and organisational tools to carry out the job. We knew of other countries who had started the process earlier and of the problems they had encountered, but felt that our model steered clear of most of these pitfalls. Now, looking back, we can see that although parts of our urban renewal experience have been good, there were also problems arising partly from unforeseen side effects. These can be classified in three groups.

### Effects mainly caused by the general economic development in the country

At the end of the 1970s several parts of the housing market were strictly regulated. It has already been mentioned that rent controls applied to pre-war tenancies. Housing cooperatives joined to a 'mother' housing association also had rules and regulations about who could buy shares and at what price. Nearly half of the dwellings in Oslo were controlled in one way or another.

At the same time there was quite high inflation but rent levels were relatively low. This resulted in pressure in the housing marked as the pre-war generation, most with reasonably good incomes, wanted to improve their housing standards. There was a large increase in the price of housing outside the controlled parts of the market. This led to black markets developing, with 'tricky' exchange deals set up in the controlled parts of the housing market. At the start of the 1980s, the strict controls for housing cooperatives were limited to the first seven years, covering the period of subsidised rates from the State Housing Bank.

Until the 1980s, there was a limitation on lending in ordinary banks, with a 'gentleman's agreement' between the private banks and the government which attempted to reduce luxury spending. But with the deregulation of the housing market, there was a constant pressure on private lending, and eventually the banks were left to regulate their interest rates without interference. This led to a large increase in rates from the mid-1980s – up to 12 or 14% on housing financing with good security.

The reduced economic activity in the early 1990s produced considerably lower interest rates, down to between 6% and 8% on similar loans. Having had a booming economy, with high building activity both for commercial premises and housing, wages and prices rose steadily, and household investments were characterised by general optimism. When the economy slowed down, and unemployment started to increase (for the first time since the 1930s,) a general pessimism led to very careful consumer spending for a few years, and this particularly hit the housing market. As a result of the economic boom, there had been reforms of taxation policies, intending to reduce over-consumption making lending in general more expensive. Unfortunately, the full effect of this came at a time when economic growth was already diminishing.

### Problems arising from momentum in the urban renewal process

The urban renewal was considered very successful for the first five to six years, with dwellings in improved properties, or in new developments on cleared sites, very much in demand. Original tenants and others were given the opportunity to buy at cost price, and were able to sell their flats for profit shortly afterwards. As intended, the possibility of a profit attracted more people from outside the renewal areas which in turn created a better population mix.

Private landlords obviously wanted a share in this. The price of non-renewed properties started to increase, more than doubling in less than five years. When interest rates increased and house prices dropped a few years later, quite a few people suffered considerable losses, with resulting repossession. Because the urban renewal process was managed through the local authority, many felt that they should be reimbursed for their loss. The relatively favourable special housing allowance for urban renewal became too expensive for the local authority, because of rising costs and increasing unemployment, so was cut back by 30%. This led to further economic problems, evictions and so on, so in 1995 it was restored to its former level. Extra expenditure was incurred, especially interest charges, during the long time taken for consultation which aimed to create consensus or, at a minimum, reduce conflicts.

*Problems arising from the tools chosen.*
Both local and central authorities underestimated the real expenditure of urban renewal. In quite a few properties, the cost of purchasing and improving it or redevelopment turned out to be higher than the market value. The main principle was that the householder should be able to pay the cost price of improvement or redevelopment with a grant to cover extraordinary expenses, and a special housing allowance for low-income groups. In the end, the local authority had to cover the difference in these projects.

Because the local government guaranteed to take over the properties after renewal, by setting up housing cooperatives and providing generous housing allowances, the non-profit agencies had little incentive to keep costs down, but rather tried to keep up production. This led to a pressure on the cost limits applied by the State Housing Bank, with some projects being financed from external sources. In a situation with rising costs and rising interest rates, the non-profit agencies became dependent on an ever-increasing output in order to cover their expenses. This also contributed to non-profit housing becoming more expensive than the market value. In 1991, the local authority decided to discontinue the special implementation agency.

The need for proper housing management after renewal was underestimated. The process of turning tenants into joint owners was not without pitfalls. At least a bad landlord could weld the tenants together. Now they were forced to solve their internal problems and differences between themselves. The increase in interest rates also led to a reluctance to put aside money for maintenance. Some cooperative owners simply could not afford it and disrepair has already become a problem in some properties renewed only 10 years before.

ELEVEN

# The renewal of older urban housing in Scotland

*Nick Bailey and Douglas Robertson*

## Introduction

While this chapter is concerned with housing renewal policies in Scotland, it cannot help but make reference to the situation in England and Wales, given the constitutional link between these countries and the fact that they currently share the same law-making Parliament. Policy for renewing older urban housing in Scotland follows a broadly similar path to that developed for England and Wales, but it also displays marked differences, reflecting variations both in the nature of the physical problem and in political circumstances. Although there will be a degree of unavoidable repetition between this chapter and that covering England and Wales, the situation provides for a unique type of comparative study.

Before exploring the current policy framework, it is important to provide some background material which sets the broad urban policy context. This explores constitutional and political factors, changes within the urban system and changing tenure patterns. Consideration is then given to the tenement problem given that it has largely determined the specific policy response to urban renewal within Scotland. After this background material, the chapter goes on to examine the historical development of renewal policies, before detailing the current system and finally the impacts of renewal.

## Background: the urban policy context

### Constitutional and political factors

Although Scotland is constitutionally part of the UK, it already has a degree of autonomy in many public policy areas, the major exceptions being in fiscal, defence and foreign policy. This is because Scotland retained its separate legal system after the 1707 Act of Union with England and Wales. A separate administrative apparatus evolved which was formalised in 1885 into the Scottish Office – a territorial, rather than functional, department of the British civil service. As the role of government at all levels has increased over the last century, the power of the Scottish Office has grown substantially over a whole range of domestic policy areas (Keating et al, 1991).

This increase in the powers and responsibilities has not been mirrored by a corresponding devolution of political power from London to Scotland. Thus, while there are all the components of a nation state in Scotland, it has no legislature of its own (McCrone, 1992). Political power over the Scottish Office is determined by electoral success in the UK as a whole. Therefore although the Conservatives currently hold just 10 of the 72 Parliamentary seats in Scotland, they control the Scottish Office by virtue of their majority in England and Wales. Indeed the Conservatives have not had an electoral majority in Scotland since 1955, yet have formed the government for 29 out of the last 40 years. The last Labour government (1974-79) failed in its manifesto commitment to create a directly elected Scottish Parliament. With the election of the Conservatives in 1979 calls for political devolution were ignored, despite substantial public support in Scotland for this change. Instead the Conservative government opted to pursue the well established policy of appeasement by further increasing administrative devolution to Scotland, while shunning any constitutional change (Mitchell, 1995).

The government currently provides an annual budget to the Scottish Office, based upon an agreed formula. For the functions for which it is responsible, this gives Scotland about 10% of all UK public expenditure, roughly in line with its proportion of the total population. The Minister responsible for the Scottish Office – the Secretary of State for Scotland – is then free to divide this up between functions as determined by the political priorities set by government. Service delivery is administered by the Scottish Office itself, by local authorities or by government agencies (organisations with boards of management appointed by the Secretary of State for Scotland, rather than being directly elected). A significant feature of the last 15 years has been the growth in the number of such agencies and in the proportion of the total Scottish Office budget they control.

The precise nature of the relationship between central and local government is the subject of much debate in the UK, as elsewhere (Stoker, 1988). In some accounts, local authorities are viewed, in large part, as the agent of central government, implementing policy determined at the centre (Stewart, 1986). There is much evidence to support this view. For example, the amount which each local authority may spend annually is tightly controlled by the Scottish Office. Local authorities may incur expenditure only where they have a specific power to do so. If they go beyond their authorised level, central government has the power to penalise them by reducing their expenditure in future years. In some areas, such as housing benefit (an individual means-tested subsidy to tenants for housing costs), local authorities merely administer what is a very tightly defined nationally funded benefit scheme.

Other accounts of this relationship, however, recognise the ability of local authorities to shape national policy at the local level and to adapt national programmes to take account of local circumstances and priorities (Ham and Hill, 1993). The local authority is seen to possess a degree of autonomy and policy is seen as the result of dialogue between the various members of the 'policy community', including both central and local government. Indeed the increasing use of central government controlled agencies may be seen as a reaction to the partial independence of local government and as an attempt to assert greater control of the actual administration of policy (Rhodes, 1988). So far as renewal policy is concerned this latter model provides a far more useful framework for characterising the relationship in Scotland, as this chapter will illustrate.

In housing, responsibility is split between local authorities and the government's national housing agency, Scottish Homes. Most local authorities own and manage a significant stock of housing, mostly built between 1950 and 1970. Local authorities are also responsible for administering renovation grants to private owners (owner-occupiers and private landlords) to encourage the improvement and repair of older sub-standard housing in accordance with nationally determined rules and regulations. Scottish Homes has particular responsibilities for funding and monitoring the work of housing associations which are involved in providing social rented housing through either new build or rehabilitation. It also has powers to fund private sector housing providers, whether they construct or rehabilitate dwellings for rent or owner occupation (Scottish Homes, 1995).

## Changing urban system

The process of industrialisation and de-industrialisation in urban Scotland is not unique in Europe. Yet both its speed and intensity are worthy of note. Scotland began to industrialise early from 1790 onwards but the pace really picked up in the late 19th century at which point the major cities grew rapidly. Glasgow, the dominant industrial centre, saw its population quadruple between 1841 and 1914 (Gibb, 1983). The great bulk of the new housing was constructed in dense tenemental developments, which contained small flats, typically one or two rooms, and no internal basic amenities such as toilets or baths.

The country's industrial base had always been narrow, focused almost exclusively upon textiles, coal, iron, steel and heavy engineering. Such specialisation could be sustained by the trading privileges which accrued from the British Empire. Once the Empire collapsed, following the end of the Second World War, many Scottish industries found themselves unable to compete in world markets and went into terminal decline (Harvie, 1981). Manufacturing employment in Glasgow fell by 60% between 1961 and 1991 (Census of Employment). Other urban centres, notably Dundee, witnessed a similar decline, although Edinburgh and Aberdeen managed to retain population through growth in financial services, and in oil and gas industries respectively.

Much of the decline reflected a growing decentralisation of population. Suburbanisation, which had started with the development of suburban rail lines in the early 1900s, gained pace in the inter-war years. From the 1960s onwards, with the growth in the ownership of private motor cars, the process became one of de-urbanisation. Major urban centres, and in particular Glasgow, began to lose both population and employment to smaller centres. This process was accelerated by the ambitions of the postwar economic planning system pursued by the Scottish Office (Robertson, 1995). The central plank of this approach was the development of New Towns and the phased scaling-down of both manufacturing activity and population within the cities, and especially Glasgow. New inward investment, particularly American capital – of which Scotland was the biggest recipient in Europe in the late 1950s and early 1960s – was steered to these New Towns.

In parallel with these shifts, Glasgow embarked upon a massive programme of housing clearance and redevelopment, which at one time included some 30% of the city's entire urban area and much of the older tenemental stock (Gibb, 1983). While much new municipal housing was constructed within the city's boundaries, many people were relocated in overspill housing in the New Towns. This ambitious redevelopment plan was never fully implemented but it did create severe problems of planning blight for the tenements under threat. With whole neighbourhoods scheduled for demolition at some unspecified point in time, any investment within this already poor stock soon disappeared. Where possible, the private landlords who dominated these areas sold out to owner occupation. Those buying often did so in the hope of being rehoused when the bulldozers finally arrived; they often had little desire or ability to invest in the stock themselves.

## Changing tenure patterns

An understanding of changing tenure patterns is fundamental to understanding Scottish, and British, housing policy. Over the 20th century, private renting has declined dramatically, from 90% of the housing stock in 1914 to just 7% currently. It has been replaced by owner-occupation, now 58% in Scotland and rising, and the social rented sector (primarily local authority housing) which accounted for 54% of the total at its peak in 1978, and was, in 1995, 32%.

A number of reasons have been put forward to explain the decline of the private rented sector in Britain. Much emphasis has been placed upon the effects of regulation, of both rent levels and security of tenure. Although introduced as a temporary emergency measure during the First World War, they were only removed for new lettings in 1988. These controls were seen to reduce both profitability and liquidity, thus encouraging investment to flow out of private renting into other housing tenures and non-housing investments. They also created a marked difference in the value of tenanted and non-tenanted property (Hamnett and Randolph, 1988).

A number of other factors, however, were also at work. At the beginning of the 20th century, other investment opportunities were opening up with the development of new financial products to compete with investments in rented accommodation (Kemp, 1988; Nevitt, 1966). Private renting suffered further from discriminatory tax treatment when compared to other businesses (Nevitt, 1966). The private rented sector also experienced subsidy and taxation disadvantages when compared to other tenures. Subsidies to council housing, while altering greatly since their introduction in 1919, have placed private renting at a distinct disadvantage, given similar subsidies were never made available to private landlords. Owner-occupation has also received preferential subsidy treatment. Most significantly, the tax treatment of owner-occupied property since 1963 has created a major fiscal incentive for owner-occupation. This, in turn, created a valuation gap which ensured that, if a rented property fell empty, it was more likely to be sold for owner-occupation than remain within the private rented sector (Hamnett and Randolph, 1988). In addition to this disinvestment, landlords have been discouraged from investing adequately in repairs and maintenance. Not surprisingly, the incidence of substandard housing is four times greater in this sector than in any other (Scottish Homes, 1993).

By contrast, owner-occupation has long been the favoured tenure of successive governments, especially the Conservatives. In the 1930s, the Conservative party's aim was the creation of 'a property owning democracy' as a bulwark against the 'spectre of communism' (Malpass and Murie, 1982). The expansion in owner-occupation has come partly through the private construction of new housing, predominantly in suburban or non-urban locations. In the older urban areas, there has also been a shift from private renting to owner-occupation as private landlords sought to disinvest. This process has been assisted by the government not just through its regulatory control on the private rented sector, but by its encouragement to building societies to provide cheap mortgage finance and, more directly, by the provision of grants to owners for improvement and repair on a large scale.

Finally, in the last 20 years there has been a notable tenure shift with the growth of housing associations. These new providers of social housing are non-profit organisations, which initially specialised in the provision of new housing for special needs groups. From 1974, with the provision of generous capital subsidies from central government, a new group of housing associations came into being which specialised in the rehabilitation of older property. This development had cross-party support. The Conservatives viewed housing associations as being non-public sector, thus representing a new type of private landlord, while the Labour Party saw them as a useful means to tackle the physical problems associated with private landlordism (Back and Hamnett, 1985). Within Scotland, as will be detailed later, the use of housing associations within defined renewal areas was a key component of the renewal strategy for older urban neighbourhoods (Robertson and Bailey, 1995). Housing associations currently own 4% of the total stock, but 8.6% of older urban housing (Scottish Homes, 1993).

## Tenement housing

In Scotland, unlike England or Wales, the dominant form of older urban housing is in flatted blocks called tenements. The physical form of this type of housing creates greater interdependence on the part of the various occupiers or owners than is the case with the brick-built terraces of England and Wales and this has important implications for renewal policy. The tenement developed in response to the feudal system of land ownership in Scotland, where building to a higher density brought a better financial return to the land owner (Robinson, 1984; Worsdall, 1979).

Although the tenemental housing form in Scotland dates back to the 15th century, the major boom coincided with the industrial revolution (Robinson, 1984), with the majority of the older tenemental neighbourhoods constructed between 1860 and 1910. Their original construction is characterised (in the main) by being four-storey stone-built blocks, with a common internal stair leading to 8 to 16 small flats. Typically toilet and clothes washing facilities were located outside the block in the common back court (Robinson, 1986; Worsdall, 1979). The majority were located close to the early industrial sites, now generally the inner areas of towns and cities. While some tenements were built for the upper classes with a large number of spacious rooms, most were for the working classes and consisted of just one or two rooms.

Tenement blocks were built speculatively and sold to private landlords or trusts, administered for small investors, the individual flats being let out on an annual lease. Day-to-day management of the blocks was usually contracted to property management agents or factors. Factors tended to manage all tenemental property within a given locality. They collected the rent, allocated property, organised the necessary repairs and paid the owners their return. As private renting declined nationally throughout the century, so the tenements suffered from a sustained lack of investment in both fabric repairs and improvements.

Legal responsibility for the various elements that make up the tenement block can be divided between the owners in a variety of different ways. Most commonly, however, the roof, external walls, common stairs and entrance, foundations and the land on which the tenement stands are communally owned (Gilbert and Flint, 1992). Repairs to these various elements required the various owners to cooperate, hence the development of factoring where landlord holdings were small or scattered. As ownership became more fragmented, with flats being sold for individual owner occupation, the factoring arrangements began to break down (Thornley, 1977; Young, 1969).

More generally, tenement housing in Scotland has suffered from a very negative image. Tenements were equated with slums which could never be transformed into attractive and acceptable housing. Population densities were too high, the housing small and squalid and there was insufficient public open space. Tenements were thus considered "an unfashionable remnant of an industrialised past" (Robertson, 1992). Antipathy towards the private landlordism associated with tenement neighbourhoods strongly influenced professional, political and public attitudes towards the tenement structure itself. While debate raged over whether they should be replaced with an English 'garden suburb' style of housing, new tenements or modernist high-rise blocks, the case for renovating these older tenement districts was rarely articulated in the 1950s and 1960s.

## The development of Scottish renewal policy

Housing policy in the immediate postwar period sought to address the severe shortages of accommodation resulting from bomb damage and the lack of maintenance work carried out during the period of hostilities, and to cope with the rapid postwar 'baby boom' (Merrett, 1977). The objective of meeting severe housing shortages gave way in the 1960s to a focus upon slum clearance and the provision of new municipal housing for the displaced families. The housing legacies of the old industrial era were to be cleared away and a new modern environment constructed. In pursuing this modernising agenda, the use of industrial housing systems became the norm. Throughout the postwar period the construction sector was used by government as a means to regulate the national economy.

Nowhere was the problem more acute than in Glasgow. A study carried out in 1965 had noted that 85% of Glasgow's housing was tenemental, and 33% of the stock was either one- or two-roomed flats. Taking Glasgow's stock of dwellings as a whole, 40% had no fixed bath or shower, 20% no internal toilet and 40% had no adequate hot water supply (Cullingworth, 1968). Glasgow also had a very high level of overcrowding, in part related to the small size of tenement flats. While the level of overcrowding (more than 1.5 persons per room) was 10.7% in Birmingham and 6.4% in Manchester, the figure for Glasgow was 34.3% (Office of Population Censuses and Statistics, 1961). It was little surprise, therefore, that Glasgow was considered to be the worst urban environment in Britain and one of the worst in Europe at that time.

The plans for rapid redevelopment, however, quickly ran into major financial problems with the balance of payments crisis of 1967 (Merrett, 1977). There then followed a period of rapid retrenchment, marked in housing terms by the policy shift away from clearance and municipal house construction, to that of improvement. The 'discovery' of the negative impacts of clearance and rehousing on the affected communities (most famously in Young and Wilmott, 1957) is cited as a factor in the shift from clearance to rehabilitation (Gibson and Langstaff, 1982). There is, however, a danger that this aspect is overplayed. In most cases there was a strong desire among slum residents to escape from what they saw as poor housing conditions and restrictive social networks (Glendinning and Muthesius, 1994; Paris and Blackaby, 1989). Concern with the preservation of existing communities was less important in bringing about the switch to improvement than economic reasons, although it did provide a useful justification for this change.

The shift to improvement was given a significant boost with the publication of *Scotland's older houses* (SHAC, 1967) which articulated the need for a comprehensive policy. The impetus for this report, produced by Barry Cullingworth, was not indigenous, rather it mirrored developments occurring in England and Wales (CHAC, 1966). The report found that the previous estimates of the scale of Scotland's housing problems had to be dramatically revised. Official local authority returns estimated that there were 100,000 unfit houses in Scotland. Cullingworth called for the rapid demolition of 273,000 houses, and advised that another 193,000 should go within 15 years. In total this represented a quarter of Scotland's entire housing stock. With the scale of the problem revised, and still regarded as an underestimate, the rate of slum clearance, which stood at 15,000 units per annum, was seriously questioned. Further, in recognition that many families would have years to wait, the report called for "an urgent re-assessment of the need for improving those houses which must, of necessity, stand for a considerable number of years and a much more adequate policy aimed at preventing deterioration" (SHAC, 1967, para 85).

The Cullingworth Committee had been established to examine the statutory provisions relating to the determination of inadequate housing and to make recommendations for amendments. The Committee took the view that 'unfitness', a concept based on 19th-century ideas of public health, had to be replaced with a standard based upon considerations of convenience, amenity and socially acceptable conditions. Two standards of fitness were proposed, a 'satisfactory' standard to act as a target, and the 'tolerable' standard, below which houses should not be allowed to exist. The Committee also broke new ground by recognising 'a satisfactory environment' as a prerequisite for 'a satisfactory house' (SHAC, 1967, para 115).

Having addressed its remit, the Committee went on to consider what measures were required to initiate the improvement of inadequate housing. It found that the vast bulk of improvement work was carried out by owner-occupiers, yet private landlords were still the dominant owners of tenemental property. To encourage an increase in improvement works undertaken by landlords, Cullingworth suggested it would be necessary to ensure they received a reasonable return on their properties. This proposal was not acted upon within the resultant legislation and therefore the renewal of tenements has required a large-scale change in ownership.

Enhancing grant levels, for both owner-occupiers and landlords, was another part of the proposed improvement strategy. For improvement to succeed, it was also seen as essential that local authorities were given stronger and simplified powers to initiate such work, and that they were made responsible for ensuring the eradication of unsatisfactory housing within an acceptable time period.

The Scottish legislation in 1969 which resulted from this report was markedly different to its English and Welsh equivalent. For the latter, improvement legislation placed an emphasis upon flexibility, persuasion and help. The Scottish legislation, on the other hand, opted for compulsion and strong sanctions, backed up with grant assistance. Local authorities were given the power to declare blocks of substandard housing as 'Housing Treatment Areas'. Within such areas the local authority had the power to compulsorily purchase housing in order to improve it if, in their opinion, the owner would not carry out the work themselves even with improvement grants.

The legislation proved to be relatively ineffective, in itself, but provided local authorities and central government with the opportunity to learn from their mistakes (Robertson, 1985). Where local authorities sought to implement improvement in the same way as they had implemented clearance (through large-scale compulsory acquisition), resistance from residents was such that the programme ground to a halt. Owners who did wish to improve, encountered difficulties both in relation to making the necessary technical arrangements and in finding the resources to pay their share of costs. It was acknowledged that there was a need for an organisation which could help to coordinate the technical aspects of the work and experiments in Glasgow established a useful model approach (Robertson, 1985). In addition there was a general interest within the planning profession at the time in finding mechanisms for involving local residents in the planning process, following the Skeffington Report (MHLG, 1969). The mechanism which emerged was thus under the control of local residents. There was also a recognition of the need to provide higher grants within these poorer targeted improvement areas.

In 1974, new legislation was introduced which established the current improvement framework. It was this which led to the distinctive Scottish approach to the renewal of older tenement neighbourhoods, described in detail below. Before that, there is a short description of the characteristics of the current stock of older urban dwellings.

## The present stock of older urban dwellings

According to the results of the first Scottish House Condition Survey in 1991, there are some two million occupied dwellings in Scotland, of which 83% have been classified as being within urban locations (Scottish Homes, 1993 – as are all the figures in this section). Of the urban stock, 18% was constructed before 1919 – a total of just over 300,000 dwellings. Very little of this stock (less than 5%) is in the public sector compared with 42% of the urban stock as a whole. The great majority is in the private sector, with 72% owner-occupied and 15% privately rented. The proportion privately rented is particularly high, reflecting the previous dominance of older housing by private landlords.

One half of all older urban dwellings are flats in tenements, with a further 10% flats in converted houses. Older urban dwellings are less likely to be houses than average. They are also much more likely to be small; 32% have just one to three rooms, compared with 17% of all urban dwellings. Nevertheless, a larger proportion of older urban dwellings than average has seven or more rooms. Thus while there are a significant number of large houses, the bulk of the older urban stock is comprised of small flats in the private sector, mostly owner-occupied but with a significant proportion privately rented.

## Current renewal policy mechanisms

Many of the policy mechanisms operating in Scotland result from British legislation and are therefore identical to those employed in England and Wales. This is particularly true of fiscal policies to regulate tenures. There are, however, significant differences in some policy areas, particularly in relation to grants for private owners. While the grant system in England and Wales underwent fundamental reform in 1990, the system in Scotland remained unchanged. However, at the time of writing this, the government has expressed a desire to see similar changes adopted in Scotland (Scottish Office, 1988). In other areas, while the policy mechanisms have been similar to those south of the border, they have been employed in quite different ways.

### Regulation of tenure

As noted above, tenure objectives, in particular the promotion of owner occupation, have been the dominant concern of British housing policy for the last 40 years. While public sector housing has been supported through direct subsidies by central government, in the private sector 'regulation' has occurred through differential tax treatment of owning and renting. In general, these policies have not been designed to encourage the private rehabilitation of property, however, and have acted as general consumption subsidies.

The primary subsidy to owner occupation flows through the tax relief on mortgage interest payments. The justification for such tax relief is that mortgages are seen as borrowing for investment. In line with the treatment of other forms of investment, this tax relief was originally offset by taxation of the 'income', or benefit, which owner-occupiers received from their asset (namely, from living in their home) the 'imputed rental income tax'. When this tax was abolished in 1963, the tax relief was left in place. This arrangement is different to the treatment of private landlords; they too receive tax relief on borrowings for investment, but are taxed on their (real) rental income. Thus owner-occupation benefits from a clear tax advantage. In many other European countries, including The Netherlands, Spain, Denmark, Norway, Finland, Greece and Sweden, owner-occupiers are given both tax relief on mortgage interest and are taxed on imputed income. In France and Germany, however, the treatment is the same as the UK (OECD, 1989).

During the 1980s and early 1990s, progressive steps have been taken to limit the tax income lost by government in granting tax relief on mortgage interest as the cost of this arrangement had spiralled. In Scotland, the cost increased by a factor of three in real terms between 1979 and 1990, declining slightly thereafter to just under £350 million in 1992 (Robertson and Bailey, 1994). This compared with £121 million in the form of grants given by government to the private sector in 1992/93 specifically for improvement and repair.

For private landlords, some incentive to invest in their property is provided through tax relief on the cost of repairs. However, this is only applicable where the landlord pays others to carry out the work, not where they carry out repairs themselves. This arrangement therefore ignores much of the informal repair activity carried out by smaller landlords themselves. In Scotland, private landlordism is predominantly a small-scale activity; half of the sector is controlled by individuals or companies owning less than ten properties (Kemp and Rhodes, 1994).

While fiscal policy has encouraged the decline of private renting and the growth of owner-occupation, it has not sought to directly address housing quality issues. Furthermore, house prices do not appear to adequately reflect house conditions. Investment in repairs and maintenance is not seen to provide an economic return. The recently introduced sales tax on all repair and maintenance work acts as a further disincentive. New build property, on the other hand, continues to be tax exempt.

*Indirect regulation*

The government makes a variety of grants available for the repair and improvement of property, the amount is calculated as a percentage of the cost of the work, up to certain maximum limits. Depending on the type of grant, the percentage is between 50% and 90%, and may also depend to some extent upon the individual's circumstances. The maximum levels of grant are only increased infrequently. They are not index linked, and so between rises the real value is eroded by inflation; at the time of writing this, current grant levels were last revised in 1988. Local authorities may apply to the Secretary of State for permission to exceed the maximum levels and this practice has become increasingly common. The present maximum limits should therefore be regarded as 'notional' levels.

The first grants were introduced in 1949 and the system has developed and evolved in a piecemeal fashion since then. Initially, grants were made available only for specific works of improvement: the installation of basic amenities such as a bath or shower, or an inside toilet. Over time, grants have been extended to cover the cost of repair works associated with improvements and, later, to cover works of repair alone. Specific grants have been introduced to encourage the replacement of lead piping for drinking water, the installation of heat insulation, the conversion of large dwellings into smaller units and the adaptation of dwellings to meet the needs of disabled occupants. In general, where individuals are required to undertake certain works by the local authority, they will be entitled to receive a higher grant. The limit on expenditure is higher for older dwellings, reflecting higher works costs.

Periodically, the government has increased the amount of grant awarded for certain types of work. Between 1971 and 1972, the uptake of improvement grants soared, as the percentage of costs covered by grant was increased from 50% to 90% in all development areas. The Conservative government used this as a means to stimulate economic activity, and adopted the same approach between 1982 and 1984, when the percentage allowable for both Improvement and Repair Grants was raised from 50% to 90%. As a result grant activity also spiralled.

While the range of grants has steadily increased, the government has placed increasing controls on local authorities' overall expenditure. Although individuals may apply for grants, they are only entitled to receive an award by right in specific circumstances. Those applying for discretionary awards must wait until resources become available. Some local authorities are still trying to find the resources to pay for grants awarded during the 1982 to 1984 boom.

In 1995, Repair Grants covered 50% of costs up to a maximum expenditure of up to £7,800 for older tenement properties; less if the property was more modern. Improvement Grants started at 50% of costs, with a maximum expenditure limit of £12,600. Where the local authority required improvement, the grant could cover between 75% and 90% of costs, with an expenditure limit up to £19,700 in older tenements. In very complex tenement improvement schemes, it has not been unknown for the expenditure to increase to £100,000 per flat, with the grant covering £90,000, although this is unusual.

## Direct regulation

Local authorities have a number of powers to deal with 'sub-standard' properties; that is, properties below the minimum tolerable standard or lacking one or more standard amenities. The tolerable standard was first put forward in 1967 (SHAC, 1967) and has not been revised since then. The standard amenities have even earlier origins. The two overlap to some degree, as can be seen from Table 11.1. There is some pressure to revise this minimum standard. The major criticism is that, while a dwelling may meet the minimum standards, it may still not provide adequate accommodation by present standards. For instance, it may be difficult or expensive to heat or suffer from problems of condensation.

For individual dwellings, local authorities have the power to order the demolition of substandard dwellings or, if the dwelling forms just part of a building, the closure of a dwelling to prevent its use. Since 1978, the

**Table 11.1: The tolerable standard and the standard amenities**

A dwelling meets the tolerable standard if it:

- is structurally stable;
- is substantially free from rising and penetrating damp;
- has satisfactory provision for natural and artificial lighting, for ventilation and for
   heating;
- has an adequate piped supply of hot and cold water within the house;
- has a sink provided with a satisfactory supply of hot and cold water within the house;
- has a water closet available for the exclusive use of the occupants of the house and suitably located within the house;
- has an effective system for the drainage and disposal of foul and surface water;
- has satisfactory facilities for the cooking of food within the house;
- has satisfactory access to all external doors and outbuildings.

The standard amenities, which must be for the exclusive use of the occupants of the home, are:

- a sink with a satisfactory supply of hot and cold water;
- a WC;
- a fixed bath or shower with a hot and cold water supply;
- a wash hand basin with a hot and cold water supply.

Source: Robertson and Bailey (1995)

authority has also had the power to order that a dwelling is improved to the tolerable standard, provided with the standard amenities and put into a good state of repair. Where such an Improvement Order is made, the owner becomes entitled by right to an Improvement Grant at higher levels than normally apply (75% of eligible costs, rather than the normal 50%, up to a maximum expenditure of £12,600). In cases of financial hardship, the grant rate may be increased to 90% and, as mentioned above, the maximum limit is frequently exceeded, sometimes quite considerably.

In addition, local authorities have powers aimed at whole areas of substandard dwellings. Where the majority of dwellings in an area are substandard, the local authority has the power to declare a Housing Action Area (HAA). This is, in effect, a collective Improvement Order and derives from the legislative framework established in 1974. This measure was specifically developed to enable authorities to adopt a coordinated approach for improving areas of older tenemental housing, following the Cullingworth Report and the failure of the earlier Housing Treatment Areas. The HAA may require that some or all of the dwellings are demolished but, more usually, the requirement is that they are improved up to the specified standard, that is, above the tolerable standard given the standard amenities put into a good state of repair. Declaration of an HAA is a two-stage process, during which the local authority must consult with local residents and explain the implications of the declaration. This process was designed to promote resident cooperation after the conflict over Housing Treatment Areas. As with Improvement Orders, owners in HAAs are entitled to enhanced levels of grant, which can then be used quite flexibly for such works of improvement or repair as are necessary.

To back up both the individual Improvement Order and the collective HAA, the local authority has strong powers to compulsorily purchase dwellings where owners are either unwilling or unable to improve within a reasonable period of time. It may then arrange improvements itself, subsequently renting the property out or selling it on, or it may sell the dwelling unimproved. In general, compulsory purchase is not widely used but its presence may encourage many owners to sell voluntarily rather than improve their property.

In addition to these powers aimed at substandard housing, local authorities have a number of powers to tackle problems of disrepair. Where a building is in 'serious disrepair', they may issue a Repairs Notice, requiring specific works to be carried out. As previously, owners receiving such notices are automatically eligible for Repair Grants. If the notice is not complied with, the authority has the power to carry out the works itself and to charge the costs to the owner. Other, similar powers exist under general civic government legislation. Local authorities also have specific powers regarding dangerous buildings.

While local authorities have clear powers to intervene where a problem exists, they are virtually powerless to prevent problems arising and/or to ensure that buildings are adequately maintained. Indeed, the existence of a grants system can be said to discourage maintenance, precisely because grants are only available once buildings have deteriorated sufficiently. The only condition attached to grants is that the dwelling is maintained in a good state of repair for five years, otherwise the grant may be reclaimed. As owner-occupation has become the norm in tenements, the old factoring arrangements have been broken down, unable to cope with the difficulties of ensuring that every owner pays their contribution.

## Impacts of the renewal legislation

### Housing associations and Housing Action Areas

A key feature of Scottish renewal policy has been the involvement of housing associations on a large scale in the renewal of areas of older housing. As mentioned above, housing associations are eligible for a capital subsidy to enable them either to construct new housing or to acquire and renovate older housing. The capital subsidy is controlled by the government's housing agency, Scottish Homes (previously the Housing Corporation). In Glasgow, a particular approach developed whereby the local authority and the Housing Corporation worked closely together to target the subsidy on areas of older substandard housing (Robertson, 1988). The local authority declared HAAs, requiring all the owners to improve their housing to the specified standard and provided grants to those willing to improve. If owners were unable or unwilling to improve, they could sell their dwelling to a housing association set up to carry out the necessary rehabilitation works. Where the association acquired privately rented stock, the tenants transferred to the association. Former owner-occupiers were also rehoused as tenants. If dwellings were compulsorily purchased by the local authority, they too were transferred to the housing association. After improvement, the associations rented out dwellings at below market rents.

Since 1974, HAAs had affected some 70,000 dwellings, of which 17,000 have been lost through demolition or amalgamation, and 45,000 have been improved. Housing associations have been responsible for the improvement of half of the total. Owner-occupiers have improved one quarter and private landlords one sixth (Robertson and Bailey, 1995). In Glasgow, which has accounted for half of the total HAA programme, associations accounted for 80% of all dwellings improved. In addition to improving dwellings which they owned, associations coordinated improvements for a great many private owners as well, arranging the technical works and helping owners to apply for grants from the local authority.

This approach was favoured by Glasgow City Council because it enabled the city to gain access to new resources for renewal which were seen to be vital given the scale of the city's problems (Robertson, 1988). While the local authority provided the resources to private owners who wished to carry out improvements through the grant mechanisms, the finance for housing associations came from central government. Associations acquired a large part of their stock from private landlords and this was seen as an additional benefit by the local authority opposed to private landlords on political grounds.

The work of these housing associations has been seen to represent a very successful model for the renewal of the housing stock. They have not only succeeded in achieving significant improvements in the physical fabric but are perceived to have had a number of additional 'spillover' benefits. Housing associations are seen as having acted as 'growth poles', bringing housing investment back to large areas of the inner core. In areas where associations have carried out renewal work, private developers have followed, constructing new housing on vacant inner-city sites for the first time in many years (albeit sometimes encouraged by subsidies). Private owners outwith the HAAs have also invested in repair and modernisation, encouraged by grants and by the rise in house prices resulting from the housing association investment. Indeed, the rise in house prices is so marked that housing associations are finding it increasingly difficult to acquire stock. To a degree, they have become "the victims of their own success" (MacLennan, 1985).

Not all local authorities have encouraged housing associations to the same extent. In Scotland's capital, Edinburgh, the formerly Conservative controlled local authority saw the promotion of owner-occupation as the priority. For this authority, housing associations represented a form of "municipalisation" (Robertson and Bailey, 1995). Different approaches to implementing HAAs were therefore developed, which tried to ensure maximum participation by individual owner-occupiers (SDD, 1983). In order to do this, owners were given greater control over the extent of improvement work carried out, resulting in a lower cost and lower standard of improvement.

These two approaches have had different impacts. Where housing associations have acquired large portfolios of stock, very different patterns of socioeconomic change have been recorded than in areas where grants have been targeted on private owners. In the latter, significant changes in the characteristics of the local population have been recorded following renewal, as owner occupation replaces private renting and more affluent groups moved in: a process often referred to as 'gentrification'. Where associations have been active, however, they have provided a mechanism which ensures that lower income groups continue to have access to housing in the neighbourhood even after renewal, since association dwellings are allocated administratively to those in 'need', rather than through market processes. Associations can thus facilitate the retention of local communities. Furthermore, the process of establishing and running a housing association is seen as strengthening social networks, providing a focus for the community and a voice to represent it. Since one of the justifications for a switch from clearance to rehabilitation was that it would prevent the destruction of local communities, the housing association approach offers a successful example of a socially sensitive renewal mechanism.

From the government's perspective, one concern with the impact of housing associations is that they are perceived as displacing owner-occupation, particularly at the bottom end of the market. This is reflected in several earlier attempts to evaluate the impacts and to find ways of encouraging owner-occupiers to participate in the improvement process rather than selling to a housing association (SDD, 1980; 1983).

A more recent evaluation suggests that this process has been somewhat exaggerated (Robertson and Bailey, 1995). In general, the growth of housing association ownership has come at the expense of private landlords. This sector was on the decline in any case, although the presence of housing associations looking to acquire run-down stock may have provided landlords with an alternative exit strategy. While associations have acquired some stock from owner-occupiers, this is offset by the creation of other opportunities: new private developments for owner-occupiers have been attracted in to these areas; the associations themselves provide some dwellings for sale; and the process of private landlords selling to individuals continues and has been accelerated by the process of renewal.

While housing investment clearly played an important role in the physical regeneration of these areas, it would be simplistic to ascribe all that has been achieved to date to this alone. Other forces have been at work. Demographic changes resulting in the rapid growth in the number of smaller households have greatly increased demand for the type of housing offered in these neighbourhoods. In 1971, 47% of households consisted of just one or two people, but this had risen to 61% in 1991 (Census Data for Scotland). The location of the housing close to city centres has also proved attractive to these predominantly younger households. Further, there has been a general increase in the availability of mortgage finance for owner-occupiers as a result of government action to broaden building society lending. Building societies expanded their lending into these neighbourhoods for the first time during the early 1980s. Finally, it should be noted that some investment was occurring in these poorer neighbourhoods even before the intervention of HAAs and that house prices were already rising as a result of the lifting of the threat of clearance and the improved prospects for the older tenemental neighbourhoods (Robertson and Bailey, 1995).

## Use of statutory powers and uptake of grants

In general, local authorities have relied upon threatened rather than actual use of their statutory powers to ensure improvements or repairs are carried out, preferring to encourage investment through the take-up of grants. Outwith HAAs, 29,000 dwellings were served with Improvement Orders or Repairs Notices between 1979 and 1994, but local authorities record that 83,000 substandard dwellings were improved to meet the minimum standards (Scottish Office, 1994). Within HAAs the use of Compulsory Purchase Powers was also relatively rare, yet an estimated 56,000 substandard dwellings have been tackled, with the great majority being improved (Robertson and Bailey, 1995).

Local authorities have approved grants on a total of some 387,000 dwellings between 1979 and 1994: two fifths of the Scottish private sector stock. Of these, 238,000 were grants for repair works, while 129,000 were for improvements (SDD, 1986; Scottish Office, 1994). There were also a small number for the conversion of properties or for the installation of specific amenities. The take-up of Repair Grants peaked in the early 1980s, when the grant rate was temporarily increased from 50 to 90% and restrictions on local authorities' overall expenditure were eased. Since returning to the previous 50% level, the number of Repair Grants approved had dropped dramatically, but still remains ahead of the number of Improvement Grants.

From 1982 to 1985, only some 4% of Repair Grants were for dwellings below the tolerable standard. For Improvement Grants in the same period, some 63% went to substandard dwellings (SDD, 1986). Unfortunately no comparable figures exist for later years. In HAAs, some 80% of dwellings affected were substandard, indicating the degree to which this approach targeted particularly severe housing conditions (Robertson and Bailey, 1995).

Figures for total expenditure are difficult to collect. Within HAAs, it has been estimated that approximately £1 billion has been invested by housing associations, local authorities and private owners since 1979 (Robertson and Bailey, 1995). Outside these areas, an 'educated guess' would put the figure for investment through grants to individuals at between £2 and £3 billion.

## Impact on substandard housing

One means of tracing the overall impact of renewal policy is to look at the proportion of dwellings regarded as substandard at different points in time. There are a number of difficulties with the data in Scotland, due to the lack of a regular national house condition survey. In the past, local authorities' figures were based upon a variety of sources. As they have been encouraged, more recently, to undertake systematic surveys so their estimates of the extent of sub-standard housing have increased, suggesting significant undercounting in previous years.

Nevertheless, the total number of dwellings regarded as substandard fell significantly from 1979 to 1994: 124,000 to 89,500 respectively (Scottish Office, 1994). Moreover, the proportion of those which are older urban dwellings has also fallen. While the incidence of substandard dwellings within the pre-1919 stock remains higher than average, especially within the private rented sector, there is now a growing concern with conditions in other sectors, especially public housing (Scottish Homes, 1993).

The problem which the current framework was established to address, that of obsolescence and the need for comprehensive improvement of the older stock, has been very substantially reduced. In its place, a new problem of disrepair in older housing is emerging. While the pre-1919 stock constitutes 21% of the total stock, it accounts for 50% of the estimated need for repairs (Scottish Homes, 1993). On average, older urban flats required £1,860 spent on urgent repairs, a figure far higher than the national average (Scottish Homes, 1993). It is likely that the Housing Action Area programme is coming towards an end. The next challenge for renewal policy for older urban tenements is finding the means to encourage adequate investment by owner-occupiers in repairs and maintenance. As yet, no adequate answer to this problem has been found.

## Conclusion

Scottish housing renewal policy is firmly located within wider tenure policies. The long-standing discrimination against private renting discouraged investment in this sector, which for many years dominated the older urban neighbourhoods. Thus a precondition for renewal was either a change of attitude towards private renting (as recommended by the Cullingworth Report [SHAC, 1967]) or a change of tenure within these areas. In the end, it was the latter approach which was adopted.

Renewal policy targeted resources to owner-occupiers and housing associations. Owner-occupation has received political (and fiscal) support for many years now. While grants for repair and improvement were also available to private landlords, few felt able to make use of them given the financial disincentives of the tax and subsidy system. Housing associations were favoured by the Conservatives as they provided an alternative to local authority housing, whereas Labour viewed associations as an acceptable replacement for private landlords. This convergence of political interest has, from 1975-95, provided housing associations with a relatively favoured position.

In 1994/95, however, the Conservatives' support for owner-occupation has shown signs of weakening. Tax relief on mortgages was sharply reduced, and support for unemployed homeowners was also limited. In an already weakened housing market, there is a danger that the newly revitalised older urban neighbourhoods may slip into decline as overall demand for owner-occupation falls.

The key characteristics of the Scottish approach to renewal (at least in contrast to England and Wales) have been a reliance upon strong compulsory powers for local authorities to ensure a coordinated response to the problems of tenemental housing, and the involvement of locally-controlled housing associations which act as a coordinator of the rehabilitation work, a conduit for large-scale subsidies and as a barrier to 'gentrification'. Many claims have been made for the great successes of this interventionist approach, most notably that it represents a model for 'housing-led regeneration'.

In physical terms, a measure of that success might be the massive reduction in the number of dwellings lacking the standard amenities: 200,000 households lacked a fixed bath or shower in 1971, but this had fallen to just 9,000 in 1991 (Census data). Other problems have, however, not gone away. Disrepair has emerged as an issue, but it is not a new problem, merely one that was previously masked by obsolescence. While the problem of dwellings lacking certain amenities can be tackled effectively through a one-off injection of cash, repair and maintenance is a continuing issue. The central problem remains that of the overall affordability of housing (including adequate maintenance) for those on lower incomes. Solutions, therefore, do not lie in one-off grant mechanisms, but rather in reforms of the overall housing finance system, as it affects the private sector.

In broader terms, renewal policies are often seen as having brought about not just physical renewal, but social and economic regeneration of many older urban neighbourhoods. While the achievements of the housing association have been remarkable in transforming some of Europe's most notorious slums, housing investment has not been the only factor; planning policies, demographic changes and increases in mortgage availability have all contributed. The scale of subsidy involved should also not be underestimated. Nevertheless, the housing associations pioneered this area-based approach to renewal and, where they led, further investment followed through market processes (albeit often encouraged by further subsidies). Furthermore, the future of these neighbourhoods remains tied to that of the wider urban areas within which they are located; the area-based approach cannot isolate these neighbourhoods from broader economic and social policy changes operating at the UK and European scale.

Finally, it is worth stressing that the approach to renewal should not be seen as a uniform one. The national framework has been utilised in a variety of ways in response to different local conditions. Most importantly, where local political support for renewal was a secondary concern to the need to facilitate the growth of owner-occupation, the role played by housing associations was markedly less significant. In turn, this led to quite different impacts. This illustrates an important lesson for comparative studies such as this. Comparisons must address not just the formal policy positions of nation states, but also the effective local policies resulting from their implementation.

TWELVE

# Housing rehabilitation and urban renewal in Europe: a cross-national analysis of problems and policies*

*Hans Skifter Andersen*

It may seem from the preceding chapters, that public policies for housing rehabilitation vary enormously between countries. Indeed, the conclusion reached in *Urban renewal policy in a European perspective* (Priemus and Metselaar, 1992), based on questionnaires answered by government agencies in nine countries, was that there was little agreement on the meaning and concept of 'urban renewal' and the kind of problems and activities it involved. It was also concluded that "goals and motives of urban renewal policy differ to no small extent per country" (p 18), and that "urban renewal legislation in the countries cannot be described by means of a generally applicable model" (p 24).

So why is there such a large discrepancy between Western European countries concerning policies and practice in this field?

As already observed in Chapter One, urban renewal and housing rehabilitation reflect several different but connected problems and activities. Thus the way in which different countries have chosen to deal with the situation has been dependent upon their particular context.

Another possible cause of divergence between countries is a general uncertainty among policy makers (and researchers) in Europe on the fundamental causes of urban problems and what role the public sector should play in defeating them. There are no clear answers to the basic questions of why market forces are not always able to create the necessary

---

* Germany is also included in this analysis based on Hansen and Skifter Andersen (1993).

renewal of housing and urban areas, and how governments can regulate the market efficiently so that renewal takes place. Consequently, urban renewal has sometimes been organised as an isolated public task, planned and implemented by public agencies as if market forces did not exist. Even though all the countries discussed have found it necessary to establish special subsidy programmes and public regulation of urban renewal and housing rehabilitation, it seems that in many countries there has been a lack of clear understanding of the purpose of these policies and the extent of their application.

This was also mirrored in the above-mentioned study (Priemus and Metselaar, 1992), which showed that it was difficult for governments to give precise information on the need for urban renewal activities in their countries or a clear picture of what policies they were going to follow in the future. Urban renewal and housing rehabilitation policies seem to some extent to be ad hoc measures aimed at urban problems which are recognised but hardly understood.

## Main features in the historical development of urban renewal and housing rehabilitation in Europe

The development of public involvement in urban renewal and housing rehabilitation since the Second World War is shown in broad outline in Figure 12.1. Just after the war, the dominating problem in all European countries was housing shortage – especially in the countries where a large share of the housing stock has been demolished. This had two consequences. First, the public interest and resources were directed at increasing the housing supply through new building, with little attention paid to improvement of the existing stock. Second, there was a continuation of the strict control on rents in private and public housing that had been introduced during the war. This rent control had, to a varied extent, a negative impact on maintenance and improvement activity in rented housing. France was one country where the government tried to take action against maintenance problems by introducing a national fund for supporting improvement and maintenance of housing, financed by a charge on rented property.

Some countries tried in the 1950s and 1960s to solve slum problems by passing legislation on minimum standards for housing with the purpose of putting pressure on private owners of bad housing. But this instrument only seems to have had limited importance for housing renewal. It would

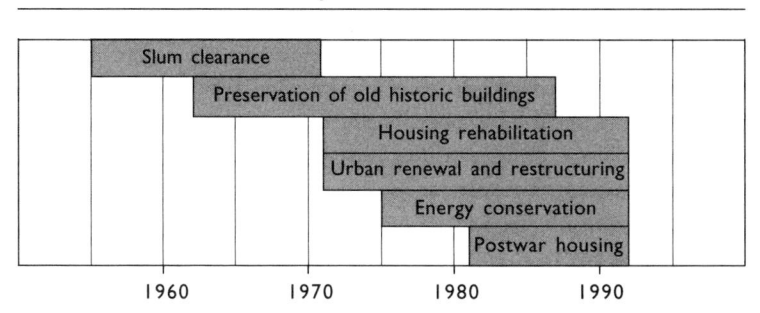

**Figure 12.1: The historical development of urban renewal and housing rehabilitation in Western Europe**

| 1960 | 1970 | 1980 | 1990 |
|---|---|---|---|

- Slum clearance (c. 1955–1970)
- Preservation of old historic buildings (c. 1965–1985)
- Housing rehabilitation (c. 1970–1990)
- Urban renewal and restructuring (c. 1970–1990)
- Energy conservation (c. 1975–1990)
- Postwar housing (c. 1985–1990)

often imply economic losses for owners to meet the demands if no public subsidies were involved.

The first real urban renewal activity, which took place from the middle of the 1950s, was slum clearance – that is, demolition across whole urban areas and construction of new buildings. This activity was often combined with a reorganisation of traffic systems where new streets were constructed across the existing urban structure.

Partly because of these brutal interventions in cities, an interest in renewing and preserving old historic buildings and districts emerged in the 1960s, often with the introduction of special programmes. In some countries this was combined with planning regulations aimed at making it difficult to demolish these buildings or to change their use.

The 1960s saw a boom in housing investments which also created an increase in private investments in housing rehabilitation. It was first of all in the owner-occupied sector that housing improvement took place, while the rented sector came staggering up. The activity in the rented sector depended to some extent on the development in rent control systems. Most countries continued a form of regulation in the 1960s, while Germany and the UK for a period had a free rent setting, which was succeeded by a new and weaker form of control in 1971.

From the late 1960s there was, in many countries, an increasing opposition to slum clearance from residents in the areas concerned and from the public in general. This led to a gradual shift in urban renewal policies and practices in the 1970s towards preservation and renewal of buildings and urban areas in cooperation with the residents. Another possible explanation for this change in policy could in some countries (such as the UK) be found in a need for expenditure cuts.

The willingness of governments to give economic support for housing rehabilitation was affected by the economic depression in the late 1970s. The strong decline in the construction of new housing made governments in some countries increase the subsidies for urban renewal and housing rehabilitation as a measure to defeat unemployment. The political arguments for this were supported by a change in the focus of housing policy from quantitative aspects of housing supply to the quality of the existing housing stock.

As industrialism moved to post-industrialism, many cities experienced a change in their economic conditions and the use of land. Industries declined or were moved out, leaving behind unused areas and empty buildings, while unemployment increased and the economic situation of many cities worsened. This led to a public involvement in urban restructuring and revival of city centres. At the same time, increasing traffic and pollution brought a growing pressure on local authorities to improve the urban environment.

A new and unexpected field of urban renewal emerged in the 1980s in large postwar social housing estates. Increasing problems in these areas caused by technical defects and social unrest made it necessary for public authorities to intervene. In some countries this experience caused a change in the concept of urban renewal from that of a finite task to remove or renew old and obsolete housing to a continuous effort to solve problems of combined social and physical decay in vulnerable neighbourhoods. Moreover, it has in most countries produced a stronger consciousness of the social processes at the root of urban decay. The interplay between physical and social agendas in relation to renewal has, to an increasing extent, come into focus leading to new policies which try to develop an integrated approach.

Development in the 1980s in many countries was also influenced by the general trend of privatisation in housing policy, which brought reduction in rent control and other regulations of the housing market which could hamper housing rehabilitation. Most of the heaviest slums in the cities had by now been removed, which meant a change in the role of urban renewal policies. New tasks for housing rehabilitation gained importance such as energy conservation and accessibility for old and disabled people. Less importance was attached to direct public involvement and more to making private investment in urban renewal and housing rehabilitation attractive by changing the market conditions, by direct cooperation between public and private agents or by giving subsidies. An effort was made to replace or simplify existing legislation to make it more efficient.

The nine countries compared deviate in various ways from this general picture, and the chronological order described has not been quite the same in all cases. Switzerland seems to be most at odds from the norm with very weak rent control which means an almost free rent setting from the end of the 1960s and little public involvement in urban renewal and housing rehabilitation. Denmark, Austria and Sweden have hardly begun the privatisation phase which in many other countries occurred in the 1980s.

The extent of involvement by the state has, however, been quite different in the nine countries. In most of them urban renewal just after the war was entirely in the hands of local government, with the legal basis of their activities in planning legislation or, in some countries, in special powers to remove or compel buildings for slum clearance (for example, the UK and Sweden). In most countries special legislation on urban renewal was passed from the end of the 1950s onwards, but at very different times and to different degrees. The first countries to pass national laws on slum clearance were Denmark and France in 1958, followed by Norway, Germany and Austria around 1970 and The Netherlands in 1981. Sweden also introduced slum clearance legislation at the start of the 1970s, but this law was never very significant as other and more flexible legislative tools were available and subsidies were not linked to the law. In the UK, some legislation was passed in the late 1970s that gave local authorities measures to control urban renewal, but an all-embracing piece of legislation was never formulated. In Switzerland and in Finland (see Hansen and Skifter Andersen, 1993) there was never a special national urban renewal legislation.

Before the development of national legislation, however, many of the countries introduced economic support from central governments for urban renewal activities to be carried out by local authorities. Just after the Second World War in Sweden, for example, a subsidy system was set up aimed at new building, slum clearance and housing rehabilitation, meaning that Sweden had probably the most extensive slum clearance activity in Europe in the 1950s and 1960s. Similarly, governments in The Netherlands, Austria and the UK introduced major subsidy schemes for urban renewal from the beginning of the 1970s.

In most countries new national subsidy programmes were introduced in the 1970s for various kinds of housing rehabilitation outside declared urban renewal areas and often without the involvement of local government.

In the late 1980s there was a trend towards decentralisation in some countries where national governments to some extent handed over the responsibility of urban renewal to local government or gave them greater freedom to choose courses of action (France, The Netherlands, Norway, Denmark). In other countries the regional authorities always had a great influence (Germany, Austria and Switzerland).

## Problems of urban decay and housing deterioration

The physical problems at which urban renewal and housing rehabilitation policies are directed involve obsolete dwellings which are not improved or removed from the housing stock, deteriorated buildings which are not kept in a satisfactory repair, and worn-down urban areas with an outdated infrastructure which are not renewed.

Most properties undergo regular maintenance and improvement that compensates for wear and tear and provides the house with up-to-date facilities. However, sometimes this process has not taken place, or has been inadequate. This tends to happen in certain parts of the housing market often concentrated in particular districts of the cities which we could call 'areas of problematic deterioration'. The problems of decay and obsolete housing in these areas have led all Western European countries to implement programmes and regulations to promote urban renewal and housing rehabilitation.

The fundamental causes of these urban problems in Europe are not very well illuminated in the research literature. For example, why are market forces not able to facilitate the necessary change and renewal? And why do governments have to intervene?

If the housing market were functioning as is presumed for a market within general economic theory, problems of bad and inadequate housing could only be a consequence of failing demand, mainly because of excessively low incomes. Demand subsidies would then be the only effective way in which to remove bad housing, while supply subsidies and market interventions would be ineffective.

Throughout Western Europe there has in general been much government intervention in the rental housing market in the form of

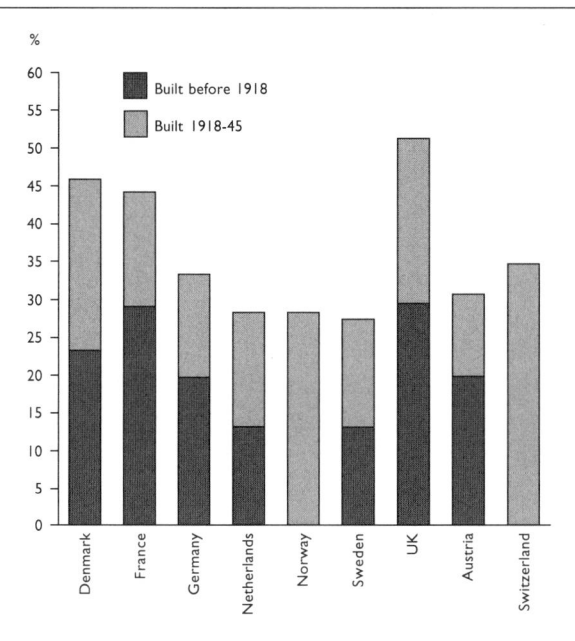

**Figure 12.2: The share of dwellings built before 1945 in nine countries**

[Bar chart showing percentages of dwellings built before 1918 and between 1918-45 for Denmark, France, Germany, Netherlands, Norway, Sweden, UK, Austria, and Switzerland]

rent control and other measures. Many economists have pointed to this intervention as the main reason for a badly functioning market and an important indirect cause of failing maintenance and housing improvement.

However, the extensive research on the large problems of urban decay in the US, which has quite an unregulated housing market, shows that there are other causes of housing deterioration. In principle buildings can be maintained indefinitely, but fundamental social and economic mechanisms exist in the market which create self-perpetuating processes of social, economic and physical decline in vulnerable city neighbourhoods (see Skifter Andersen, 1995a). The American experience also shows that a renewal of obsolete and worn-down housing without public support often means demolition and the construction of new buildings. Improvement and preservation seldom take place without public support and if they do, it tends to mean that the residents are replaced and the area 'gentrified'.

The extent of urban problems in different countries in Europe depends, among other factors, on the degree of social inequality, differentiation and segregation in each country. A highly segregated housing market with a high concentration of people with low incomes and social problems in certain urban areas leads to larger problems of urban decay. Unfortunately we do not have information about the differences between the countries in this matter.

The general economic and legal conditions for private maintenance and improvement of dwellings have also been a decisive factor. The fundamental economic conditions are not the same in different tenures and vary from country to country. Thus differences in the composition of the housing market and the public regulation of tenure play an important role.

As already discussed in Chapter One and the following chapters, the most problematic sector is private rented housing (with the exception of the UK), both because of the inherent tension between landlords and tenants, but also the lack of financial initiative for landlords to carry out adequate maintenance. Problems in social housing tend to focus on the social and physical aspects of high-rise estates of the 1960s and 1970s as well as lack of maintenance on the older estates. Meanwhile, the situation regarding rehabilitation in owner occupied housing, including flats, has deteriorated (for instance, in the UK), particularly in areas of declining demand or those with a high concentration of low-income residents.

Urban problems have had variable significance depending partly on the composition of the housing stock. As an example it can be seen from Figure 12.2, that some of the countries – Denmark, France and the UK – have a much larger share of old dwellings built before 1945. France and the UK in particular have an old housing stock, while the dwellings in Sweden, Norway and The Netherlands are quite new.

The extent of the problems has also changed over time depending on the general economic development of the country and the public response to the situation. As an example we can look at the development in obsolete housing lacking a bathroom (Figure 12.3). In 1980 in most of the countries less than 10% of the dwellings did not have a bath. Although in The Netherlands and UK there were already very few dwellings without a bath, in three countries – Austria, Denmark and France – more than 15% of the dwellings still lacked a bathroom in 1980. Austria and France achieved quite a large reduction of the problem during the 1980s while Denmark only improved a few dwellings in the period.

So far we have touched on some of the problems in cities and housing which have led governments to implement policies for urban renewal and housing rehabilitation. We now list the main physical and social

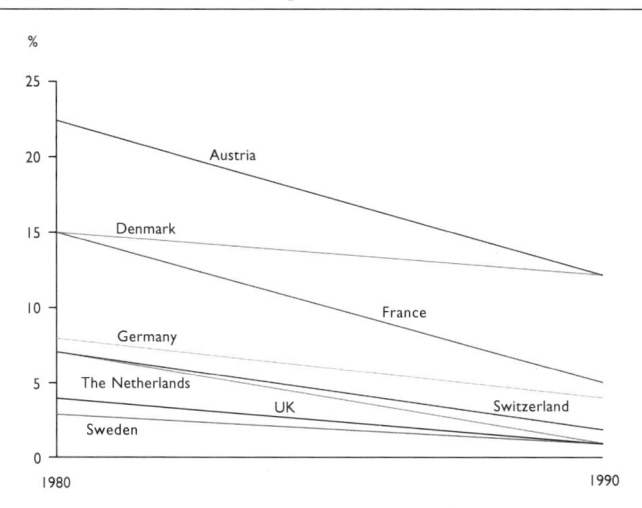

**Figure 12.3: The share of dwellings without a bathroom**

```
%
25

20           Austria

15   Denmark

10                              France
     Germany
 5   The Netherlands
                        UK              Switzerland
     Sweden
 0
    1980                                        1990
```

problems and try to assess their significance in different countries in the period after 1980.

### Threatened destruction of historic buildings and neighbourhoods, largely in old inner-city areas

This is often closely linked with the industrial and commercial development of these areas. In most countries there had been an extensive effort to preserve historical buildings during the 1960s and 1970s so that there is no longer such a pressing need.

### Lack of improvement of obsolete housing from the last century and the beginning of this

As can be seen from Figure 12.3, very obsolete housing is most frequently found in Denmark and Austria and to some extent in France and Germany. These problems are often combined with the following.

## Severe problems of social and physical decay in certain older urban areas in pre-1920s housing

There is a concentration of people with low incomes and social problems combined with unsatisfactory maintenance and deterioration in the housing stock. This has mainly been the case among high-density blocks of flats or row houses with a lack of open space and dwellings with substandard sanitation which have often become seriously run down.

These problems have been found to varying degrees in all the main urban areas in Europe. In Sweden this had been virtually solved by 1970 through extensive slum clearance. As in Switzerland, which also seems to have less significant problems, the older urban areas were not as large as in other countries. The countries with the most extensive renewal needs if this kind after 1980 have been Austria, Denmark, Great Britain, France and The Netherlands. Again the problem was less in Germany, where a large part of such areas were destroyed during the Second World War, and in Norway, where the cities are relatively smaller.

## Less serious problems with social and physical decay in housing from 1920 to 1950

These are usually well-built properties, but either lacking certain basic amenities or in need of modernisation or replacement of standard amenities such as kitchens and sanitary installations. Deterioration is usually not pronounced; but it has accelerated in some areas with a preponderance of residents who expose the dwellings and estates to particularly hard wear and tear. Some countries have not experienced such problems (for example, Switzerland, Sweden).

## The need to restructure economic activity and reorganise the use of land inside cities

This is where the use of former industrial areas has to be transformed to accommodate housing or commercial enterprise. Increasing environmental problems in the cities concerning noise, pollution and traffic have also played their part. This has especially been the case in highly populated and industrialised urban areas in Germany, the UK and The Netherlands, and to some extent also in France, Austria and Switzerland. It has not been so pressing in the Nordic countries.

## Special problems in social housing from the 1960s and 1970s built as large, multi-storey housing estates

These dwellings, typically with good-standard installations but a poor architectural appearance, tend to have serious structural defects for which the remedy will require relatively heavy investment.

The deterioration is often due to the dwellings being less attractive than others in the area. Disadvantaged residents may be referred to this housing causing heavy wear and tear on the buildings. In addition, the repair of structural defects may make the dwellings disproportionately expensive, compounded by a loss of rental income due to a high tenant turnover rate.

All the countries have experienced this kind of problem, but they seem to be have been most serious in France, The Netherlands and the UK, where there has been a high proportion of immigrants. In Norway this was limited to its cooperative postwar multi-family housing; Austria also had fewer problems in this area. In Switzerland there have been similar problems in newer private rented housing and in owner-occupied flats.

## Deterioration of single-family houses in rural fringe areas or those occupied by low-income households

Regions suffering decline typically have a low demand for the poorest dwellings, unless they are attractive as holiday homes. There is also deterioration in owner-occupied housing in urban areas inhabited by people with low incomes who cannot afford to pay for sufficient maintenance.

Deterioration of housing in fringe areas has been a particular problem in mountainous parts of Switzerland, France and Norway. In the UK a large part of the former private rented housing of bad quality has been sold to low-income households who have not been able to keep the buildings in good repair. In Norway and Denmark problems of disrepair are found in some owner occupied flats.

Table 12.1 gives a general view of the assessments of urban renewal and housing rehabilitation problems in the countries as mentioned above. It appears from this that Sweden, Switzerland and, to some extent, Norway had the least problems after 1980, while Austria, Denmark, France, The Netherlands and the UK still had extensive renewal needs.

Of great significance for the choice of urban renewal policies is the extent to which the problems are connected to single properties or to a

Table 12.1: Assessment of the extent of urban renewal and housing rehabilitation problems after 1980

|  | A | CH | D | DK | F | GB | N | NL | S |
|---|---|---|---|---|---|---|---|---|---|
| Destroyed historic building | • | •• | •• | • | • | • |  | • | •• |
| Obsolete dwellings | ••• | • | •• | ••• | ••• | • | •• | • | • |
| Decay areas before 1920 | ••• | • | •• | ••• | ••• | ••• | •• | ••• | • |
| Decay areas 1920-45 | • | • | •• | •• | •• | • | ? | • |  |
| Needs of urban restructuring | •• | •• | ••• | • | •• | ••• | • | ••• | • |
| Deterioration in postwar buildings | • | •• | •• | •• | ••• | ••• | • | ••• | •• |
| Deterioration in owner-occupied stock |  |  |  | •• | • | • | •• | ••• | • | •• |

whole housing area or urban district with many different properties and owners. An urban renewal approach which tackles several properties at once is more appropriate in the case of problems with urban restructuring or when dwellings in a whole area are deteriorating simultaneously. Germany had substantial urban restructuring needs, as did Switzerland, Denmark and, to some extent, Norway had large older housing areas in decay, while Austria, France, The Netherlands and the UK had both kinds of problems. Only Sweden had less need for an area approach to urban renewal in the older parts of the cities once the slum clearance programmes had been completed.

## Objectives of urban renewal and housing rehabilitation policies

It is to be assumed that the design of policies in some way reflects political objectives concerning the purpose of public involvement. In this section we try to identify the main political objectives and interests that drive public intervention in urban renewal and housing rehabilitation in the countries concerned.

As stated earlier it looks as though governments have quite different goals and motives. One reason for this is that political objectives, which affect housing rehabilitation and urban renewal policies in Europe, often originate from other policy areas such as:

- general housing policy;

- general urban economic and social policies;

- energy conservation policies;
- social policies for elderly and handicapped people;
- general health policy.

Another reason for the variation is, as shown above, that the spectrum of problems of decay and inadequate renewal of housing and urban areas has been different in each country, in turn giving relevance to different objectives.

In principle, the objectives appear to concern the following:

- the specific problems, as those described above, which should be eliminated;
- the desired consequences of the renewal: preservation or demolition of buildings and districts, consequences for the residents and for the housing market, changes in the functioning of cities and housing areas;
- the way the renewal processes is to be organised: the role of local authorities, influence for the owners and tenants;
- other consequences: employment in and the use of resources of the building sector, economic development of cities.

As also stated by Priemus and Metselaar (1992), it seems that many of the countries lack a pronounced clarity about the goals of urban renewal. The political objectives are sometimes expressed more or less clearly in official documents or in the political debate. Sometimes they are not expressed explicitly but can be deduced from the way programmes and regulations are formulated.

It has thus been difficult to determine those objectives which have been central to the design of policies in the field. However, we have identified the following:

1. Economic revitalisation of cities and districts leading to better opportunities for industries and other commercial activities.

2. Improvement of the utilisation of urban infrastructure.

3. Better quality of life and environment in the cities.

4. Social renewal of districts with a concentration of social problems.

5. Preservation and enhancement of historic buildings.

6. General improvement of housing standard.
7. Maintenance of a supply of cheaper housing.
8. Transfer of rented dwellings to owner-occupiers or cooperatives.
9. General preservation of older buildings and districts to maintain the character of the cities, instead of demolition and new building.
10. Energy conservation.
11. Better housing for elderly and handicapped people.
12. Guarantee for residents to stay after renewal.
13. Influence for residents on the renewal process.
14. Decentralisation of power to local government.
15. Involvement of the private sector and public–private partnerships.
16. Employment in the building sector.

In Table 12.2 we indicate those objectives which have been of particular importance in different countries. If one compares this with Table 12.1 it appears – as expected – that those countries with special urban restructuring needs also have economic revitalisation of their cities as an important objective (Austria, Germany, France, The Netherlands and the UK). Some have also attached weight to improving the utility of the infrastructure. Similarly, the improvement of the environment and the general quality of life in cities have been of special importance in countries such as Austria, Switzerland and Germany.

One of the objectives emphasised in nearly all countries is to improve conditions in those areas of cities which have a preponderance of social and economic problems. This might apply to the older parts of the cities or to new social housing as in Sweden.

Housing rehabilitation is part of a policy which in general has as its goal the improvement of housing conditions. One way to do this is to improve the existing stock. It must be assumed that this objective has some importance in all the countries concerned, although this has not always been formulated explicitly and it seems that only four countries have done this (Denmark, France, Sweden, the UK). In some countries it has also been of special importance to make dwellings more convenient for elderly and handicapped people (Norway, Sweden).

Table 12.2: Objectives of urban renewal and housing rehabilitation used in the countries

| | A | CH | D | DK | F | GB | N | NL | S |
|---|---|---|---|---|---|---|---|---|---|
| Economic revitalisation | • | • | | | • | • | | • | |
| Infrastructure | • | • | | | | | | | • |
| Quality of life, environment | • | • | • | | | | | • | • |
| Social renewal of district | • | | • | • | • | • | • | • | • |
| Historic buildings | • | • | • | • | • | | | • | |
| Better housing in general | (•) | | (•) | • | • | • | | | • |
| Keeping cheaper housing | • | • | | | | | | | |
| Promote owner-occupation, etc | | | | | | | • | | |
| Preservation not demolition | • | • | • | • | • | ? | • | • | • |
| Energy savings | (•) | • | ? | • | • | ? | • | • | • |
| Provision for elderly and handicapped | | | | (•) | | | • | | • |
| Residents to stay | • | | | • | | | | • | • |
| Influence for residents | • | | | | | • | • | | • |
| Decentralisation to local gov | | | • | • | | | • | • | • |
| Public-private cooperation | | | | | | • | | | |
| Building sector employment | | | • | • | | | | | • |

In Austria and Switzerland it has been a special objective to keep a supply of cheaper dwellings among the older housing stock. In Switzerland the problem has been that much of the old housing stock would have been demolished or transformed for other use if the public had not intervened. In Norway it is a particular goal to give tenants the opportunity to buy their dwelling – often as a part of a cooperative – as part of the rehabilitation process.

In nearly all countries it has been a declared objective since the 1970s to preserve as much as possible of the older housing areas instead of demolishing them and constructing new buildings on the sites. In the UK this has not been a declared national objective, but local authorities have often wished to preserve old housing. At an earlier stage, it had also been a special goal to preserve historic buildings, but this seems to have lost importance in many countries in recent years as stock of the greatest cultural value has been renewed.

A matter of conflict in most countries has been the risk of displacing residents with low incomes from renewed dwellings. It seems that only four countries have explicitly expressed the objective that residents should be able to stay after a rehabilitation programme has been carried out (Austria, Denmark, The Netherlands and Sweden). In the UK a wish to retain existing communities and social networks was a justification for the switch to rehabilitation even if this was not expressed formally in the legislation. It is to some extent these same countries which have emphasised the residents' right to be informed and have a say in the renewal process (Austria, Denmark, Norway, Sweden and the UK).

In some countries it has been a particular intention to shift responsibility for urban renewal from central to local authorities (Austria, Denmark, France, The Netherlands, Norway and Sweden). These are not necessarily countries with a tradition of strong local government (see Table 12.1). Thus this objective does not say anything about the absolute extent of power for local governments, only that the former division of responsibilities should be changed. In the UK it has been a special objective to involve the private sector in urban restructuring through private–public partnerships.

Finally it has been a prime consideration for the willingness of governments to provide subsidies for urban renewal in Switzerland, Denmark and Sweden that the process will reduce unemployment in the building sector and keep up building capacity in times of depression. This is particularly true of those countries which had a turbulent economy in the 1980s (see Table 12.1).

## National strategies and policies

A national strategy for urban renewal and housing rehabilitation can be defined as a set of policies with the combined aim of preventing the physical surroundings in our cities and dwellings from severe dilapidation and obsolescence. In principle such a strategy can comprise policies which are either preventative or curative. The preventative policies aim at supporting running maintenance, improvement and renewal of dwellings and urban structures, made by private actors, to forestall urban decay. The curative policies are put into work when the preventative policies have failed and problematic deterioration and obsolescence have occurred in certain dwellings and urban areas.

Looking at the descriptions of the nine countries contained in this book it is striking that none of them seem to have developed a complete national strategy and that it is mostly the preventative policies that are missing. The different regulations and programmes put into use have generally been aimed at curing specific cases of deterioration and obsolescence, while few policies exist with the purpose of facilitating maintenance and improvement activities without public support in different tenures.

A possible explanation is that the awareness of and knowledge about the fundamental causes of urban decay and housing deterioration in a market-led society (see Skifter Andersen, 1995a) has not been sufficiently extensive to provide a basis for the formulation of preventative policies. Policy makers have taken note of the problems and done something about them, but often the needs of renewal, for example in housing from the last century, has been seen as a finite and limited project that solved the problems once and for all. Sometimes there has been an awareness of specific causes of increased deterioration – for example, rent control which limits incentives for landlords – but for other political reasons it has not been possible to do anything about it.

Important to the design of policies and the instruments chosen is the weight attached to broader urban problems and the extent to which housing deterioration and obsolescence are seen as part of general social and economic processes in geographical defined urban areas. The main question is whether it is feasible to renew individual buildings in urban areas with large social and economic problems or if the problems in an area have to be tackled simultaneously in order to stop deterioration. In the latter case urban renewal projects have to comprise a whole urban area and housing rehabilitation has to be combined with physical, social and economic measures for the whole neighbourhood.

In some countries such problems of urban decay have been treated in an unusual way for societies based on a market economy. Urban renewal has in these cases contained elements of a planned economy, where it has been delegated to public authorities to initiate, plan and carry through the renewal. This kind of practice usually involves two important features. The first is that it requires instruments to either force private owners to assist in the renewal or to make it possible to acquire the property under compulsory order. The second is that the use of such powers often requires heavy economic compensation for the owners as well as large subsidies. In such countries, powers to compel owners to renovate buildings appear in legislation on eliminating security and health problems in buildings and sometimes local authorities can formally order the maintenance of deteriorated buildings. These powers, however, seldom seem to be used in practice.

In other countries the merits of using compulsory orders has not been recognised and policies have instead been based on voluntary participation by the owners, using different types of incentives such as subsidies. In theory, this approach should cost less as only those owners who are sufficiently motivated will participate. In order to achieve the coordinated renewal of a whole neighbourhood, however, larger subsidies are likely to be needed in order to obtain voluntary participation from those residents with low incomes in the most problematic housing. Ironically this might well amount to more than the cost of compulsory participation.

A way out of these problems and a method of making urban renewal programmes cheaper for the public is to direct support towards selected dwellings or groups of the population. Typically there are different programmes or rules for different tenures, but there could also be targeting of dwellings in special parts of the country, in selected cities or in selected areas inside cities. The age and quality of buildings are normally used as criteria for support. In some countries public support does not depend on the residents or owners of the concerned property. In others there is a means test concerning, for example, income, age or physical condition of the residents or owners.

At the Danish Building Research Institute we have earlier, in connection with comparative studies of urban renewal policies in the Nordic countries and in Germany (Hansen and Skifter Andersen, 1993; Skifter Andersen, 1992), identified three main types of public regulation of urban renewal and housing rehabilitation. The difference between these categories concerns to what extent the policies are preventative or curative and whether compulsory orders are used by public authorities to force owners to participate.

## Types of public regulation

### Regulation of tenure

In this case, the authorities establish a general regulatory framework for the properties, their maintenance and improvement, with no direct involvement in the actual renovation work. The purpose is to prevent dilapidation and obsolescence. This form of regulation could, for example, be embodied in tax legislation, rent acts, building codes, finance conditions relating to loans for renovation, rules for the organisation of social housing, owner occupied flats, and so on.

A strategy based on regulation of tenure leaves any decisions to renovate the property and the content of the renovation to be taken by the individual property owner. Where government subsidies are involved, these are normally given indirectly in the form of general housing allowances or tax deductions.

**Indirect regulation**

Here the authorities try to make it more attractive for owners to renovate their properties and to preserve them instead of demolishing them. This is usually done by way of subsidies, but may also take the form of advisory services delivered by local authorities or special agencies, general improvement of the environment – for example, better open areas – or restrictions on exploitation of the area so that demolition is no longer a viable option. This kind of regulation can have a preventative purpose, but is mostly used to cure problems which have become or are going to be urgent even if they are seldom the most heavy and complex problems of decay. Although the decision to renovate is taken by the owner, the authorities may demand that the renovation has a specific content or extent in order to be eligible for a subsidy.

**Direct regulation**

Here the authorities may directly order the renovation of a property or a district. In this form of regulation the authorities – normally represented by local government – can, in principle, compel the owners to renovate, having the following instruments at their disposal: expropriation, orders, restrictions on use, and preemptions. Direct regulation often features subsidies that make compulsory action more acceptable to the owner. It is normally the authorities who take the initiative. This form of regulation is used to cure heavy and complex problems of housing deterioration and urban decay.

**Regulation of tenure – preventive policies**

In our earlier comparative studies of urban renewal strategies in different countries at the Danish Building Research Institute (Hansen and Skifter Andersen, 1993; Skifter Andersen, 1992) we have observed a number of measures which governments could take to improve general conditions for maintenance and improvement of housing. Some of these measures are a part of the housing policy; some are included in tax policies or general monetary policies. Mostly objectives for improving housing quality are not central to these policies and sometimes they even directly impede housing rehabilitation, for example, rent control.

The most important measures to look at are:

- Building codes: to what extent do they demand a certain building quality and what powers do they give public authorities to compel owners to keep their properties in repair?

- Provision of loans for renewal: what kind of security is demanded for cheaper real estate loans, especially if there are problems in owner-occupied flats or shared ownerships?

- Tax rules: rules for deduction of interest on loans for renewal in owner-occupied housing, deductions for maintenance expenditure, depreciations on investments in improvement.

- Rules for the organisation of owner occupied flats or shared ownership in terms of decisions about maintenance and improvement and the distribution of costs among residents.

- Rules for administration of social housing, that is, for collection of funds from rents for future rehabilitation, for taking decisions on maintenance and renewal and tenants' rights to change their dwelling.

- Regulation of private rented housing, ie, rent control that impedes or allows rent increases in connection with improvements, gives incentives for maintenance or to secure appropriate savings. This also includes rules for tenants' rights to improve their dwelling.

- Demands on housing quality as a condition for conversion of private rented dwellings into owner-occupied flats.

- General housing allowances which reduce the increase in housing costs in connection with improvements.

The chapters in this book only give limited data on these measures. More detailed information is available from the studies of Germany and the Nordic countries made at the Danish Building Research Institute and from other general sources of housing policy.

In general it does not seem that any country has tried to formulate a comprehensive policy to prevent housing deterioration by a coordination of the above named measures. But in some countries the effects of maintenance and improvement have been taken into account through different pieces of legislation.

All countries have building legislation which requires a certain standard of building quality for safety reasons. Often this legislation is only of limited importance, because the authorities seldom want to use force against private owners without economic compensation and only take action in the most severe cases.

Tax rules are also of importance to the economic conditions surrounding housing rehabilitation. As mentioned earlier, interest on loans for improvements in owner occupied housing can usually be deducted from the taxable income of owners. In the UK and France there are certain ceilings on how much can be deducted; on the other hand there is no taxation on imputed rental income as in the other countries. In Germany there is no deduction of interest, but the investment can be written off for depreciation, and the depreciation rates are most favourable in the first years (normally 5%, by energy-saving investments 10%). In none of the countries can owners deduct expenses for maintenance. Tax benefits in Germany and in France are to some extent means tested and families with children get higher tax reductions.

In private rented housing, landlords can deduct expenses for maintenance, but these are normally outweighed by taxation of the rental income which is required to cover the expenses. In Germany, and to some extent in Sweden, all building investments can be written off, which has been of great importance especially in Germany. In Denmark only depreciation on investments in certain installations are allowed.

In the cooperative sectors it is normally not possible to deduct interest, an exception being Norway, where expenses for maintenance can also be deducted.

In all housing, except owner-occupied one-family houses, several parties are involved in the decision of and payment for housing rehabilitation. Rules for how these parties take decisions and share the costs are often of great importance to renovation activity in different tenures.

In owner-occupied flats and in cooperatives there is a question of the size of majority necessary to make a decision on rehabilitation of common parts of the building. If this is set too high, decision making becomes impractical. This seems to have been a problem in Norway, for example, where a majority of two thirds is demanded. The method of obtaining security against losses from missing payments from residents also becomes important.

The situation with multiple-ownership buildings is made more difficult where different tenures are involved, which is especially the case where rented dwellings are converted to owner-occupied flats, and there are conflicting interests between the different parties.

In private rented housing there have been problems caused by rent legislation or other legislation regulating this tenure. Here the objective of promoting housing rehabilitation has often been in conflict with other interests, especially the protection of tenants.

In general it is essential that landlords have sufficient incentive to maintain their properties and to invest in improvements. The type and strength of the applied rent control is of fundamental importance in this regard. The most restrictive system is where rents can only be increased a certain amount per year as fixed by the government. Such a system applies in The Netherlands, in two of the largest cities in Norway, in the older housing stock in France and in parts of the stock in Austria (see Wiktorin, 1993; Skifter Andersen, 1995c). Denmark has a special system, where rents are determined by the cost of operating each property plus a fixed capital yield. A less rigorous approach is when the tenants can complain of a rent increase fixed to landlord and then a tribunal or court which can reduce the rent if it exceeds a level calculated in accordance with certain rules. Here it is of importance the extent to which rents determined by these rules deviate from market rents. It appears that the rents fixed by such a system are most different from market values in Sweden, in French dwellings built before 1948 and in English dwellings rented before 1988. Less so are rents in Norway outside the two cities, in new tenancies in France and parts of Austria and in continuing tenancies in Germany. For new tenancies in Germany and for all tenancies in Switzerland and in the UK entered into after 1989, there are no restrictions on rents.

According to these criteria, it seems that the incentives for landlords to invest are best in Switzerland, Germany and the UK, followed by Norway and the majority of the French sector. The most restrictive systems are found to be in The Netherlands, in parts of the Austrian, French and British housing stock, followed by Denmark and Sweden.

It does help, however, if the rent control system makes it possible for landlords to increase rents in order to pay for expenses for maintenance and improvements. In Norway, landlords can – within certain limits –

collect a higher rent to cover expenses for greater maintenance works. In France, tenants with special contracts pay directly for maintenance. In Denmark, it is a part of rent setting rules to collect a certain amount per square metre which is transferred to a maintenance account for the property. This arrangement secures savings for maintenance and at the same time gives landlords incentives to use the money for maintenance. Most of these countries with rigorous rent control systems also have rules for increasing rents after improvements. In France and Denmark, contributions from rents are paid into a central fund from which landlords can obtain subsidies and cheap loans for rehabilitation, that is, a kind of collective savings system.

Sometimes residents want to improve their dwellings and the landlords do not want to assist, in which case rights for tenants to carry out improvements could be of importance. Such rights are to be found in Denmark, Austria and Germany, with rules as to when tenants can decide to make improvements and how big a share of the investment will be refunded to them on moving out.

The main problem in social housing is to ensure savings for future maintenance work. This can partly be done in each housing association or by collective savings in a fund, such as the system in Denmark. Not much is known about these rules in the different countries, but it seems to be a common problem that many newer social housing estates from the 1960s and 1970s have not collected enough resources to solve their maintenance problems.

*Direct and indirect regulation – curative policies*

Direct regulation is often connected with an area approach to urban renewal and housing rehabilitation, but there are also examples of direct regulation in programmes for renovation of single properties. Indirect regulation of housing rehabilitation is mostly used in connection with single properties, but in some countries area renewal is also based on indirect regulation with no compulsory measures.

Table 12.3 gives an overview of the main differences between the urban renewal strategies in the nine countries. The main characteristics of these strategies are as follows:

- Do combined programmes for urban revitalisation/restructuring and housing rehabilitation exist or are these tasks divided between different programmes?

- Are housing rehabilitation programmes directed towards areas or single properties?
- Are programmes directed towards special building works?
- Is housing rehabilitation regulated directly or indirectly?
- To what extend are the programmes directed or limited to certain dwellings, tenures or geographical areas?
- To what extent is public financial support limited to certain parts of the population, for example, means tested?

In four countries (Austria, Germany, The Netherlands and the UK) programmes of housing area renewal have been integrated into broader programmes of urban restructuring/revitalisation. These are four of the five countries which attach special importance to economic revitalisation of cities in their objectives for urban renewal as shown in Table 12.2. Only the last of the three countries, France, has chosen to establish

Table 12.3: Characteristics of urban renewal strategies

|  | A | CH | D | DK | F | GB | N | NL | S |
|---|---|---|---|---|---|---|---|---|---|
| **Types of programmes** | | | | | | | | | |
| Combined programmes | (D) I |  | D |  |  | I | (D) | D? | |
| Separate urban restoration/rev pr |  |  |  |  | • | • |  |  | |
| Separate housing renovation |  |  |  | D | I | I | D |  | |
| Programmes for single properties | I | I | (I) | I | I | (D) I | D I | I? | (D) I |
| Programmes for special works | I |  |  | (I) | I | I | (I) |  | I |
| **Programmes for selected dwellings** | | | | | | | | | |
| Tenures |  |  |  | NS? | NS | O,P, S,NS | O,P, S,NS | P, NS | O,P, S |
| Geographically selected |  |  | • |  |  |  | • | (•) | |
| Building age quality | • | • | ? | • | • | • | • | • | |
| **Means-tested programmes** | | | | | | | | | |
| Income |  |  |  | • |  | • | • | • | |
| Other means test |  |  |  |  |  | • | • | • | • |

Note: Regulations: D=direct; I=indirect regulation; Tenures: O=owner occupied; P=private rented; S=social housing in general; NS=newer social housing estates.

separate programmes for urban restructuring and for housing area renewal. The UK has both combined and separate programmes.

In Norway the focus has been on housing renewal, but the area renewal programme also has elements of a broader urban renewal. Denmark has only used a separate housing area renewal programme and there are no special government programmes for urban restructuring and revitalisation — a task which has been completely in the hands of local government. Finally it appears that Sweden and Switzerland never had any government programmes for urban area renewal or for housing or urban restructuring. In Sweden, however, local authorities have been equipped with strong legal instruments within planning and other legislation to carry through area renewal, and there has been easy access to subsidies from the general housing finance system.

In most countries the prepared legislation for area renewal has provided local authorities with instruments for direct regulation such as powers to compel owners to renovate or sell their properties. Only in the UK and France area renewal has not been equipped with such powers. In the UK, however, local authorities have quite strong powers through other legislation to compel private landlords to make their properties fit for habitation.

Programmes for renovation and improvement of single properties, inside or outside defined renewal areas, are found in all countries — not at the national level in Germany and Austria but in some of the *Länder* and cities. In nearly all countries these programmes are framed as indirect regulation, which means that the participation of owners is always voluntary. In Norway the special legislation on housing rehabilitation also allows local authorities to compel owners outside renewal areas to renovate, but it is seldom used. Similarly to the UK, local authorities in Sweden have strong powers to force through renovation by use of planning legislation.

In most of the countries there are either special programmes directed towards individual properties for support to special building works or the general programmes have limitations on which works can get public support. The UK in particular has developed a wide range of such programmes such as so-called 'Enveloping' or 'Group Repair Schemes', which aim at repairing fundamental structural problems of the buildings like roofs and walls. Other special grants are given for all work bringing the dwellings up to a certain standard of fitness for human habitation or to make them suitable for handicapped people. Such programmes are also found in Norway and Sweden. In Austria special grants exist for the basic improvement of amenities or for other improvements. In France one programme only supports improvements; another is only for basic repairs. Denmark has also got a new scheme for housing rehabilitation limited to a set of fixed building works.

## Prioritising policies

As shown in the section above, problems of housing deterioration and obsolescence differ in different parts of the housing stock and from country to country. Obviously the problems and need for public support are not equal in all dwellings even if they were built simultaneously. In the cases where differences are systematic, it is necessary to have different programmes and regulations for different dwellings. Table 12.3 indicates those countries in which separate housing rehabilitation programmes for different tenures are found.

France and the UK have developed the most differentiated systems with separate programmes for owner-occupied dwellings, for private rented housing and for social housing in general. Moreover, as in several other countries, they have a special programme for newer social housing estates with problems. In The Netherlands there are also special rules for each of the tenures within the general urban renewal legislation. In other countries, programmes for housing rehabilitation usually include all tenures and rules for public support do not differ. The exceptions are that of Denmark and Norway which have both had special programmes for new social housing. Norway also had special support for private rented dwellings in multi-family houses; Denmark has a form of special indirect regulation which does not include owner occupied housing.

An order of priority can also be made by a geographical selection of dwellings. This is found in Switzerland, which had a special programme for housing in mountainous regions. In Norway the funds for area renewal are limited to the three largest cities. In The Netherlands, funds are distributed between municipalities in accordance with a 'urban renewal key', which is calculated on the basis of statistics on the size and properties of the municipalities. Such a system has also been used in Denmark, but only as guidance, as the distribution of money between local authorities is based on applications for funds.

In most of the countries there are also fixed rules which limit the supportable part of the housing stock by criteria of quality or age of the buildings.

Another way of prioritising programmes is to use a means test to direct public subsidies to people who have special needs or who are not able to pay for rehabilitation by themselves. In the UK all support for housing rehabilitation is means tested (except in new social housing estates) by fixed income limits for residents or landlords. In France there are smaller subsidies for households with lower incomes in owner-occupied housing. In Norway there are income limits for recipients of support for housing rehabilitation.

In all three countries, and in Sweden, there are also special programmes or rules which aim at improving dwellings inhabited by elderly or handicapped people. In Denmark this is made through social security programmes rather than legislation.

As it appears from the above examination some countries have chosen a strategy based on a centrally fixed order of priority, evident through a complex system of programmes aimed at specific building works in dwellings in certain parts of the housing stock inhabited by special people with low income or with special needs. This could be called a *strategy of strong central priorities*. The UK in particular has followed this strategy, but also France and to some extent The Netherlands and Norway. Two reasons for this strategy can be identified. One is a general wish to reduce public involvement and use of resources by trying to make subsidies as focused as possible, as has been the case in the UK and Norway. The other reason could be that in not wanting to surrender the power to make priorities to local authorities, some governments make detailed rules about the use of subsidies. This is a possibility in France, The Netherlands and the UK, where local government traditionally has a weak position.

The other five countries can be divided into two groups. The first consists of Austria, Denmark and Sweden, where, to some extent, housing is seen as a public good and there is a tradition of strong public involvement. This tradition is manifested through programmes for housing rehabilitation which are directed at a broad part of the housing stock and of the population, with few special priorities or means tests, that is, a *strategy of general housing improvement*. It is also the case in these countries that more powers are handed over to local government.

The last group consists of Switzerland and Germany. There housing is regarded more as a private good and the role of the public sector is limited to special social and physical problems. The focus is more on making the market work by regulating (or by abstaining from regulation) the form of tenure and by tax incentives (Germany) to prevent housing deterioration. Thus the total public involvement in urban renewal through direct and indirect regulation is limited. The present programmes are quite general but it is left to local authorities to prioritise distribution of limited resources to the buildings and people most in need. This could be called a *strategy of limited public involvement*.

## Evaluation of national strategies

Urban renewal and housing rehabilitation policies are complicated public interventions in urban and housing systems which are also influenced by the general social and economic forces in each country. It is therefore not an easy task to evaluate the concrete performance of the strategies performed in each country and it is even more difficult to compare them. In the following evaluation, three different points of view are used. Firstly, we look at the physical results of the national policies as they can be observed in the actual quality of cities and housing and in remaining problems of urban decay, housing deterioration and obsolescence. Secondly, we analyse the policy instruments used in the different countries in the light of their expected economic efficiency and social consequences. Thirdly, we summarise the internal critique formulated in each country regarding the policy in operation.

As was shown in the above section, there are large differences between the countries concerning remaining problems of urban decay and housing deterioration. Some of these are due to general conditions in the countries outside the reach of urban renewal policies, for example, the degree of urbanisation, general economic conditions, housing policy, and so on. But it is also possible to connect some of the problems with the choice of national strategy for urban renewal and housing rehabilitation. Differences in the needs of urban restructuring and in problems of newer social housing estates can mainly be assigned to differences in external conditions. Problems of obsolete and deteriorated housing in the older stock are much more a result of faulty preventative or curative housing rehabilitation policies as defined above.

In five countries (Austria, Denmark, France, The Netherlands and the UK) we found larger problems in the older housing stock; in three of them (Austria, Denmark and France) there were also many obsolete dwellings, for example, dwellings lacking a bathroom. In most of the countries (all except the UK), the bulk of problems are found in private rented housing subject to regulation that has increased deterioration and hampered improvement. In these countries the preventative policies achieved through regulation of tenure seem to have been absent or have failed. In the UK, most deteriorated dwellings are found in owner-occupied housing, the main causes of which are social inequality, segregation and a defective social housing policy. If we look at the curative policies it looks as though the Dutch, French and Austrian programmes have had the strongest effect, while the Danish and UK strategies have not been so successful.

Norway has also had problems in private rented housing due to inadequate regulation, but the extent of the problems are much smaller than in the above mentioned countries. The curative policies seem to have been quite effective during the 1980s, at least in the first half of the decade.

Among the remaining three countries, Sweden and Switzerland seem to have reached the highest housing quality but with quite opposite strategies. In Switzerland, the strategy has been to limit public involvement, and the preventative policies, if that is what they are, seem to be successful. However, housing renewal in Switzerland has been favoured by a very low interest rate and an easy access to capital. In Sweden there has been an extensive and costly public involvement and only in a few cases have houses been rehabilitated more extensively without public support.

In Germany, also, the market has created good conditions for housing rehabilitation. This is partly due to favourable economic conditions (low interest rates and favourable tax depreciation) but also because of effective regulation of private rented housing. The remaining problems in the older housing stock in Germany are mainly related to the needs of restructuring of the big industrial cities and some of their housing areas. It seems that, until recently, the German urban renewal programme has been quite slow working.

The strength of housing rehabilitation programmes can be due to whether governments have used a large amount of money to support the activity, as has been the case in Sweden. It can also be due, however, to the economic effectiveness of the regulations in terms of the private investment generated.

It is obvious that those regulations which are the most economically effective are those based on indirect regulation where only the most motivated property owners voluntarily apply for subsidies and where they are also more willing to invest their own money. In contrast, direct regulation means that some of the owners have to be compelled to carry out renovation and experience tells us that politicians and local authorities in Western European countries seldom want to do this without substantial compensation. It is more difficult to generate private investment in relation to direct regulation and the economic efficiency is lower, partly because there are more administrative and planning procedures involved. However, some countries cannot do without direct regulation because they have districts in their cities with a high concentration of social and physical problems needing attention. It is difficult to achieve renewal in such areas when some of the property owners can refuse to participate. In most cases it is also difficult to activate owners of the poorest part of the housing stock through programmes of indirect regulation and it is not sometimes possible to avoid the use of direct regulation.

Economically efficient ways of organising public support for housing rehabilitation also come into conflict with some of the objectives for urban renewal. If an extensive rehabilitation programme is carried out with a low share of public subsidy it usually means that rents or housing costs will be raised considerably and residents with low incomes will be expelled and replaced with more well-to-do people, that is, 'gentrification' will take place. In countries where an objective of allowing residents to stay in their dwellings has been formulated, this has forced governments maintain a level of subsidy that is probably higher than absolutely necessary just to carry through renovation of the properties in a way that makes them competitive on the open market.

Another way of making programmes more economically efficient is through means tests; that is, the targeting of subsidies towards dwellings or people in most need where rehabilitation without public economic support seldom takes place. A variant of this is to direct the support at repair works which are most often neglected. In this way the unnecessary subsidy of self-reliant housing rehabilitation is avoided.

However, means tests can impose problems, especially in cases where area renewal is needed. It is more difficult to get all the property owners in an area or all residents in a tenement to accept renewal when some of them only get minimal support (see, for example, the English experience of block renewal schemes).

Finally, it can make urban renewal more efficient if responsibility for and control of programmes are decentralised to local government. Local authorities are able to direct the support towards those urban areas and parts of the housing stock where they are most needed and can better judge which level of subsidy is necessary in each case. This presupposes, however, that local authorities have incentives to economise on resources, which will only be the case if they have to finance a share of the public expenses. Otherwise they will be happy to spend state money.

## Comparing strategies in operation

Having divided the country strategies into three main groups – a strategy of general housing improvement; a strategy of strong central priorities; a strategy of limited public involvement – we now attempt to draw some conclusions from the performance of strategies.

### Strategies of general housing improvement

In the countries in the first group – Austria, Denmark and Sweden – the lack of, or minor importance of, means tests and other ways of directing limited resources results in a relatively high subsidy and the support of some activity which, strictly speaking, does not need public support. The economic efficiency of these systems are greater, however, if the local authorities are strongly motivated to economise on resources.

In Denmark and Austria a strong preference for area renewal has been one of the reasons why these countries have chosen to use direct regulation, which also tends to be more expensive. Moreover, all three countries have given a strong priority to the protection of sitting residents, which implies relatively high subsidies to keep down rent increases. The problem of this strategy has been that the renewal activity has been too restricted because of limited resources and there is still a considerable amount to be tackled. These countries, have, in recent years, implemented some new programmes based on indirect regulation in single properties to attract more private investment and speed up the renewal activity.

In Sweden the main problems were solved years ago with the help of significant public support. However, there is concern that the system has encouraged renovation work which is more extensive than necessary and has not always reflected the architectural values of older buildings. Moreover, the easy access to subsidies has prevented landlords from carrying out maintenance themselves because it has worked in their favour to let the properties deteriorate and then have them repaired more thoroughly with help from public money. In recent years Sweden has begun to cut down on subsidies. However, it has been done in such a way that it has created serious uncertainty among investors because the conditions for renewal have been changed several times without any warning.

**Strategy of strong central priorities**

The second group of countries – France, Norway, The Netherlands and the UK – have developed complex systems with many different programmes directed towards different parts of the housing stock. In France, Norway and the UK there has been a widespread use of indirect regulation using means tests resulting in a more economical use of public resources but also making it more difficult to carry through area renewal.

Norway also has a separate programme with direct regulation for area renewal but with limited resources. The economic effectiveness of the programme was originally based on the idea that increasing property prices made it possible to buy the estates more cheaply compared to when renewal was finished. However, the fall in property prices in the late 1980s meant a crisis of this system and a sharp decline in activities. The high price of renewed dwellings has made it difficult to sell them to the residents – an objective of the Norwegian system – and the high housing costs have prevented new owners from carrying through adequate maintenance in the following years which means that new problems of deterioration can be expected. Thus the relatively low level of subsidies for area renewal in the Norwegian programme has created new problems and resulted in the displacement of residents.

UK urban renewal has also been hampered by a shortage of public resources. This has prompted local authorities to try to limit the demand for grants through various measures and has prevented local authorities from actively surveying their areas to identify unfit dwellings. The extensive means tests and complex rehabilitation schemes in England seem to make it difficult for local authorities to fulfil a rational strategy for the renewal of cities. The rules for means tests sometimes lead to a situation where some property owners in need are prevented from getting support either because they cannot pay their part of the expenses or because the test of resources compares income to a notional set of allowances rather than actual outgoings.

In France the sole use of indirect regulation may imply a relatively high economic efficiency, with a quite centralised system and local authorities only a limited influence from local authorities. However, this must have made it difficult for local government to direct resources towards properties in most need and to carry through area renewal. There has also been a tendency for the renewal to result in a rent level which has been too high for residents with lower incomes leading to an exclusion of these groups.

The Dutch strategy seems to be something of a cross between the English/French strategies and the systems used in Denmark and Austria. Direct regulation is possible in the urban renewal legislation, but at the same time there are special subsidy programmes for different tenures which make it possible to differentiate subsidy and thus involve more private resources. As in Denmark there is a combination of central and local responsibilities which involves local authorities in the use of resources and makes it possible for them to carry through a rational and planned renewal of cities. There does not seem to have been a lack of public resources involved. It has been a policy objective to allow residents to stay in their dwellings but it is not known to what extent this goal has been fulfilled. The political objective is to reduce the level of subsidies by involving more private capital in urban renewal.

**Strategy of limited public involvement**

This leaves the two countries with limited direct public involvement in urban renewal and housing rehabilitation – Germany and Switzerland. The problems of housing deterioration have for reasons described above been limited in these countries and the needs of direct or indirect public regulation have thus been smaller.

Some of the *Länder* in West Germany still have their own housing rehabilitation programmes using indirect regulation which are quite economically effective but do not always reach the worst part of the housing stock. The German urban renewal law implies direct regulation and concerns some of the urban areas where renewal is most needed but affects only a relatively small number of dwellings. It is the local authorities which in every case decide the amount of subsidies given to a renovation project, with the public only paying that part of the expenses which could not be covered by an increase in the market value of the property. In principle this system implies a minimum of public expense, but this is dependant on whether the authorities are able to make a correct judgement of the necessary public support. The German urban renewal law also requires that a social plan is worked out for the renewal areas, but it is the responsibility of the local government to finance this plan and pay allowances for tenants. The social consequences for the tenants therefore vary between municipalities depending on local government policy. In general the liberal rent control in Germany has led to relatively high housing costs for low-income tenants (see Skifter Andersen and Munk, 1994).

Switzerland has implemented the most market-oriented system with very little public involvement and a high degree of decentralisation. One of the objectives was to keep some of the older and cheaper rental dwellings in the older housing stock, but it does not seem that this has been achieved. In general, rents and housing costs are relatively high in Switzerland in spite of a low interest rate and small capital costs.

## Lessons for UK housing renewal policy

This book is not, of course, intended for exclusive consumption by a UK-based readership and it is hoped that the material will be of interest to policy makers and academics from many countries within Europe and elsewhere. However, some useful conclusions can briefly be drawn which are of relevance to UK policy makers and academics in the context of current debates on housing and urban renewal policy.

The preceding chapters illustrate the wide range of national and local housing and urban renewal problems which are to be addressed in different countries. It is clear from this that problems can arise in widely differing segments of the housing stock, in different tenures, and for different types of occupant. For example, poor housing conditions are not restricted to the privately rented sector but may also be found in social rented housing and in the owner-occupied stock. Owner-occupation may be thought of in some countries as a relatively unproblematic tenure but, as more low-income households become owners and as the age of the owner-occupied dwelling stock increases, problems of physical decay may be anticipated. The recent focus within the UK on the regeneration of social rented housing areas risks failure if it ignores the problems found in areas of private housing often adjacent to these areas and closely linked to them in social and economic terms.

Problems may affect many different types of household, but those on low incomes are most at risk. In the social rented sector, where housing is in theory allocated on the basis of need, it is not clear why the link between poor housing and low incomes persists. Differences in the types of housing allocated to people seeking housing through different routes might be significant, however, as might rent differentials. There is a tendency to underestimate the problems of physical condition in social rented housing and to lay emphasis on broader social problems as more significant influences on the quality of life of occupants. However, this overlooks the very substantial levels of investment required either to renovate or to demolish and, if appropriate, rebuild areas of social rented housing which do not provide a satisfactory physical environment for their occupants. Securing the necessary resources for this investment, whether through public or private sources and in ways which retain affordability for tenants, is the challenge which social landlords face in coming years. There are examples in this book of initiatives which could be drawn on.

In the private rented and owner-occupied sectors, those on low incomes experience poor conditions because they cannot afford higher rents, because they can only afford to purchase dwellings in the poorest condition, or because they cannot afford the ongoing costs of maintenance, repair and periodic modernisation. Measures to deliver better conditions will not be effective in the longer term unless they also assist these households to meet the ongoing costs associated with improved conditions, whether this takes the form of increased rent levels or future maintenance costs. Failure to address this problem will result either in changes in the social composition of renewal areas or in a return to poor conditions in the medium and sometimes the short term. In the UK, a narrow focus on physical housing renewal and a failure to look at ongoing assistance with housing costs have led to the decline of previously renovated areas and the need to revisit these areas often after relatively short intervals.

Poor housing conditions may arise in many different locations, including both urban and rural settings and in inner-city and more suburban areas. They are always problematic for the individuals affected and should not be ignored wherever they arise. In the private sector, considerable reliance can be placed on market processes to generate adequate investment in most housing areas, even if this is somewhat cyclical and associated with house purchase and mobility.

However, there are clearly some situations in which market processes do not provide adequate solutions. Concentrations of private housing in poor condition in particular locations pose special problems which have long been recognised in the UK by area-based housing renewal policies. However, the longer-term lesson is that investment in housing renovation is not in itself sufficient to secure the regeneration of run-down neighbourhoods, although it at least has the merit of improving the quality of life for some of those resident in these areas. Although the broader Renewal Area approach to area-based renewal in England and Wales recognises the need for a wider context to housing interventions, it is not clear that this is yet fully integrated into regeneration initiatives.

Areas of pre-1919 housing were referred to in Britain in the 1960s as 'twilight areas' implying that the end of their days was approaching. News of the end in most such areas was exaggerated, however, and many are likely to provide a living environment for a large number of households well into the next millennium. Most inner-city areas of older privately-owned housing have experienced two or three decades of considerable stability and significant investment by both the state (through housing associations and the provision of grants to private owners) and on a major scale by private owners themselves. This stability has in large part been accounted for by the transfer of these areas into owner occupation and the part played by mortgage lenders in the creation of a viable housing market.

However there are now clear warning signs that some inner-city areas can look forward to more rapid neighbourhood decline of the kind which has long been a fact of life in the US. In the UK this phenomenon – reflected in falling property values, high levels of vacancies, incipient abandonment and dereliction and high levels of vandalism – is less familiar, but becoming increasingly significant, especially in northern cities and other areas of low demand including more rural communities based around former mining or manufacturing industries. Dealing with this process, whether through positive action to secure regeneration or through the effective management of decline is emerging as one of the main challenges facing policy makers in the UK.

There are a variety of justifications for state intervention to deal with poor housing conditions. These include the provision of decent housing conditions for all households, the long-term preservation of the housing stock, the prevention of health problems caused by substandard housing, the provision of savings to social care services, and making a contribution to broader regeneration programmes. These all have different implications in terms of the mechanisms required to achieve each objective and the role of the state in doing so.

Two processes of change over time are particularly evident from this book. The first is a shift from direct interventions to secure better conditions such as compulsory high-standard renovation or policies to secure transfers of ownership from private to socially-orientated landlords, often directly mainly at private landlords, towards more hands off and indirect approaches. The latter are intended either to limit negative consequences for tenants, or to adopt the less prescriptive approaches seen as appropriate or politically necessary when dealing with individual owner-occupiers. These shifts have been paralleled by and steered by wider economic pressures to reduce public spending and seek solutions based mainly on private investment, in both public and privately owned stock.

The second process is the recognition that state sponsored housing renewal forms only one part of the broader task of urban regeneration, reflected most obviously in the diversion of resources from general housing renovation programmes into more targeted areas of spending. Again this process has been evident in relation to both spending on the public stock (in the UK the shift of funding from housing estate regeneration to economic and environmental regeneration) and in provision for private sector renovation (as evidenced by the growth in spending on grants to disabled people for adaptations and grants to older people for minor repairs). Effectively, there has been a refinement and narrowing of the state role in housing renewal away from the acceptance of a broad and long-term state responsibility for the housing stock towards a more residual and selective responsibility with interventions designed to assist the poorest households in the most extreme circumstances, often motivated by the potential for cost savings for other programmes such as health and social care. As yet these changes remain little-explored and only partially implemented, but we may expect to see them pursued more explicitly in years to come.

# References

Adams, C.T. (1987) 'The politics of privatization', in B.Turner, J. Kemeny and L.J. Lundqvist (eds) *Between state and market: Housing in the post-industrial era*: Stockholm: Almqvist & Wiksell International.

Ambrose, P. (1992) 'The performance of national housing systems – a three-nation comparison', *Housing Studies*, vol 7, no 3, pp 163-76.

Back, G. and Hamnett, C. (1985) 'State housing policy formation in the UK and the role of housing associations in Britain', *Policy and Practice*, vol 13, no 4, pp 377-98.

Blomberg, I., Schönning, K. and Wikström, K. (1985) 'Ombyggnad' (Renovation), in S.Thiberg (ed) *Bostadsboken*, Stockholm: BFR.

Boelhouwer, P. and van der Heijden, H. (1992) *Housing systems in Europe Part I: A comparative study of housing policy*, Housing and Urban Policy Studies No 1, Delft: Delft University Press.

Bostadsstyrelsen (1969) *Kommunal bostadspolitik* (Municipal housing policy), BOS 1, Stockholm: Bostadsstyrelsen.

Boverket (1992) *Svensk bostadsmarknad in internationell belysning* (The Swedish housing market in international comparison), Report No 2, Karlskrona.

Carlén, G. and Cars, G. (1991) 'Renewal of large-scale post-war housing estates in Sweden: Effects and efficiency', in R. Alterman and G. Cars (eds) *Neighbourhood regeneration: An international evaluation*, London and New York, NY: Mansell.

Cars, G. and Hårsman, B. (1991) 'Housing policy in transition', in A. Fredlund (ed) *Swedish planning in times of transition*, Stockholm: The Swedish Society for Town and Country Planning, pp 52-3.

CBS (Centraal Bureau voor de Statistiek) (1994a) *Nationale rekeningen 1993* (National Accounts 1993), 's-Gravenhage: Centraal Bureau voor de Statistiek, Sdu Uitgeverij.

CBS (1994b) 'Inkomen en vermogen', *Sociaal-economische maandstatistiek* (Socioeconomic monthly statistics), 11 December, 's-Gravenhage: Centraal Bureau voor de Statistiek, Sdu Uitgeverij.

CBS (1995) *Statistisch Jaarboek* (Statistics Yearbook), 's-Gravenhage: Centraal Bureau voor de Statistiek, Sdu Uitgeverij.

Central Statistical Office (1992) *Family spending: Report on the Family Expenditure Survey 1991*, London: HMSO.

CHAC (1966) *Our older homes: A case for action*, Report of the Sub-Committee on Standards of Housing Fitness (Dennington Committee), London: HMSO.

Cullingworth, B. (1968) *A profile on Glasgow housing 1965*, Occasional Paper No 8, Glasgow: Department of Social and Economic Studies, University of Glasgow.

De Vries-Heijnis, G.E. (1990) Wet op de Stads- en Dorpsvernieuwing (Urban and Village Renewal Act), Editie Schuurman en Jordens No 186, Zwolle: W.E.J. Tjeenk Willink.

Dickens, P., Duncan, S., Goodwin, M. and Gray, F. (1985) *Housing, states and localities*, London and New York, NY: Methuen.

Dieleman, F. (1993) 'Social rented housing, valuable asset or unsustainable burden?', Paper presented at the ENHR Conference, 'Housing policy in Europe in 1990s', Budapest, Hungary, September.

DoE (Department of the Environment) (1993) *English House Condition Survey 1991*, London: HMSO.

DoE (1994) *Annual Report 1994*, London: DoE.

Duncan, S. and Barlow, J. (1991) *Marketisation or regulation in housing production? Sweden and the Stockholm-Arlanda growth region in a European perspective*, D 13, Stockholm: Swedish Council for Building Research.

Egerö, B. (1979) *En mösterstad granskas. Bostadsplanering i Örebro 1945-75*, BFR T26, Stockholm: Swedish Council for Building Research.

Ekström, M. (1994) *Residential relocation, urban renewal and the well-being of elderly people: Towards a realist approach*, Comprehensive Summaries of Uppsala Dissertations from the Faculty of Social Sciences No 42, Uppsala: Department of Sociology, University of Uppsala.

Elander, I. (1991) 'Good dwellings for all: the case of social rented housing in Sweden', *Housing Studies*, vol 6, no 1, pp 29-43.

Elander, I. (1994a) 'Paradise lost? Desubsidization and social rented housing in Sweden', in B. Danermark and I. Elander (eds) *Social rented housing in Europe: Policy, tenure and design*, Delft: Delft University Press.

Elander, I. (1994b) 'Policy communities, public housing and area improvement in Sweden', *International Journal of Public Administration*, vol 17, no 5, pp 1789-824.

Elander, I. (1995) 'Policy networks and housing regeneration in England and Sweden', *Urban Studies*, vol 32, no 6, pp 913-34.

Elander, I. and Schéele, A. (1989) 'Evaluating housing renewal policy in Sweden: an interest-oriented approach', *Journal of Urban Affairs*, vol 11, no 4, pp 397-410.

Elander, I. and Strömberg, T. (1992) 'Whatever happened to social democracy and planning? The case of local land and housing policy in Sweden', in L.J. Lundqvist (ed) *Policy, organization, tenure: A comparative history of housing in small welfare states*, Scandinavian Housing and Planning Research Supplement No 2, Oslo and Stockholm: Scandinavian University Press.

Folkesdotter, G. (1981) *Störtas skall det gamla snart i gruset: Bostadssociala utredningens syn på äldre bebyggelse* (Soon the old to the dust will topple), Gävle: Swedish Council for Building Research.

Folkesdotter, G. and Vidén S. (1974) *Stadsomvandling i plan och verklighet*, BFR rapport R53, Stockholm: Swedish Council for Building Research.

Gibb, A. (1983) *Glasgow: The making of a city*, London: Croom Helm.

Gibson, M. and Langstaff, M. (1982) *An introduction to urban renewal*, London: Hutchinson.

Gilbert, J. and Flint, A. (1992) *The tenement owner's handbook*, Edinburgh: Royal Incorporation of Architects in Scotland.

Glendinning, M. and Muthesius, S. (1994) *Tower block: Modern public housing in England, Scotland, Wales and Northern Ireland*, New Haven: Yale University Press.

Gustavsson, S. (1980) 'Housing, building and planning', in L. Lewin and E. Vedung (eds) *Politics as rational action*, Dordrecht: Reidel.

Ham, C. and Hill, M. (1993) 'The policy process and the modern capitalist state', 2nd edn, Hemel Hempstead: Harvester Wheatsheaf.

Hamnett, C. and Randolf, B. (1988) *Cities, housing and profit: Flat break-up and the decline of private renting*, London: Hutchinson.

Hansen, K.E. and Skifter Andersen, H. (1993) *Strategier for regulering av bolig- og byfornyelsen i Norden – en tvaergående sammenligning* (Strategies for regulation of housing and urban renewal in the Nordic countries – a cross national comparison), SBI-meddelelse 99, Hørsholm: Danish Institute for Building Research.

Harloe, M. (1994) 'The social construction of social housing', in B. Danermark and I. Elander (eds) *Social rented housing in Europe: Policy, tenure and design*, Delft: Delft University Press.

Harvie, C. (1981) *No gods and precious few hero's: Scotland 1914-80*, London: Edward Arnold.

Hatje, A.-K. (1978) *Bostadspolitik på förändrade villkor. En studie om den statliga bostadspolitikens mål och medel under 1940- och 1950-talen*, Rapport nr 5, Stockholm: KTH.

Headey, B. (1978) *Housing policy in the developed economy: The United Kingdom, Sweden and the United States*, Andover: Croom Helm.

Heclo, H. and Madsen, H. (1987) *Policy and politics in Sweden: Principled pragmatism*, Philadelphia: Temple University Press.

Hedman, E. (ed) (1992) *Bostadsmarknad i förändring. Årsbok 1992* (Housing market in transition. Yearbook 1992), Karlskrona: Boverket.

Johansson, B. and Ödmann, E. (1974) *Kommunal markpolitik i tre norrlandsstäder 1950-1970*, BFR rapport 24, Stockholm: Swedish Council for Building Research.

Johansson, J. (1994) 'Is there still a Swedish model?', in I. Elander, B. Zhikharevich and A.-C. Wikström (eds) *Local government, housing and urban policy in Russia and Sweden*, Örebro: Centre for Housing and Urban Research, University of Örebro.

Keating, M., Midwinter, A. and Mitchell, J. (1991) *Politics and public policy in Scotland*, London: Macmillan.

Kemeny, J. (1993) 'The significance of Swedish rental policy: cost renting: command economy versus the social market in comparative perspective', *Housing Studies*, vol 8, no 1, pp 3-16.

Kemp, P. (1988) *The private provision of rented housing: Current trends and future prospects*, Aldershot: Avebury.

Kemp, P. and Rhodes, D. (1994) *Private landlords in Scotland*, Research Report No 39, Edinburgh: Scottish Homes.

Khakée, A., Elander I. and Sunesson, S. (eds) *Remaking the welfare state? Swedish urban planning and policymaking in the 1990s*, Aldershot: Avebury.

Kirby, K. and Sopp, L. (1986) *Houses in multiple occupation in England and Wales: Report of a postal survey of local authorities*, London: HMSO.

Kuiper Compagnons (1990) *Voortgang stadsvernieuwing, onderdeel woningverbetering, Arnhem* (Progress in urban renewal, the dwelling improvement component).

Leather, P. and Mackintosh, S. (1994) *Encouraging housing maintenance in the private sector*, Bristol: SAUS Publications.

Lewin, L. (1994) 'The rise and decline of corporatism: the case of Sweden', *European Journal of Political Research*, vol 26, pp 59-79.

Lundqvist, L.J. (1988) 'Corporatist implementation and legitimacy: the case of privatization in Swedish public housing', *Housing Studies*, vol 3, no 3, pp 172-82.

Lundqvist, L.J., Elander, I. and Danermark, B. (1990) 'Housing policy in Sweden - still a success story?', *International Journal of Urban and Regional Research*, vol 14, no 3, pp 468-89.

MacLennan, D. (1985) 'Urban housing rehabilitation: an encouraging British example', *Policy & Politics*, vol 13, no 4, pp 413-29.

Malpass, P. and Murie, A. (1982) *Housing policy and practice*, London: Macmillan.

McCrone, D. (1992) *Understanding Scotland: The sociology of a stateless nation*, London: Routledge.

Merrett, S. (1977) *State housing in Britain*, London: Routledge and Kegan Paul.

MHLG (1969) *People and planning*, Committee on Public Participation in Planning (Skeffington Committee), London: HMSO.

Ministerie van VROM (1981) *Nota over de stads- en dorpsvernieuwing* (Memorandum on Urban and Village Renewal), Tweede Kamer der Staten Generaal, vergaderjaar 1980-1981, kamerstuk 16713, Nos 1 and 2, 's-Gravenhage: Staatsuitgeverij.

Ministerie van VROM (1989) *Nota Volkshuisvesting in de jaren negentig* (Memorandum on Housing in the 1990s), The Hague: Ministerie van Volkshuisvesting, Ruimtelijke Ordening en Milieubeheer.

Ministerie van VROM (1990) *Evaluatienota Stadsvernieuwing jaren '80* (Evaluation Memorandum on Urban Renewal in the 1980s), Ministerie van Volkshuisvesting, Ruimtelijke Ordening en Milieubeheer, Tweede Kamer der Staten Generaal, vergaderjaar 1990-1991, kamerstuk 21894, Nos 1, 2 and 3, 's-Gravenhage: SDU Uitgeverij.

Ministerie van VROM (1992) *Nota Beleid voor stadsvernieuwing in de toekomst* (Memorandum on Future Urban Renewal Policy), Ministerie van Volkshuisvesting, Ruimtelijke Ordening en Milieubeheer, 's-Gravenhage: SDU Uitgeverij.

Ministerie van VROM (1993) *Ontwerpnota Verdeling rijkssteun voor stadsvernieuwing in de toekomst* (Draft Memorandum on Distribution of Government Support for Urban Renewal in the Future), Ministerie van Volkshuisvesting, Ruimtelijke Ordening en Milieubeheer, 's Gravenhage: SDU Uitgeverij.

Ministerie van VROM (1994) *Volkshuisvesting in cijfers 1994* (Housing in figures 1994), The Hague: Ministerie van Volkshuisvesting, Ruimtelijke Ordening en Milieubeheer.

Mitchell, J. (1995) *Strategies for self government*, Edinburgh: Polygon.

Nesslein, T. (1988) 'Housing: the market versus the welfare state model revisited', *Urban Studies*, vol 25, April, pp 95-108.

Nevitt, A. (1966) *Housing, taxation and subsidies*, London: Nelson & Sons.

NIHE (Northern Ireland Housing Executive) (1993) *Northern Ireland House Condition Survey 1991: First report of survey*, Belfast: NIHE.

Niva, M. (1989) *Bostad, politik och marknad: En jämförande studie av bostadspolitiken i efterkrigstidens Sverige och Finland* (Housing, politics and market: a comparative study of housing policy in post-war Sweden and Finland), Avhandling 8, Stockholm: Nordplan.

OECD (Organisation of Economic Cooperation and Development) (1989) *Urban housing markets*, Paris: OECD.

Office of Population Censuses and Statistics (1961) *Household composition tables*, London: HMSO.

Öresjö, E. (1994) *Råslätt: igår, idag, i morgon. En retrospektive studie i ett storskaligt miljonprogramsområde* (Råslätt: yesterday, today, tomorrow. A retrospective study on a large-scale Million Dwellings Programme estate), (unpublished report), Lund: Department of Building Function Analysis, University of Lund.

Papa, O. (1992) *Vergelijkende studie naar volkshuisvestingssystemen in Europa: financiële instrumenten* (Comparative study of housing systems in Europe: financial instruments), DGVH- publikaties No 22, The Hague: Minsiterie van Volkshuisvesting, Ruimtelijke Ordening en Milieubeheer.

Paris, C. and Blackaby, B. (1979) *Not much improvement: Urban renewal policy in Birmingham*, London: Heinemann.

Patton, M.Q. (1984) 'Qualitative methods in the evaluation of legal reforms', in C. Edlund and G. Hermerén (eds) *Evaluation research: Proceedings from the MURA Symposium*, Lund: Studentlitteratur.

Priemus, H. (1990) 'Changes in the social rented sector in the Netherlands and the role of housing policy', Paper presented at the ENHR Conference 'Housing debates and urban challenges', Paris, July.

Priemus, H. and Metselaar, G. (1992) *Urban renewal policy in a European perspective: An international comparative analysis*, Housing and Urban Policy Studies No 5, Delft: Delft University Press.

Priemus, H., Bentvelsen, T., Meijer, F., Spaans, M., Teule, R. and Wassenberg, F. (1991) *Evaluatie van de grote-stadsvernieuwing* (Evaluation of large city renewal), Technisch-Bestuurskundige Verkenningen No 11, Delft: Delft University Press.

Rehn, K. (1990) Unpublished notes based on data collected from three Swedish municipalities, Örebro: Centre for Housing and Urban Research, University of Örebro.

Rhodes, R.A.W. (1986) '"Power dependence": theories of central-local relations: a critical reassessment', in M. Goldsmith (ed) *New research in central–local relations*, Aldershot: Gower.

RIGO (1990) *Stadsvernieuwing in cijfers, het voortgangsrapport Belstato* (Urban renewal in figures, the Belstato progress report), Amsterdam: RIGO Onderzoek en Advies.

Robertson, D. (1985) *Revitalising Glasgow: Glasgow's improvement experience 1964-74*, Discussion Paper No 3, Glasgow: Centre for Housing Research.

Robertson, D. (1988) 'Glasgow rehab: An examination and evaluation of tenement improvement in the City of Glasgow 1964-84', PhD thesis, Glasgow: University of Glasgow.

Robertson, D. (1992) 'Scottish home improvement policy, 1945-75: coming to terms with the tenement', *Urban Studies*, vol 29, no 7, pp 1115-36.

Robertson, D. (1995) 'Scotland's new towns: a modernist experiment in state corporatism', in A. Macinnes, S. Foster and R. MacInnes (eds) *Scottish power centres*, Edinburgh: Cruithne Press.

Robertson, D. and Bailey, N. (1994) *Investment in Scottish housing*, Working Paper, Edinburgh: Scottish Homes.

Robertson, D. and Bailey, N. (1995) *An evaluation of Scotland's housing action areas*, Research Report No 44, Edinburgh: Scottish Homes.

Robinson, P. (1984) 'Tenements: a pre-industrial urban tradition', *Review of Scottish Culture*, no 1, pp 32-64.

Robinson, P. (1986) 'Tenements: an industrial legacy', *Review of Scottish Culture*, no 2, pp 71-83.

Schéele, A., Elander, I. and Rundlöf, B. (1990) *När olika världar mötas: om samordnad boendeservice och områdesförnyelse* (The crossing of two worlds: On coordinated housing services and area improvement, Report No 69, Stockholm: Ministry of Housing.

Schön, L. (1993) '40-årskriser, 20-årskriser och dagens ekonomiska politik' (40-years crises, 20-years crises and current economic policy), *Ekonomisk Debatt*, vol 21, no 1, pp 7-18.

Schubert, K. and Jordan, G. (1992) 'Introduction', *European Journal of Political Research*, vol 21, no 1-2, pp 1-6.

Scottish Homes (1993) *Scottish House Condition Survey 1991: Survey Report*, Edinburgh: Scottish Homes.

Scottish Homes (1995) *Strategic Plan, 1995-98*, Edinburgh: Scottish Homes.

Scottish Office (1988) *Private housing renewal: The government's proposals for Scotland*, Edinburgh: Scottish Office.

Scottish Office (1994) *Statistical bulletin, Housing Series*, HSG/1994/6, Edinburgh: Scottish Office.

SDD (Scottish Development Department) (1980) *Housing Action Areas, First Report*, Edinburgh: SDD.

SDD (1983) *Phased Tenement Improvement Project*, Edinburgh: SDD.

SDD (1986) *Statistical Bulletin – Housing Series*, HSIU No 25, Edinburgh: SDD.

SHAC (Scottish Housing Advisory Committee, Sub-Committee on Unfit Housing) (1967) *Scotland's older houses* (Cullingworth Committee), Edinburgh: HMSO.

Skifter Andersen, H. (1992) 'Regulation of the private rented housing market – some Danish experience', *Scandinavian Housing and Planning Research*, no 9, pp 41-5.

Skifter Andersen, H. (1994) *Den private boligfornyelse i ældre andelsboliger og private udlejningsboliger* (The private housing rehabilitation in older cooperatives and private rented housing), SBI-meddelse No 105, Hørsholm: Danish Building Research Institute.

Skifter Andersen, H. (1995a) 'Explanations of urban decay and renewal in the housing market: what can Europe learn from American research', *Netherlands Journal of Housing and the Built Environment*, vol 10, no 1.

Skifter Andersen, H. (1995b) *Privat byfornyelse - vurdering af en lov med samarbejde mellem udlejer og lejer* (Private renewal - evaluation of a law implying cooperation between landlords and tenants), SBI-rapport No 250, Hørsholm: Danish Building Research Institute.

Skifter Andersen, H. (1995c) *Regulering af private udlejningsboliger i den 'ldre boligmasse i 7 europ'iske lande* (Regulation of private rented housing in the older housing stock in seven European countries), Report for the Danish National Commission on Rent Legislation.

Skifter Andersen, H. and Hansen, K.E. (1994) *A framework for comparative studies of urban renewal and housing rehabilitation policies in Western Europe*, Hørsholm: Danish Building Research Institute.

Skifter Andersen, H. and Munk, A. (1994) 'Comparison and evaluation of housing policies in Denmark and West Germany', *Scandinavian Housing and Planning Research*, vol 11, no 1, pp 1-25.

Skifter Andersen, H., Munk, A. and Hansen, K.E. (1992) *Boligpolitik, socialt boligbyggeri og byfornyelse i Tyskland* (Housing policy, urban renewal and social housing in Germany), Hørsholm: Danish Building Research Institute.

Slootweg, S. (1989) *Stadsvernieuwing onder de 1 promille* (Urban renewal under 0.1%), Serie Bestuurlijk en stedebouwkundig onderzoek No 83, 's-Gravenhage: Ministerie van Volkshuisvesting, Ruimtelijke Ordening en Milieubeheer, Directoraat-Generaal van de Volkshuisvesting.

SOAB (1992) *'n Extra zorg om achterstand* (Extra care for arrears), Gezamenlijke uitgave van 23 grotere stadsvernieuwingsgemeenten, Breda: Onderzoek- en adviesbureau SOAB.

SOU (1945) *Slutbetänkande avgivet av bostadssociala utredningen I* (Government Commission Report), 1945:63.

SOU (1947) *Slutbetänkande avgivet av bostadssociala utredningen II* (Government Commission Report), 1947:26.

Stewart, J. (1986) *The new management of local government*, London: Allen & Unwin.

Stoker, G. (1988) *The politics of local government*, London: Macmillan.

Strömberg,T. (1992) 'The politicization of the housing market: the social democrats and the housing question', in K. Misgeld, K. Molin and K. Åmark (eds) *Creating social democracy: A century of the Social Democratic Labor Party in Sweden*, Pennsylvania: Pennsylvania State University Press.

Teule, R. (1994) 'Social housing, social security and low income groups in The Netherlands', Briefing note presented at the Joseph Rowntree Foundation Seminar on 'Poverty, work incentives and housing costs', York, 18-20 May.

Therborn, G. (1992) 'A unique chapter in the history of democracy: the social democrats in Sweden', in K. Misgeld, K. Molin and K. Åmark (eds) *Creating social democracy: A century of the Social Democratic Labor Party in Sweden*, Pennsylvania: Pennsylvania State University Press.

Thomas, A. and Hedges, A. (1986) *The 1985 physical and social survey of houses in multiple occupation in England and Wales*, London: HMSO.

Thornley, M. (1977) 'Tenement rehabilitation in Glasgow', in R. Darke and R. Walker (eds) *Local government and the public*, London: Leonard Hill.

Trimp, L. (1994) 'Inkomensverdeling 1993', *Sociaal-economische maandstatistiek* (Socioeconomic monthly statistics), 11 December, 's-Gravenhage: Centraal Bureau voor de Statistiek, Sdu Uitgeverij.

Troedson, U. (1989) 'Nya villkor för bostadsförnyelse på 90-talet' (Housing renewal under new conditions in the 1990s), *Plan*, vol 43, no 4, pp 189-91.

van der Heijden, H. (1993) 'Volkshuisvestingsinstituties in Nederland', in H. Rietman and W. Derksen (eds) *Volkshuisvesting vergeleken: recente ontwikkelingen in België en Nederland* (Housing compared: Recent developments in Belgium and The Netherlands), Zwolle:Tjeenk Willink.

van der Schaar, J., m.m.v. A. Hereijgers (1991) *Volkshuisvesting: een zaak van beleid* (Housing: A matter of policy), Utrecht: Uitgeverij Het Spectrum BV.

van Kempen, R.,Teule, R. and van Weesep, J. (1992) 'Urban policy, housing policy and the demise of the Dutch welfare state', *Tijdschrift voor Economische en Sociale Geografie*, vol 83, no 4, pp 317-29.

van Weesep, J. and van Kempen, R. (1993) 'Low income and housing in the Dutch welfare state', in G. Hallett (ed) *The new housing shortage*, London.

Vidén, S. (1993) 'Housing renewal – with care?', in R. Froessler (ed) *From policy to practice: International perspectives on housing and social renewal*, Dortmund: AGB.

Vidén, S. (1994) *Stadsförnyelse och bostadsombyggnad* (Urban renewal and housing renovation), Stockholm: Kungl, Tekniska Högskolan.

Vidén, S. and Lundahl, G. (eds) (1992) *Miljonprogrammets bostäder: bevara, förnya, förbättra* (Housing of the Million Dwellings Programme: Maintain, rehabilitate and improve), Stockholm: BFR.

Vier grote steden (1992) *De stadsvernieuwing in de grote steden afmaken* (Finishing urban renewal in the large cities), Wethouders voor stadsvernieuwing in de gemeenten, Amsterdam, 's-Gravenhage, Rotterdam and Utrecht: Dienst Stedebouw+Volkshuisvesting, Gemeente Rotterdam.

VNG (1992) *Stadsvernieuwing te voet verder?* (Urban renewal one step further?), 's-Gravenhage: Vereniging van Nederlandse Gemeenten.

Welsh Office (1988) *Welsh House Condition Survey 1986*, Cardiff: Welsh Office.

Welsh Office (1994) *The Government's expenditure plans 1993-94 to 1995-96: A report by the Welsh Office*, Cardiff: Welsh Office.

Wiktorin (1993) *An international comparison of rent setting and conflict solution*, Gavle: Swedish Institute for Building Research.

Wilcox, S. (1995) *Housing finance review, 1995/96*, York: Joseph Rowntree Foundation.

Worsdall, F. (1979) *The tenement: A way of life*, Edinburgh: Chambers.

Young, M. and Willmott, P. (1957) *Family and kinship in East London*, London: Routlege.

Young, R. (1969) 'Public participation in planning', BArch Thesis, Glasgow: University of Strathclyde.

# Index

[please note: tables/figures are indicated by italics, unless there is related text on the same page]

## A

Aaen, Solveig 203-16
age
  of householders
    in Switzerland 123
    in UK 81-2
  of properties *see* older dwellings
'Agreed housing renewal' 113
AL 170, 171
ALF 170, 171
allowances, housing
  in France 170-1
  in Netherlands 179, 180
ALS 170, 171
amenities: in dwellings
  lack 248, *249*
  in Denmark 98, 99-100, 110-11
  in France 160, *161,* 162
  in UK/Scotland 70, 224, 239
  in Vienna 142, *143,* 147
  standard (Scotland) 231
Amsterdam 183-4, 191, 194, 197, 199
ANAH 155, 164
  subsidies 166-7, *168,* 169, 173
ANPE 170
apartments *see* flats
APL 169, 170-1
area renewal 11-12
  in France 169-70
  in Scotland 232, 233-6, 237, 238
  in UK 86, 92, 275-6
  and urban restructuring 264, 265

in Vienna 145-7, 150, 151
Austria 11-12, 23, 141, 271
  Vienna 141-53

## B

backyards: in Switzerland 132, 136, 138
Bailey, Nick 217-40
bathrooms *see* amenities
Bern: traffic reduction 132
Birmingham: overcrowding 225
*Blocksanierung* 146, 151, *151*
*bostadsförnyelse* 25
budget deficit: in Sweden 54, *63*
building code: in Norway 213
building sector employment: and renewal 256
  in Denmark 101, 108
  in Sweden 26-7, 44, 46
  in Switzerland 130
building societies: in Scotland 236
Bundesamt für Konjunkturfragen 131
Bundesamt für Wohnungswesen 131

## C

cantons: and renewal 117, 121, 126
Care and Repair agencies 86
'careful rehabilitation': in Sweden 25, 26, 37, 43-4, 52, *61*
CDC: partnership scheme 170

291

central heating
　in Denmark 111
　in France 160, *161,* 162
　in UK 71
*central priorities, strong see under*
　strategies
CIV: role 169
clearance *see* demolition
comfort: and housing quality (France) 162
communes: and renewal
　in France 171
　in Switzerland 117, 121, 126
community policing: in France 170
compulsory purchase 213, 232, 236
condensation: in UK houses 69, 70
conservation, energy 244 *see also under* environmentalism
conservation areas: in France 156
Conservatives
　in Sweden 33
　in UK 218, 222, 230, 238
construction *see* building
cooperatives, housing 22
　in Denmark 103-4
　in Norway 209, 210-11, 214, 216
　in Sweden 32, 53
　in Vienna 142
costs
　of housing
　　in Netherlands 180, *201, 202*
　of land: in Netherlands 192-3
　of renewal
　　in Netherlands 187-8, *189,* 196-7
　　in Norway 216
　　in UK (repair costs) 65, 67, 68, 70, 72, 74-5

council houses *see* social housing
country *see* rural housing
Cullingworth Report 225-6, 238

**D**

dampness: in UK houses 69-70
Danish Building Research Institute 258, 259, 260
decentralisation 11, 18, 19, 246, 256, 271
　in France 171
　in Netherlands 181, 186
　in Switzerland 117, 121
　in UK 219
delinquency: in France 170
demolition
　in Switzerland 134-5
　in UK 87, *90,* 93, 231
　*see also* slum clearance
Denmark **95-113**
　tenure regulation 101-5
　urban renewal
　　history 95-101
　　and housing rehabilitation policy 14, 23, 110-13, 271
　　programmes 11-12, 105-10
Dennis Highway Project 44
desubsidisation: in Sweden 33, 44, 50, 51
deterioration: of housing 246-52, 257
　in Denmark 98, 99-101
　in France 160
　in Norway 205-7
　in Scotland 232-3, 238, 239
　in Switzerland 122-3
　in UK 74, 75-7
de-urbanisation: in Scotland 220
disabled people: in Sweden 42

disrepair *see* deterioration
double glazing: in UK 220
drug addicts: in Switzerland 124
Dwelling-linked Subsidies Order 184

**E**

economies, national: and housing 19-20
  Denmark 96
  Netherlands 176
  Norway 204-5
  Sweden 63
Edinburgh 220, 234-5
*Einzelverbesserungen* 146
Ekström, M. 47-8
Elander, Ingemar 25-64
elderly people: in Sweden 42
Energy Action Grants Agency 86
English House Condition Survey (1991) 65-7, 81-2, 83-4
'Enveloping' 265
Environment, Department of (UK) 86
environmentalism 250
  in Denmark 101
  in France 156, 163
  in Netherlands 194, 195
  in Sweden 43, 44
  in Switzerland 116, 131-2, 136, 138-9
  as energy conservation 120, 122, 125-6, 135, 139
  in Vienna 152
*Erhaltungsarbeiten* 146
ethnicity: and housing (UK) 83-4
Europe: and housing 17-24
  problems: urban decay 246-52

renewal policies/strategies 7-8, 9-15, 256-68
  evaluated 268-74
  history 8-9, 242-6
  objectives 252-6
  and UK: implications 274-7
  expenditure *see* investment

**F**

factors/factoring 223, 224, 233
FAS: partnership scheme 170
FAU 157
Finland 245
fitness: for human habitation
  in France 162-3
  in Scotland 65, *66,* 226, 231
  in UK: standards 65, *66,* 85
  *see also* unfitness
flats/apartments
  owner-occupied: maintenance 9, 238
  in Denmark 100, 104
  *see also* HLMs; tenements
FNAH 155
Folkesdotter, Gärd 35
foreigners *see* immigrants
Forschungskommission Wohnungswesen 131
Förster, Wolfgang 141-53
France: housing policy 14, 24, **155-73**
  and market 158-60, *161*
  postwar plans 155-8
  regulation: mechanism 164-5
  on rehabilitation 12, 13, 14
  and area renewal 169-70
  needs 162-4, 173
  programmes 165-9
  and tenure 160, *161,* 242

293

rent support 170-1
results 171-3, 272-3
Fribourg, Anne-Marie 155-73
Friggebo, Birgit 33
*Future Urban Renewal Policy* 186

**G**

*Gebietsbetreuungen* 146, 150
*general housing improvement:* strategy 11-12, 15, 267, 271-2
gentrification 247, 270
  in Scotland 235
Germany: housing policy/strategies 13-14, 24, 269, 273-4
  and tax allowances 20, 24, 261
ghettoisation: in Sweden 49, 57n6
Glasgow 220-1, 224-5
  and HTAs/HAAs 227, 233, 234
grants/subsidies
  in Denmark 97, 106-7, 108-9, 112
  in France 165-9, 171-3
  to local authorities 245-6
  in Netherlands 179-80, 183-5, 188, *189,* 193-4, 199
  in Norway 210
  in Scotland 219, 226, 228, 233, 236-7
  in Sweden 44-5, 46, 50, 51, 55
  in Switzerland 128-30
  in UK 65, 86, 87, *89,* 91-2, 229-30
  in Vienna 144-6, 147
  in Wales *87,* 91
group repair schemes: in UK 92, 265

**H**

Haari, Roland 115-40
Hague 183-4, 191, 194, 197, 199
Halmstad: radon problem 55-6
Hansen, Knud Erik 95-113

heating: of houses
  in Denmark 111
  in France 160, *161,* 162
  in UK 70-1
HLMs 155, 157, 158-9
HMOs: in UK 71-2, 84-6
Home Energy Efficiency Scheme 86
homeless, housing of (UK) 80
House Condition Surveys *see* English; Scottish
households: in poor housing
  in Denmark 98, 99
  in Switzerland 123-4
  in UK 78-85
Housing Act (Netherlands: 1901) 176
Housing Act Dwellings 179
Housing Action Areas (HAAs) 232, 233-5, 237, 238
housing associations
  in Britain/Scotland 222-3
  in Denmark 98
  in Netherlands 178, 179
  in Norway 212, 214
  in Scotland 219, 233, 238, 239
  *vs* owner-occupation 234, 235-6
  in UK 86, 93
  in Vienna 142
Housing Corporation (UK) 86-7, 93
  *see also* Scottish Homes
Housing Improvement Programme (Sweden) 38-41, 44
*Housing in the 1990s memorandum* 178
housing markets *see* markets
housing policies *see* policies

Housing Rehabilitation Act (Vienna: 1984) 145
Housing Renovation Act (Sweden: 1973) 37
housing stock
  in Europe 242, 247, 248, 254
  in Scotland 67, 69, 80, 227-8
  in Switzerland 119, 122-3, 139-40
  in UK 276
  in Vienna 142, 143
  see also older dwellings
Housing Treatment Areas 226, 232
HSB 32, 53

**I**

immigrants/ethnic minorities
  in Sweden 49, 57n6
  in Switzerland 119, 123-4
  in UK 83-4
Improvement Grants (UK) 230, 232, 237
Improvement Orders 232-3, 236
imputed rental income tax 228, 229, 261
incomes
  low
    and poor housing 274-5
    in UK/Scotland 78-80, 239
    and renewal 256
  in Netherlands 176, 177
  and housing costs 180, 201, 202
inflation 20
  in Netherlands 176
  in Norway 204
infrastructure: in Netherlands 193, 195
insulation, thermal: in UK 71
interest rates 20

in Netherlands 176
in Norway 215
*Interim Saldo Regeling (ISR)* 181
intervention *see* regulation
investment: in housing/renewal 23-4
  in Denmark 23, 108-10, 111
  in France 24, 171, 172
  in Netherlands 23, 184-5, 187-8, 189, 196-8
  in Norway 24, 211, 214-16
  in Sweden 23, 37, 44, 46, 62
  in UK 24, 91
  in Vienna 142

**L**

land
  costs: and building revenues (Netherlands) 192-3
  scarcity: and housing 17, 18
  use: in Switzerland 116, 117, 131
landlords
  in Norway 208-9
  in Scotland 229, 235
  and repairs 222, 226, 229, 234
  in Sweden: as policy actors 53, 54
  and tax rules 228, 229
landlords, private
  in France 165, 168, 169
Law on Housing Amelioration (Vienna: 1969) 143
Leather, Philip 65-94
*limited public involvement:* strategy 13-14, 268, 273-4
'Liverpoolisation': in Sweden 49
loans: for renewal
  in Norway 210-11
  in Sweden 50, 51, 59n, 60
  in Vienna 147

local authorities 11, 13, 18, 19, 256, 271
   in Denmark 101, 105-8, 109-10
   in France 158
   in Netherlands 181, 186, 188, 191-2
     and dwellings purchase 183-4, 194, 199
     and funding 182-3, 197-8
     and social housing 178, 179
   in Scotland 219, 236-7
     statutory powers 226-7, 231, 232-3, 239
   in Sweden 50
   in Switzerland 117, 121, 126, 134-7
   in UK 85, 86, 219
     under-funding 91, 92, 229-30
   Vienna 141-53
Local Government and Housing Act (UK: 1989) 85, 91
low incomes *see under* incomes

**M**

maintenance
   and grants: in Scotland 233
   of owner-occupied flats 9, 238
   in Denmark 100, 104
   regulation: in France 165
   and rent control 262-3
Malraux law (France: 1962) 156
Manchester: overcrowding 225
markets, housing: *vs* policies 1, 21-4, 245-6, 247, 248
   in Denmark 97-8, *99*
   in France 158-60, *161*
   in Netherlands 176-80, *201, 202*
   in Norway 14, 24, 205
   in Scotland 221-3, 227, 235, 238
   in Sweden 56n3, 59
   in Switzerland 14, 117-21, 129
   in UK: renewal problems 72-4, 79-80, *82,* 274
   in Vienna 142, 143, 144-5
means tests 12, 267, 270
   in UK 92, 267, 272
*Memorandum on Urban and Village Renewal* (1981) 181, 199
renewal definition 185, 186, 191
Metselaar, G. 241, 242, 253
Million Dwellings Programme 25, 37
mould growth: in UK houses 69, 70
mountains: and housing 251
   in Switzerland 117, 128
municipalities *see* local authorities

**N**

National Association of Municipal Housing Companies (SABO) 32, 53
National Board of Health and Welfare 52
National Board of Housing (Building and Planning) 36, 45, 46, 50, 52, 53
National Board of Labour Market 46
National Federation of Tenants' Associations (Sweden) 32, 53
National Fund for the Improvement and Maintenance of Rural and Urban Housing (France) 155
National Science Foundation 131
Netherlands 23, **175-202**
   housing: and market 176-80, *201, 202*

renewal 180-6, 198-200, 273
  future: to 2005 192-6
  investment 184-5, 187-8, *189,*
    196-8
  1980s: achievements 187-92
New Towns: in Scotland 220, 221
Nora Report (France) 156-7
Norway **203-16**
  housing policy/market 14, 24, 205
  problems: urban decay 205-7
  renewal: policy/strategies 12-13,
    265
    evaluation 214-16, 269, 272
    goals 207-8
    implementation 208-14

## O

older dwellings *247,* 248
  in Denmark 98, 99-101
  in Norway 206-7
  in Scotland 227-8
  in Sweden 39-40, 46-7, 55
  in Switzerland 122
  in UK 74, 75-6, 93, 94
  and urban decay 248, 249-50
  in Vienna 142, *143*
OPAHs 157, 165-6, 169
  effects 157, 171, 172-3
orders, compulsory 257-8
  for improvement 232-3, 236
  for purchase 213, 232, 236
Örebro 36
Öresund bridge 44
Oslo 203-4, 205, 211-12, 213
Oslo Urban Renewal 211-12, 213
owner-occupation 9, 21, 248
  in Britain 75, 222
    and poor housing 76, 77, 79, 80,
      93-4, 274

and tax rules 228-9, 238
in France: and PAH 164, 167-8
in Netherlands 177
  and housing costs 180, *202*
  and subsidies 184, 193
in Norway 205, 206, 208
in Scotland 80, 221, 233, 238
  and housing associations 234,
    235-6
  and improvements 226, 234

## P

PAH 164, 167-8, 173
PALULOS 166, *168*
planning: in Switzerland 132, 135-6
planning blight
  in Norway 204
  in Scotland 221
policies, housing/renewal 9-11
  curative 10, 256, 257, 259, 263-6
  evaluation 47-9
  and housing markets 1, 21-4, 245-
    6, 247, 248
  objectives 4-5, 252-6
  preventative 10, 256, 257, 258-63
  prioritising 266-7
  and strategies 11-14, 267-8
  *see also under named countries*
'policy network': in Sweden 53-4
pollution *see* environmentalism;
  traffic
Popular Movements Coalition 32
population: and housing 17-18, 19
  in Denmark 96
  in France 158
  in Netherlands 176
  in Norway 204
  in Switzerland 115, *116*
post-industrialism 244

preservation: of buildings 243, 244, 255
  in Netherlands 194
  in Switzerland 126
Priemus, H. 241, 242, 253
private dwellings: renovation
  in Denmark 102-3, 108
  in France 157, 163-4
  in Netherlands 183-5, 193-4, 199
  in Norway 208-9
  in Scotland 231-3, 234, 235
  in Switzerland 118, 121, 123, 139
  in UK 87, 91, 92
private renting 9, 22, 248
  in Denmark 98, 100, 102-3
  in France 160, *161,* 164
    and renewal/maintenance 165, 166-7, 168, 169
  in Netherlands: subsidies 194
  in Norway 206, 208-9
  in Scotland 222, 223-4, 226, 227-9
  in Switzerland 117, 118-19, 127
  in UK 73, 75, 79-80, 92, 221-2
Private Urban Renewal Act (Denmark) 108, 112, 113
privatisation: in policy 244, 245
PST projects 167, 169
public housing *see* social housing

**R**

radon: in Sweden 55-6
recession: in Switzerland 116
regulation/intervention 1, 5, 10-11
  direct/indirect 5, 10-11, 259, 263-6, 270
  in Scotland 229-33
  of tenure 5, 9, 11, 228-9, 258-63
  in Denmark 101-5
rehabilitation, housing *see* private

dwellings; urban renewal; *and under named countries*
renewal *see* policies; strategies; urban renewal
renewal areas: in UK 86, 275-6
Rental Act (Vienna: 1917) 145
rents/renting
  and allowances
    in France 170-1
    in Netherlands 180, *201*
  control 242, 262-3
    in Denmark 97
    in Norway 206
    in Switzerland 118, 120, 127
    and renovation 127, 129
  in Vienna 145
  *see also* housing associations; landlords; private renting; social housing; tenants
repair costs *see* costs: of renewal
Repair Grants (UK) 230, 232, 237
Repair Notices 232-3, 236
research: role
  in Switzerland 130-4
  in Vienna 152
restructuring/revitalisation, urban 2, *255,* 264, 265-6
rights: of residents
  in Denmark 106, 112, 113
  in Sweden 38, 50, 57n5
  in Vienna 142, 143, 152-3
Robertson, Douglas 217-40
Rotterdam 183-4, 191, 194, 197, 199
rural housing 251
  in France 156
  in Switzerland 119, 120, 122

**S**

SABO 32, 53

# Index

Saltsjöbaden Agreement 27
*sanering:* in Sweden 25, 36-7
Schön, Lennart 29-30
Scotland **217-40**
  fitness standard 65, *66*
  government 217-19
  housing stock 67, 69, 80, 227-8
  tenements 220, 223-4
  renewal policy/strategies 228-33
  for areas 232, 233-6, 237, 238
  development 224-7
  grants 219, 226, 228, 233, 236-7
  legislation: impact 233-8
  tenure patterns: changes 221-3
  urban system: changes 220-1
Scottish Homes 219, 233
Scottish House Condition Survey 69, 80, 81, 227
Scottish Office 218
Skifter Andersen, Hans 1-15, 17-24, 95-113, 241-77
slum clearance 8, 225, 243, 245
  in Denmark 95, 105-7
  in Glasgow 220-1, 224-5
  in Netherlands 181, 198
  in Sweden 25, 34-7, 245
  in Vienna 142
Social Democrats: in Sweden 28
  housing policy 32, 33, 46, 53-4
  on social housing 33, 38
social flats (France) *see* HLMs
social housing 22
  in Denmark 98, 104-5
  estates: problems 9, 244, 248, 251
  in France 157
  in Sweden 37, 39-40, 41, 49, 55
  in France 155, 157, 158-9
  rehabilitation 164, 173

maintenance: problems 263
  in Netherlands 177, 178-9, 184
  in Scotland 219, 221
  in Sweden 33, 37-43, 49, 55, 56n3
  in Vienna 142, 145
Social Housing Commission 34-5
Social Life and Housing 157, 158
social problems
  in France 169-70
  in Sweden 54-5
  in Switzerland 123-4
  *see also* social housing: estates
*Sockelsanierung* (basic renewal) 144, 145, 146, 147, *148*
'soft urban renewal' 144, 146
space, living
  in Glasgow 224-5, 227-8
  in Sweden 31
  in Switzerland 117-18, 119
speculation: in Vienna 153
*stadsförnyelse* 25
State Housing Bank (Norway) 205, 210, 211, 213
State Rental Act (Austria) 142
Staying Put agencies 86
strategies: for renewal
  *general housing improvement* 11-12, 15, 267, 271-2
  *limited public involvement* 13-14, 268, 273-4
  *strong central priorities* 12-13, 15, 267, 272-3
subsidies *see* grants
suburbanisation: in Scotland 220
sustainable development *see* environmentalism
*Svenska Riksbyggen* 32, 53
Sweden **25-64**

housing policies 23, 31-4
non-socialist government 31-2, 51, 53
renewal 11, 12, 14, 26-7, 47-54, 265
  in future 54-6
  during 1990s 43-7
  slum clearance 25, 34-7, 245
  of social housing 37-43, 49
  state support 41-2, 44-5, 50, 51, 55, 271-2
welfare state model 27-9
  decline 29-31, *63, 64*
Switzerland **115-40**
  housing market/policy 14, 117-21, 129
  legislation 118-19, 128-30, 136-7
  problems: urban decay 121-5
  renewal policy/strategies 13, 125-6, 245
  effects 137-9, 269, 274
  regulations/programmes 121, 126
  cantonal/communal 134-7
  federal 127-30
  research 130-4, 140

**T**

tax
  allowances
    in France 166
    in Germany 20, 24, 261
  rules: and tenure 228-9, 238, 261
Tenancy Act (Austria: 1919) 141, 145, 152-3
tenants
  in Denmark 98-9
  and maintenance: in France 165
  in Netherlands 180, *201*
  and policy: in Sweden 53, 54

rights
  in Sweden 50, 57n5
  in Vienna 142, 143-4
  services: in Sweden 41-2
tenements
  in Denmark 98, 100, 104
  in Scotland 220, 223-4
  in Switzerland 120, 137
tenure *see* markets, housing; *and under* regulation
Teule, René 175-202
'tolerable standard': of fitness 65, *66,* 226, 231
*Totalsanierungen* 146
traffic
  in Netherlands 195
  in Switzerland 120, 125, 135, 138-9
  research 131, 132

**U**

UK 24, **65-94**
  housing, poor 65-78
  residents 78-85
  renewal: policy/strategies 14, 85-7, *88, 89, 90,* 245
    for areas 86, 92, 275-6
    on preservation 255
    problems 13, 87, 91-3, 272, 274-7
    *strong central priorities* 12, 13
  unemployment
    in Norway 204, 210, 215
    and renewal 20, 244
    in Sweden *64*
    in Switzerland 124
    *see also* building sector
  unfitness: in UK housing 67-71
    and age/type 74, 75-7

and location 77-8
and tenure 72-4
United States 1, 247
Urban and Village Renewal Act (UVRA) (Netherlands: 1985) 181-2, 186
urban renewal definition 191, 199
urban decay 246-52, 257
　in France 160
　in Norway 205-7
　in Switzerland 121-5
urban renewal 2, 8, 241
　and housing rehabilitation
　history 8-9, 242-6
　problems: urban decay 4, 246-52
　strategies/policies 5, 10-15, 256-68
　evaluation 268-74
　objectives 4-5, 252-6
　*see also under named countries*
Urban Renewal Act/Law (Denmark: 1982) 96, 107-8, 109, 111-12
urban renewal companies: in Denmark 106, 107

urban renewal fund (Netherlands) 184
'urban renewal key' 182-3, 266
Urban Renewal Law (Austria: 1974) 144
Utrecht 183-4, 191, 194, 197, 199

**V**

vacant dwellings
　in Switzerland 118
　in UK: and unfitness 74
*varsam ombyggnad see* 'careful rehabilitation'
Vidén, Sonja 36, 39-40
Vienna: renewal **141-53**
Vienna Housing Construction Research 152
Vienna Land Procurement and Urban Renewal Fund *see* WBSF

**W**

Wales: private sector renewal *87, 91*
WBSF 146, 147, *148, 149, 150,* 151
West Germany *see* Germany